THE POLITICS OF SAMUEL JOHNSON

THE POLITICS OF

Samuel Johnson

BY DONALD J. GREENE

NEW HAVEN

Yale University Press

1960

POLITICAL TRUTH is undoubtedly of very great Importance, and they who honestly endeavour after it, are doubtless engaged in a laudable Pursuit. Nor do the Writers on this Subject ever more deserve the Thanks of their Country, than when they enter upon Examinations of the Conduct of their Governors, whether Kings, Senates, or Ministers; when they impartially consider the Tendency of their Measures, and justify them in opposition to popular Calumnies, or censure them in defiance of the Frowns of Greatness, or the Persecutions of Power.

To clear the Character of a good King from the Aspersions of Faction, or Misrepresentations of Jealousy, is the Duty of every Man who has an Opportunity of undeceiving the Deluded; but it is much more his Duty to warn a People against any intended Encroachments upon their Rights or Liberties, as the Happiness of twenty thousand is of twenty thousand times more Value than the Happiness of one.

> JOHNSON, "To Mr. Urban,"
> Gentleman's Magazine (January 1739), p. 3.

IF we consider, Sir, what Opposition of Character is necessary to constitute a Political Writer, it will not be wondered, that so few excel in that Undertaking.

> Sir Robert Walpole, in the House of
> Commons, December 2, 1740, as "reported"
> by Johnson, Gentleman's Magazine (Supplement,
> 1741), p. 673.

PREFACE

THE aim of a recent study of the political life of Oxford University in the eighteenth century, says its writer, W. R. Ward, is "to cast light . . . on one of the many varieties of eighteenth-century Toryism, of which much remains to be learned." [1] I hope that this introductory sketch—for it can claim to be little more—of the political activities, ideas, attitudes, and milieu of Samuel Johnson will cast some light on another variety, or aspect, of it.

There are many reasons why no more than a tentative outline of my subject can be drawn at the present time. A serious biography of Johnson's middle and later years, corresponding in fullness and accuracy to the work done by Aleyn Lyell Reade and James L. Clifford on his early life, has still to be written (when I say this, I am aware of the existence of a work called Boswell's *Life of Johnson*). A study of Johnson's general intellectual background, including an account of his vast reading, is badly needed. Although an edition of Johnson's writings is at last in progress, much work on establishing the canon of those writings has still to be done; substantial additions to it, and some deletions, have been made in the last few years, and there is reason to believe that this activity will continue. Though invaluable work on the political history of Johnson's time has recently appeared, important gaps remain to be filled—in particular (for the student of Johnson) the decades just before and after the period covered by John B. Owen's *The Rise of the Pelhams*. Work on the nature of Toryism in the eighteenth century, as Ward suggests, is just beginning, and is not likely to be soon concluded—what, one wonders, will be the effect on that study of Trevor-Roper's startling thesis that the small landed gentry, the "impoverished squires" of 1640 (the great-grandparents of the Tories of

Johnson's youth) were "the true revolutionaries of the Puritan Revolution, in which they appear as the Independent party"?[2] (One thinks of Johnson's familiarity with Harrington's *Oceana*, apparently a significant document for that thesis.) What effect, too, would the development of a science of political psychology, such as Harold Lasswell and David Riesman adumbrate, have on these questions? Will it some day be possible to assess the full significance of such a remark of Johnson's as "All change not evidently for the better alarms a mind taught by experience to distrust itself?"[3]

But these are problems for the future to take care of. Meanwhile, enough new information about Johnson and the political history of his times has become available for the continued currency of the simple old legend of Johnson the "blind reactionary" to be an unnecessary handicap to serious students. If the thesis that emerges from this essay is largely a negative one—if I seem too reluctant to supply new stereotypes for old—I can only plead that, at this point, anything else seems to me premature. I do permit myself, in my last chapter, to put forward some broad generalizations, but I hope these will be regarded as in the nature of working hypotheses, to be verified or rebutted by future inquiry, not as dogma. The best motto, at this stage, for the student of Johnson's ideas, and of the history of eighteenth-century thought generally, is, it seems to me, what Johnson said about the study of constitutional history: "It is . . . not by searching into past times but by searching superficially and deciding hastily that just censure is incurred. Knowledge is always promoted by inquisitive industry, and almost always retarded by systematic dogmatism. To these studies may be eminently applied that important axiom '*Qui pauca considerat facile pronunciat*,' and of antiquaries, as of other scholars, I suppose it will be found that often as their knowledge increases their confidence grows less."[4]

This work is based on a doctoral dissertation for Columbia University, completed in 1954, and bearing the same title (published on microfilm by University Publications, Ann Arbor, Michigan). But new work both in Johnson studies and in eighteenth-century British historiography that has appeared in the four or five years since that time has caused considerable modification of some of my earlier views. My chief acknowledgments of valuable advice and criticism are to Allen T. Hazen, the late J. Bartlet Brebner, and, above all, James L. Clifford, all of Columbia University, who read the work in its earlier form. I was assisted during its composition by a scholarship of the Royal Society of Canada and a faculty summer fellowship of the University of California; a grant from the Ford Foundation has aided its publication; to those bodies I express my gratitude.

D. J. G.

Waltham, Massachusetts
May 1959

CONTENTS

CHRONOLOGICAL TABLE

FLT = First Lord [Commissioner] of the Treasury (after 1714 usually, though not always, the king's chief minister). Ch. Ex. = Chancellor of the Exchequer (second-ranking member of the Treasury commission).

BRITISH HISTORY		SAMUEL JOHNSON
William III dies; Anne queen. War of Spanish Succession begins. Marlborough, Captain-General; Duchess of Marlborough, Mistress of the Robes; Godolphin, Lord Treasurer.	1702	
Battle of Blenheim.	1704	
Union of England and Scotland as Great Britain.	1707	
	1709	Born at Lichfield (7/18 Sep.).
Impeachment of Sacheverell. Godolphin dismissed. Harley (Oxford), Ch. Ex.; St. John (Bolingbroke), Secretary of State.	1710	
Oxford, Lord Treasurer. Marlborough dismissed.	1711	
Sir William Wyndham, Secretary at War.	1712	Touched by Queen Anne.
Peace of Utrecht.	1713	
Anne dies; George I king. Townshend, Stanhope, Secs. State; Walpole, Paymaster General, later FLT; Pulteney, Sec. at War.	1714	
Oxford and Bolingbroke impeached of high treason. Bolingbroke flees to France, and is attainted. Invasion of Scotland by James Edward (the Old Pretender).	1715	
Septennial Act. Alliance with France (later Quadruple Alliance).	1716	

BRITISH HISTORY		SAMUEL JOHNSON
Stanhope, FLT; Sunderland, Addison, Secs. State. Oxford's impeachment fails. Townshend dismissed; Walpole resigns.	1717	Enters Lichfield Grammar School.
Abortive Jacobite invasion.	1718	
South Sea bubble; ministry implicated.	1720	
Stanhope dies; Sunderland resigns. Walpole, FLT; Townshend, Carteret, Secs. State. Pulteney not given office.	1721	
Bolingbroke returns from France.	1723	
Carteret replaced by Newcastle as Sec. State.	1724	
	1725	At Stourbridge (meets Lyttelton?)
George I dies; George II king.	1727	
	1728	To Pembroke College, Oxford (Oct.).
Frederick Louis created Prince of Wales.	1729	Returns to Lichfield (Dec.).
Townshend quarrels with Walpole and resigns.	1730	
	1731	Michael Johnson (father) dies.
	1732	Usher at Market Bosworth school. Quarrels with Sir Wolstan Dixie.
Walpole forced to withdraw Excise Bill. Chesterfield dismissed as Lord Steward for opposing it.	1733	At Birmingham. Translates *A Voyage to Abyssinia.*
Sir William Yonge, Sec. at War (till 1746).	1735	Marries Elizabeth (Jervis) Porter.
	1736	At Edial school. Begins *Irene.*
Stage Licensing Act passed. Queen Caroline dies (Nov.).	1737	Nathanael Johnson (brother) dies. To London (Mar.). Begins work for Cave.
Inquiry into Spanish treatment of British seamen. Birth and christening of Prince George of Wales (later George III) (June).	1738	*London; Life of Sarpi; State of Affairs in Lilliput* (intro. to *Debates*); Eubulus and Pamphilus letters.

BRITISH HISTORY		SAMUEL JOHNSON
War declared on Spain (Oct.).	1739	Marmor Norfolciense; Vindication of the Licensers; tr. of Crousaz' Commentary on Pope. Extended visit to Midlands.
Sir William Wyndham dies. Anson begins voyage around the world.	1740	Lives of Blake, Drake, Barretier. Probably assisting Guthrie with Debates.
Motion in Parliament to remove Walpole (Feb.). War of Austrian Succession begins. General election; Walpole's support diminished.	1741	Sole writer of Debates. Abridgment of Monarchy Asserted. Probably contributes to "Foreign History" and discussion of wool exports in Gentleman's Magazine.
Walpole resigns; created Earl of Orford (Feb.). Carteret, Newcastle, Secs. State; Sandys, Ch. Ex.; Gower, Lord Privy Seal. Pulteney created Earl of Bath.	1742	Continues with Debates and "Foreign History." Review of Conduct of Duchess of Marlborough.
Battle of Dettingen. Controversy over use of Hanoverian troops in British army.	1743	Savage dies. Continues with Debates. Work on Harleian library. "Historical Account of Parliament" (lost).
Carteret (Granville) forced to resign over war and foreign policy. Henry Pelham, FLT; Newcastle, Sec. State; Hardwicke, Lord Chancellor; Lyttelton, George Grenville, junior ministers.	1744	Life of Savage; Harleian Miscellany; "Essay on Small Tracts and Fugitive Pieces"; (perhaps) report of debate on Hanoverian troops.
Invasion by Charles Edward (the Young Pretender).	1745	Observations on Macbeth; sermon for Henry Hervey Aston.
Granville, Bath, ministers for two days. Pelhams resume office. Chesterfield, Sec. State (till 1748); Pitt, Paymaster General.	1746	Signs contract for Dictionary.
General election; Gower-Anson group win Lichfield seats.	1747	Plan of Dictionary (dedicated to Chesterfield).
Peace of Aix-la-Chapelle.	1748	Preface to Preceptor.
	1749	Letter on fireworks; Vanity of Human Wishes. Irene produced (epilogue by Sir William Yonge).
	1750	Begins Rambler (to 1752).

BRITISH HISTORY		SAMUEL JOHNSON
Frederick, Prince of Wales, dies.	1751	*Life of Cheynel.*
Hostilities between French and British in India and America; French advance toward Ohio valley.	1752 1753	Elizabeth Johnson (wife) dies. Takes Frank Barber under his care. Contributes to *Adventurer* (to 1754).
Henry Pelham dies. Newcastle, FLT; Henry Fox, Sec. at War, then Sec. State; Anson, First Lord of Admiralty. French take Fort Duquesne.	1754	*Life of Cave.*
Braddock defeated by French. Russian and Hessian subsidy treaties attacked by Pitt. Pitt and Grenville dismissed. Lyttelton, Ch. Ex.	1755	Letter to Chesterfield. *Dictionary* published. Hon. M.A., Oxford.
Treaty of Westminster (Jan.), allying Britain and Prussia against France. War declared on France (May) (Seven Years' War). G. Townshend's first Militia Bill defeated in Lords. Admiral Byng fails to prevent French taking Minorca; court-martialed (Dec.) and executed. Newcastle resigns (Nov.). Pitt, Sec. State.	1756	Preface to Rolt's *Dictionary of Commerce;* "Further Thoughts on Agriculture." Edits *Literary Magazine* (Apr.): "Political State of Great Britain"; "Observations" on Present State of Affairs, Militia Bill, Russian and Hessian treaties, letter from Gallo-Anglus; reviews of Evans' *Middle Colonies,* pamphlets on Byng, *History of Minorca.* Life of Frederick the Great.
Pitt dismissed (Apr.). Coalition ministry (June): Newcastle, FLT; Pitt, Sec. State; Anson, Admiralty; Halifax, Board of Trade and Plantations. Clive wins Battle of Plassey (June). Unsuccessful expedition to Rochefort (Sep.).	1757	Review of Soame Jenyns' *Origin of Evil;* intro. to *London Chronicle;* "speech" on Rochefort expedition.
Louisburg taken (July). Fort Duquesne taken (renamed Fort Pitt, now Pittsburgh).	1758	Begins *Idler* (to 1760). Observations on the war in *Universal Chronicle;* "Of the Duty of a Journalist" (*Univ. Chron.*).
Battle of Minden (Aug.). Quebec taken (Sep.). French navy defeated at Quiberon (Nov.).	1759	Sarah Johnson (mother) dies. *Rasselas;* intro. to *The World Displayed.*

BRITISH HISTORY		SAMUEL JOHNSON
Montreal taken. George II dies (aged 77) (Oct.); George III (aged 22) king. Bute in cabinet.	1760	"Bravery of English Common Soldiers"; intro. to *Proceedings of Committee for Clothing French Prisoners;* review of Tytler's *Inquiry* into Mary, Queen of Scots.
Pondicherry (India) taken. French begin peace negotiations. Bute, Sec. State (Mar.). Pitt resigns (Oct.) over question of war with Spain.	1761	Assists with Gwynn's *Thoughts on the Coronation.*
Newcastle resigns (May). Bute, FLT; Grenville, Egremont, Secs. State; Dashwood, Ch. Ex. Charles Jenkinson, Bute's private secretary.	1762	Awarded pension of £300 (July).
Peace of Paris (Feb.). Bute resigns (May). Grenville, FLT; initiates policy of economy to pay war costs. Egremont, Halifax, Secs. State.	1763	Meets Boswell. Jenkinson sends papers on Peace of Paris (returned 1765).
Wilkes arrested on general warrant, over *North Briton* No. 45; freed by Chief Justice Pratt (Camden); expelled from House of Commons.	1764	Lines in Goldsmith's *The Traveller.*
Stamp Act passed (Mar.). Grenville dismissed (July). Rockingham, FLT; Grafton, Sec. State; Newcastle, Privy Seal (dies 1768). Burke, Rockingham's private secretary.	1765	Meets Thrales. Prayer on "Engaging in politicks with Hamilton." Writes election publicity for Thrale. Shakespeare edition published. LL.D., Dublin.
Stamp Act repealed (Mar.); declaratory act affirming right to tax colonies passed. Rockingham dismissed (July). Pitt (Chatham), Privy Seal; Shelburne, Sec. State; Grafton, FLT; Camden, Lord Chancellor; Charles Townshend, Ch. Ex. Riots over price of bread; embargo on export of wheat.	1766	Contributes to Chambers' Vinerian lectures. "Considerations on Corn"(?)

BRITISH HISTORY		SAMUEL JOHNSON .
Inquiry into East India Company. Chatham incapacitated (resigns 1768). Townshend sponsors duties on tea, etc., in America. Grafton, FLT; North, Ch. Ex.; Shelburne (resigned 1768), Sec. State.	1767	Correspondence with Chambers over defense of East India Company.
General election. Wilkes defeated in London, elected in Middlesex. Junius letters begin.	1768	Election publicity for Thrale.
Wilkes expelled by House of Commons; re-elected twice by Middlesex; House declares his opponent elected. Junius' Letter to the King (Dec.).	1769	Paragraph in Gentleman's Magazine concerning Sir Joseph Mawbey, Thrale's colleague as MP for Southwark.
Grafton resigns (Jan.). North, FLT. Grenville's Contested Elections Act passed. Spanish occupy Falkland Islands.	1770	The False Alarm (Jan.); concluding lines of The Deserted Village.
After diplomatic negotiations, Spanish agree to evacuate Falkland Islands.	1771	Thoughts on Falkland's Islands (Mar.). Recommended to Government by Strahan as Parliamentary candidate.
	1772	Preface to Hoole's Present State of East India Company's Affairs(?).
Act authorizing export of tea to America by East India Company. "Boston tea party" (Dec.).	1773	Tour of Scotland with Boswell.
Port of Boston closed. Quebec Act passed. First Continental Congress, Philadelphia. General election (Nov.). C. J. Fox dismissed as junior minister.	1774	The Patriot (Nov.). Election publicity for Thrale.
Burke's speech on conciliation (Mar.). Actions at Lexington and Concord (Apr.). Battle of Bunker Hill (June).	1775	Journey to Western Islands of Scotland (Jan.); Taxation No Tyranny (Mar.). Visit to France with Thrales (autumn). D.C.L., Oxford.
British evacuate Boston (Mar.). American Declaration of Independence (July).	1776	Dinner with Wilkes (May).

BRITISH HISTORY		SAMUEL JOHNSON
Burgoyne surrenders at Saratoga (Oct.).	1777	Concerned with trial of Dr. Dodd. Begins *Lives of the Poets.*
France declares war on Britain. Chatham dies.	1778	
	1779	First group of *Lives* published.
Gordon Riots (June). Dunning's motion on increase of influence of the Crown.	1780	
Cornwallis surrenders at Yorktown (Oct.).	1781	Visits Bennet Langton at militia camp at Warley. Remaining *Lives* published. Dissertation "Of Tory and Whig" for Boswell.
North resigns (Mar.). Rockingham, FLT; Fox, Shelburne, Secs. State; Burke, Paymaster. Fox and Shelburne quarrel over peace negotiations. Rockingham dies (July). Shelburne, FLT; William Pitt, Ch. Ex.; Thomas Townshend, Sec. State.	1782	
Preliminaries of Peace of Versailles signed (Jan.). Shelburne defeated in Commons by Fox-North coalition; resigns (Feb.). Fox, North, Secs. State; Burke, Paymaster; Sheridan, Sec. to Treasury. Fox's India Bill defeated in Lords. Fox and North dismissed (Dec.). Pitt, FLT; Townshend, Home Sec.; Thurlow, Lord Chancellor.	1783	
Pitt in minority in House of Commons. General election (Apr.); Fox's supporters overwhelmingly defeated. Pitt prime minister, 1783–1801, 1804–06.	1784	Unsuccessful application to ministry for grant to enable Johnson to spend winter in Italy (Sep.). Dies (13 Dec.).

Chapter One

INTRODUCTION

1. THE WHIG INTERPRETATION

SINCE we all know that Samuel Johnson was a Tory, and since we all know what a Tory is, we at once know a great deal about Johnson. We know, for instance (to quote a highly regarded modern literary history), that he was "blindly conservative"; that when he "could not stem the rising tide of democracy," he "turned shuddering from such corruptions to fly . . . to the impartial protective authority of the throne." [1] Given that Johnson was a Tory, we can immediately deduce the essential facts not only about his political opinions, but about his critical principles, which must have been authoritarian, his religion, which must have been "High," his morality, which must have been prescriptive, and many other things. It is very useful to know all this a priori, for it saves us the trouble of having to read what Johnson actually wrote on these matters. [2]

The foregoing is perhaps not too exaggerated a parody of the reasoning behind much Johnsonian commentary in the past. Recently, it is true, some parts of the amazing structure of myth that the nineteenth century (chiefly) erected around the figure of Johnson have begun to show signs of crumbling. It is growing harder for even the laziest undergraduate to continue to believe what the older histories of literature tell him, that Johnson was a pompous dogmatist in morality, an incompetent blunderer in criticism, and a maker of mechanical and pedantic verse. This change has come about because

1

modern critics (including such formidable and diverse ones as Eliot, Leavis, and Edmund Wilson) have actually read Johnson and discovered the reality to be very different from the legend. But the old version of Johnson's political position still persists; and since it constitutes (I believe) the framework of the whole structure, fragments of the rest of the myth cling tenaciously to it and continue to give trouble.

In fact, the myth of Johnson the blind and frightened political reactionary can easily be shown to be as unsubstantial as the myths of Johnson the dogmatic critic and Johnson the academic versemaker. Even a casual reading of Johnson's writings reveals much that simply cannot be reconciled with the theory of his bigoted and unbending Toryism. According to that theory, for example, we are supposed to believe that Johnson wrote his pamphlets of the 1770's—*The False Alarm, Taxation No Tyranny*, and the rest—as a partisan Tory in support of the repressive Tory government of George III. Holders of this doctrine must be surprised to find Johnson saying, in the next-to-last paragraph of *The False Alarm*, "Every honest man must lament" that the question under discussion in the pamphlet "has been regarded with frigid neutrality *by the tories*." Again, one of our firmest assumptions is that Johnson and the Tories were the implacable enemies of the Whig Sir Robert Walpole. It is therefore strange to find, in a division of the House of Commons in 1741 on a motion calling for the dismissal of Walpole, the Tory members deliberately rescuing Walpole from defeat, and Johnson, in a note appended to his report of the debate, vigorously defending their action.[3] Of Lord North, generally regarded as the chief instrument of George III's "Tory" policies, Johnson said that he was "a fellow with a mind as narrow as a vinegar cruet," and when North's ministry left office, Johnson's epitaph was "Such a bunch of imbecility never disgraced a country." [4] It is taken for granted that Johnson's Toryism must have included a fervent devotion to monarchy. Yet when one collates the various references to monarchs in his writings, one gets the impression that his opinion of the institution was, to say the least, unenthusiastic. "Kings," says Johnson, after commenting that Frederick the Great was fortunate in encountering a variety of "forms of life" during his youth, "without this help . . . see the world in a mist, which magnifies everything near them, and bounds their view to a narrow compass. . . . I have always thought that what Cromwell had more than our lawful kings, he owed to the private condition in which he first entered the world." [5] "Liberty," said Johnson, "is, to the lowest rank of every nation, little more than the choice of working or starving" [6]— the perfect anticipation of a favorite Socialist slogan of the 1930's.

Some recent students, troubled by such "anomalies," have tried to find the explanation of them in the complexity and "ambivalence" of Johnson's psychology. No one doubts that Johnson's mind was complex. Yet there is also the possibility that if it is difficult to reconcile Johnson with our notions of eighteenth-century Toryism, the source of the confusion may lie less in Johnson than in those notions; and we may be moved to ask where those notions originated and how valid they are. These questions can now be answered confidently, for they have been the subject of much excellent historical research during the past quarter-century.[7] The answers are clear: the hitherto accepted picture of Toryism and of the political structure generally in eighteenth-century Britain is myth; it was the creation, for purposes of political propaganda, chiefly of two good Whigs, Burke and Macaulay, handed on by such Whig historians as Green, Lecky, and the Trevelyans, and now embalmed in school textbooks of history. Controversial as this judgment once was, the cumulative weight of the evidence collected by modern historians is such that the

nineteenth century's account of eighteenth-century political
history can no longer be seriously entertained.[8]

The nucleus of the "Whig interpretation" of the period—
we are all familiar with it; we were brought up on it—is
this. The political history of the century was essentially a
continuous struggle between two parties, the Whigs and the
Tories, each with a well-defined political philosophy and each
having its innings at the government of the country, the Whigs
during the reigns of the first two Georges, the Tories at the
accession of George III. The Tory party represented the
"forces of reaction" and the Whig party the "forces of progress" or "democracy." The chief issue on which the two were
divided was whether the executive power of government
should rest in the hands of the king or the "representatives of
the people." Thanks to the indifference and incompetence of
the first two Georges (so the tradition goes) the principle was
established that executive power should rest with the leader
of the majority party in Parliament, Sir Robert Walpole or
one of his successors. When George III ascended the throne,
he and the Tories tried to turn the clock back and restore
power to the Crown. But, discredited by the loss of the American colonies, they at last bowed to the inevitable, and the
principle of government by a cabinet responsible to the majority party in the legislature was triumphantly reaffirmed.

Macaulay summed it up clearly: "Through the whole of
that great movement [from Magna Carta to the Reform Act
of 1832] there have been, under some name or other, two sets
of men, those who were before their age, and those who were
behind it." [9] Macaulay's postulate has an inspired simplicity,
and it is not to be wondered at that so many people, from his
day to the present, have accepted it. It is so easy to grasp, and,
based as it is on the doctrine of the inevitability of progress, so
cheerful; so useful, moreover, to political groups who wish to
identify themselves with "the wave of the future." [10] But as

far as any evidence can determine, it has no relevance to the actual events of British politics in the eighteenth century; and to try to explain the political happenings of the century in terms of such a dichotomy inevitably results in such confusion, or such suppression of inconvenient evidence, as exists in the standard treatment of Johnson.

If we abandon Macaulay and try to arrive at an accurate view of the eighteenth-century political scene in Britain, there are two main things to be kept in mind. First, we must forget Burke's and Macaulay's attempts to date the inception of the modern British constitution back to the early eighteenth century. The responsibility of the cabinet to Parliament rather than to the Crown was not accepted as constitutional until well on into the nineteenth century. The king was supposed to be the effective chief executive of the nation: most Englishmen in the eighteenth century would no more have thought of disputing this than twentieth-century Americans would dispute that the president is, and ought to be, the effective chief executive of the United States. Second, parties were not parties in the modern British sense: groups of politicians were held together, tenuously, not by allegiance to formulated principles, to platforms, but by shifting personal alliances and similarities of interest—very much as in modern America.[11]

The constitution of eighteenth-century Britain was, indeed, very similar to that of the United States as it has continued to the present day; the American constitution was, after all, an offshoot of the older British constitution.[12] In both countries, a system of checks and balances was supposed to exist, manifesting itself in an executive not removable during its term of office and not responsible to the legislature. While such an executive retains large powers of patronage independent of the action of the legislature, the rigid party discipline of modern British politics cannot be maintained, and party

lines are blurred and easily crossed. Party policies tend to be
nebulous, and when a chief executive holds office who (like
George III) refuses to identify himself firmly with any one
group, they become even more difficult to detect. A British
politician of the eighteenth century would be much more at
home in the American political scene of the 1950's than in
modern Britain: the spectacle of an unpolitical chief executive, maintained in office by his personal popularity (throughout his reign George III had the bulk of his people solidly
behind him), committed to no one group of professional politicians but carrying on the government of the country with
the help of any whom he can depend on to support his policies
(to the annoyance of career politicians who believed themselves indispensable); the spectacle of "parties" whose labels
are little more than vestigial survivals from an earlier day and
guarantee nothing regarding their owners' principles, where
wider differences of principle and temperament often exist
between members of the same "party" than between members
of different "parties," where indeed a great many members
have no discernible political philosophy at all but are frankly
motivated by expediency—all this a Duke of Newcastle or a
Charles Jenkinson, if he were alive today, would recognize
and approve. The modern student of eighteenth-century British politics would do well, if he wishes to understand what
was actually going on, to think in terms of twentieth-century
Washington rather than of twentieth-century Westminster.[13]

2. TORIES AND PSEUDO-TORIES

When we try to sort out the "party" groupings of the eighteenth century as they really existed, the first thing to strike us
is that from the accession of George I to the end of the century
no Tory, properly so called, ever held a position of power in
the central administration. Throughout the period the scene
at Westminster was dominated by Whigs of one stripe or an-

other. Indeed, a man who seriously sought power in the national arena became virtually by definition a Whig. Walpole was a Whig. The leaders of the great opposition to Walpole—Pulteney, Carteret, Chesterfield, the elder Pitt—were Whigs. Lord North, for whom Johnson wrote pamphlets and who conducted the American Revolutionary war to its (for Britain) inglorious close, was a Whig. The younger Pitt was a Whig. Lord Bute, to be sure, played too unorthodox a role in politics to be called a Whig, strictly speaking; but neither was he a Tory.[14] The great political battles of the century—between Walpole and Pulteney, Pitt and Newcastle, North and Fox, Fox and Pitt—were all battles between various Whig groups warring for power.

There *were* Tories in the eighteenth century. But they were not nearly so prominent or active in national politics as the school histories would have us think. From 1714 to 1784, perhaps a fifth of the members of the House of Commons would have so designated themselves. These were, chiefly, the "country gentlemen," men who, like some modern American grassroots congressmen, had no particular ambition for high office but whose main motive in entering Parliament was to enhance or maintain their own local prestige and influence.[15] They were usually isolationist and against the government, looking on almost any administration with suspicion as the source of wars, taxes, and general interference, regarding themselves complacently as the repository of genuine English tradition, as true-born, 100 per cent Englishmen—and insofar as a feeling that the least government is the best government is part of the Anglo-Saxon cultural tradition, perhaps they were. Occasionally some politician arose who appealed to their particular interests or prejudices, or whom they regarded as the least of a number of evils—Harley and Bolingbroke, early in the century; sometimes Bute, sometimes North, later the younger Pitt—and to him they would give fitful support. But the career politicians came and went; they, the country members, stayed, returned regularly by their faithful constituents, inarticulate, often leaderless among themselves, basically not much interested in national politics at all, but a force which could never be entirely ignored by any administration. The memorable thing about them was their independence of vested political interests and their skepticism of current political cant. Their refusal to replace Walpole with the high-sounding Pulteney was clearly explained by Shippen: it was "a scheme for turning out one minister and bringing in another. . . . it was quite indifferent to him who was in or who was out; and he would give himself no concern in the matter." [16] If all professional politicians are in business primarily for what they can get out of it, the Tories' job was to keep them reminded that they were only professional politicians and not the voice of the people.

An understanding of the position of the country gentlemen is essential in comprehending the political structure of eighteenth-century Britain. Very roughly, the membership of the House of Commons in the century can be divided into three groups: the career politicians, the leaders of factions, who continually sought power and were rewarded, when successful, with the great and lucrative offices of government and with peerages; the placemen, holders of permanent office of a vaguely civil-service nature, who voted with whatever administration might be in power; and the independents—chiefly the country gentlemen, to whom may be added a few independent merchants such as Sir John Barnard. Before 1714 the country gentlemen counted in their ranks many who considered themselves Whigs. But later, when the Norfolk Whig leaders, Robert Walpole and Charles, Viscount Townshend, attained a position of dominance among the various Whig groups, the more active "country Whigs"—men like Onslow, Cowper, and Sir Peter King—were attracted into their orbit, so that the Whiggish element of the country gentlemen began to be siphoned off into the governmental circle, leaving the remainder as the only true "Tory party" left in existence. Walpole himself was of the squirearchy by origin and taste; his constant anxiety to get away from Westminster to the delights of fox-hunting and drinking with his neighbors in Norfolk was notorious. Townshend too, in spite of his peerage, seems to have been temperamentally of the squirearchy; after he had broken with Walpole in 1730, he retired to Norfolk and contentedly raised turnips for the rest of his life. The fact that Walpole and his allies were so close to the smaller landed gentry may account for the antagonism between them and the sophisticated cosmopolitanism of the aristocratic Whig factions of Sunderland and Stanhope, and later Carteret and Chesterfield.[17] It may also account for the fact that whenever a serious political crisis developed in the 1730's, the Tories supported Walpole rather than his Whig opponents.

It is to the group whose nucleus was the country gentlemen, I believe, that Johnson normally referred when he used the word "Tory," and normally to this group that the word will be applied in this study. It might be guessed, however, that it would be difficult to show a very consistent correspondence between Johnson's political attitudes and those of the Parliamentary Tories. For one thing, Johnson's associations, in the mature part of his life, were chiefly with urban intellectual circles, which the country gentlemen seldom penetrated. For another, it is extremely difficult, and becomes more difficult as the century progresses, to trace any definite coherence in the political actions of the country gentlemen themselves. Some analysis has been done of their votes on crucial issues in the latter part of the century, and the results may startle readers with preconceived ideas about the kind of political behavior implied by the label "Tory." If anything is well established in the minds of modern students, especially American students, it is that the Tories of the eighteenth century were against American independence. Yet on the vote on the repeal of the Stamp Act, in 1766, it has been calculated that 34 Tory members of the Commons voted for repeal and 39 against.[18] On the vote on the legality of general warrants, in 1764, a vote regarded by liberal historians as crucial in the development of civil liberties, 41 Tories voted on one side and 45 on the other. In 1782, on the vote of no confidence that resulted in the resignation of North's administration, 51 county members voted against North and only 7 for him. Most striking of all is the vote on Dunning's famous motion of 1780, "that the influence of the Crown has increased, is increasing, and ought to be diminished." If there were a germ of truth in the nineteenth-century conception of what a Tory is, every Tory in the House should have voted against this resolution. As it turned out, the votes of the county members, the representatives of simon-pure "Old Toryism," were divided 61 for the motion and 9 against.

Were the term Tory used exclusively to designate the independent country gentlemen, the student would not find too much difficulty in understanding the political literature of the century. Where the confusion begins is with the introduction, as the century progresses, of various looser and less legitimate uses of the word. It came to be used around the middle of the century as a term of abuse hurled by one set of Whigs against another set of Whigs. Thus Junius says of Lord Egremont, son of the Tory Sir William Wyndham but long since attracted into the Whig orbit of the Grenvilles, "This man, notwithstanding his pride and Tory principles, has some English stuff in him." [19] Junius would have been hard pressed to define Egremont's Tory principles; but for one Whig to charge another with not being really a Whig is too effective polemics to resist.[20]

Much terminological confusion was caused by the intervention of Bolingbroke, in the 1730's, on the side of the opposition to Walpole. Before 1714, Bolingbroke was certainly entitled to the designation "Tory": he had the support of the country members and was recognized by them as one of their leaders. His career after the accession of George I is well known: he made overtures to the new king, was snubbed, and fearing impeachment, fled the country; attached himself to the Pretender; quarreled with the Pretender; later, by the grace of Walpole, was permitted to return to England, and in the *Craftsman* and other publications forged a new political philosophy that was designed to result in the overthrow of Walpole.

Bolingbroke's efforts were naturally welcomed by the various other elements of the opposition to Walpole—the interlocking opposition Whig groups; the Prince of Wales and his friends; and the "old Tories," headed by Sir William Wyndham, who had been a ministerial colleague of Bolingbroke under Queen Anne. In spite of Wyndham's domination by Bolingbroke, however, it seems wrong to think of Bolingbroke in the 1730's as representing the main Tory tradition.[21] The allegiance to Bolingbroke of the Tory members was insecure, and more than once, on critical occasions, they revolted from him to support Walpole. And Bolingbroke at this time had formally renounced for himself the label of Tory, setting himself up as a "patriot," above mere party. The most enthusiastic propagators of Bolingbroke's political theses were not the Tories but various Whig "patriot" groups, notably those around the Prince of Wales, including such writers as Thomson and Fielding.

As the century drew on, the general public seem to have contagiously picked up the word "Tory" and used it, innocently enough, to designate any opponent of the group which cried "Whig" most loudly—generally the group that considered itself the main stream of Whiggism pure and undefiled, the continuum of career politicians headed successively by Walpole, Henry Pelham and his brother the Duke of Newcastle, Lord Rockingham, and Charles James Fox, whose chief propagandist was Burke. Thus when Mrs. Thrale remarks, "Of Mr. Johnson's Toryism the world has long been witness, and the political pamphlets written by him in defence of his party are vigorous and elegant," [22] it must be remembered that Johnson's four pamphlets of the 1770's are defenses not of a nonexistent Tory "party" but of certain policies of the administrations of the Duke of Grafton and Lord North, both of whom had recently served in ministries with Newcastle and Rockingham and would have been shocked to be called Tories. Johnson himself makes this clear when in one of them, as we have seen, he condemns, by name, the position of the Tories.[23]

Mrs. Thrale was writing in the mid-1780's. By that time the historical meanings of "Tory" as a supporter of the anti-Exclusionist side in the days of Charles II and Shaftesbury, or of the pacifist side in the days of Queen Anne and Marlborough, had been almost forgotten by the public; and even its loose sense of a supporter of Bute or North as against Newcastle and Rockingham was beginning to be superseded in popular usage by its meaning of a supporter of the younger Pitt—an extension, of course, of its earlier meaning of an opponent of the Walpole-Pelham-Rockingham-Fox "connexion." But Pitt, again, was no Tory. All three of the great political figures of the end of the century, Pitt, Fox, and Burke, were, historically, Whigs. Not even the heirs of Pitt's political power—Liverpool, Castlereagh, and Wellington—seem to have readily applied the term "Tory" to themselves.[24] Around the middle of the nineteenth century any independent meaning the word might still have had disappeared with the emergence of the Conservative party, which accepts and even welcomes the nickname "Tory," though it would be difficult to prove it the historical descendant of the Tories of 1714 to 1784.

The student then should distinguish several approximate meanings of "Tory" as actually used after 1714: (1) one whose sympathies and interests were generally those of the country members of the House of Commons; (2) very loosely, a supporter of various groups opposing the Walpole-Pelham-Rockingham Whig succession; hence, after 1760, a supporter of Lord Bute or Lord North; (3) after 1784, a supporter of the younger Pitt and his successors, and so, among other things, an opponent of the French revolution and what it stood for. In considering the use of the word in connection with Johnson, it should be kept in mind that most of Johnson's biographers belonged to a later generation than Johnson's own. When Boswell, Mrs. Thrale, and Murphy use the word, its meaning is shading from (2) into (3); when Johnson himself used it, meaning (1) would be uppermost in his mind. The result, for a reader trying to get a coherent picture of Johnson's political position from Boswell and Mrs. Thrale, is often bafflement. Sir John Hawkins, who belonged to Johnson's own generation and used a similar terminology for political discussion, is much easier to follow.

3. JOHNSON AND TORYISM

It might be thought that the place to go for illumination on what Toryism meant to Johnson would be his own writings and the voluminous reports of his conversation. It comes rather as a surprise to discover that he did not often talk about his Toryism or use the word "Tory" to describe himself. To be sure, Boswell and others often called him, or as much as called him, a Tory in his presence, and his silence may be thought to have given consent; though Johnson's omissions to contradict Boswell, when Boswell is buzzing around him, are sometimes a little wearily ironic—"Sir, you *may* wonder."

Johnson made two major *ex cathedra* pronouncements on the subject of political terminology. In 1781, after being badgered by Boswell, he dictated a statement, which, since he composed it after all for the edification of posterity, deserves to be reprinted at the beginning of any serious account of his political views:

OF TORY AND WHIG

A wise Tory and a wise Whig, I believe, will agree. *Their principles are the same,* though their modes of thinking are different. A high Tory makes government unintelligible: it is lost in the clouds. A violent Whig makes it impracticable: he is for allowing so much liberty to every man, that there is not power enough to govern any man. The prejudice of the Tory is for establishment; the prejudice of the Whig is for innovation. *A Tory does not wish to give more real power to Government;* but that Government should have more reverence. Then they differ as to the Church. *The Tory is not for giving more legal power to the Clergy,* but wishes they should have a considerable influence, *founded on the opinion of mankind;* the Whig is for limiting and watching them with a narrow jealousy.[25]

Boswell prints this without further comment. Very likely it puzzled him: this was not *his* idea of the difference between a Tory and a Whig. And to any reader familiar only with post-Macaulayan conceptions of the terms, it must be puzzling, especially the clauses I have italicized. It will become more comprehensible after we have examined the record of Johnson's political actions and writings. One thing at least is clear: Johnson would have rejected any suggestion that he was a high Tory, who makes government unintelligible.

Johnson's other official definition of "Tory" is that in the *Dictionary:* "One who adheres to the antient constitution of the state, and apostolical hierarchy of the church of England." This Boswell seemed to regard as more significant than the other. In the definition, Boswell tells us, Johnson was "introducing his own opinions, and even prejudices." Later, Boswell recalls our attention to it by expressing his wish that the editorship of the *Biographia Britannica* "had been assigned to 'a friend to the constitution in Church and State.' We should not then have had it too much crowded with obscure dissenting teachers, doubtless men of merit and worth, but not quite to be numbered amongst 'the most eminent persons who have flourished in Great-Britain and Ireland.' " [26] This ill-mannered *obiter dictum* called forth a protest from Kippis, the editor, which afforded Boswell an opportunity for remarking that "the expression . . . from my steady and avowed predilection for a *Tory*, was quoted from 'Johnson's Dictionary,' where that distinction is so defined."

But the practice, in which Boswell was followed by many other Johnsonian students, of taking the definitions in the *Dictionary* as largely representing Johnson's "prejudices" has recently, and rightly, been called into question. It has been shown that in the definitions of "Tory" and "Whig" Johnson was on the whole following current lexicographical tradition, and that the choice of words had no such great personal significance as Boswell thought.[27]

On another occasion Johnson seems to confess that he once had Jacobite sympathies. Boswell reports him as saying at Ashbourne in 1777, "You know, Sir, Lord Gower forsook the old Jacobite interest. When I came to the word Renegado [in the *Dictionary*] . . . I added sometimes we say a Gower." Boswell's original note of the incident, however, reads, "At night he told Dr. Taylor and me that he had put Lord Gower into his Dictionary under the word *Renegade* (alluding to his having deserted the old Jacobite interest I [i.e. Boswell] doubt not)." [28] The political maneuverings of the Leveson Gower family form a complicated chapter in the power politics of the

1740's, with which Jacobitism had little or nothing to do; Boswell knew very little of the intricacies of Midlands politics in the time of George II.

It is apparent that something, at least, of most readers' impressions of Johnson's "blind" Tory partisanship is due to the artistry of Boswell. As one reads, for instance, the passage about the *Biographia Britannica,* one unconsciously assimilates to one's picture of Johnson the churlish expression of dislike for Dissent and the irrational exaltation of the word "Tory" without noticing as clearly as one ought that all this is pure Boswell, and has nothing whatever to do with Johnson. How Boswell amended the anecdote about Lord Gower we have seen. It was Boswell who fixed on Johnson as a youth the memorable epithet of "the infant Hercules of Toryism"; it is Boswell who continually nudges us with such remarks as that Johnson, in the *Life of Waller,* "satisfies his readers how nobly he might have executed a *Tory History* of his country"; that Johnson's dedication of Zachary Pearce's *Commentary* "will tend to propagate and increase that 'fervour of *Loyalty*,' which in me, who boast of the name of TORY, is not only a principle, but a passion"; that "I ventured to say to him, in allusion to the political principles in which he was educated, and of which he ever retained some odour, that 'his mother had not carried him far enough [when she took him to London to be touched by Queen Anne]; she should have taken him to ROME.' " [29]

It is not our concern here to define the nature of Boswell's own Toryism, but it seems to have been quite a different thing from Johnson's. For one thing, Boswell was a Scot.[30] For another, the whole climate of political discussion underwent a change in the half century between the formative years of Johnson's political attitudes and those in which Boswell wrote the *Life.* In the interim people had learned to feel and to introspect; Steele and Rousseau, the sentimental novelists and the sentimental dramatists, had done their work; the romantic age had begun. Jacobitism was no longer the matter of cold steel and hard bullets it had been in 1715 and 1745; it was approaching the stage in which George IV could drape his portly form in the Royal Stuart tartan and Victoria and Albert upholster Balmoral with it. Monarchy was ceasing to be merely one of a number of alternative practical forms of government and becoming a potent symbol, inspired by which one might, like Sir Walter Scott, piously purloin a wine glass touched by the lips of George IV, or, as in France, with equal piety, guillotine the royal family. The polite and dignified language of Johnson's dedications to George III forms an instructive contrast to Boswell's accesses of fatuous enthusiasm when he addresses his sovereign.

Besides this, the temperamental differences between Boswell and Johnson are so great as to make it difficult a priori to put their fundamental political attitudes, which are so much a matter of temperament, into the same category. Boswell was a hero worshiper; no one more alien to the spirit of hero worshiping than Johnson ever lived. Johnson was basically a skeptic; belief in anything came hard to him. Boswell loved nothing more than to lose himself in an *O altitudo!* It is to be feared that one element of Boswell's Toryism was a certain amount of snobbery: Whiggism represented to him the unpolished backwoods Presbyterianism that he spent so much of his life trying to avoid—the "Scotch drink, Scotch manners, Scotch religion" of which Matthew Arnold complained. It represented "obscure dissenting teachers, doubtless men of merit and worth, but not quite . . ." There was not a particle of snobbery in Johnson's constitution.

Yet the two men had in common one important quality, which is hard to describe except by some such unsatisfactory term as warmth of heart or emotional sensitivity. It manifested itself in a dislike of "poverty of sentiment" (Mrs.

Thrale's phrase), or the application of cold calculation to human relationships.[31] To this phenomenon Johnson gave— with how much historical justification this study will certainly not presume to determine—the name of "Whiggism." No doubt the one thing that most persuades the casual reader of Johnson's "blind Toryism" is his continual raillery against "Whigs"—"Sir, I perceive you are a vile Whig"; "Sir, the first Whig was the devil"; "The dog is a Whig. I do not like much to see a Whig in any dress; but I hate to see a Whig in a parson's gown," and so on. It is clear that in such outbursts Johnson is relieving his feelings, not against a political party or a set of principles or even "negation of all principle," but against sophisters, economists, and calculators, against essential coldness of feeling masked by a specious appeal to "rational humanitarianism." Sir Andrew Freeport in the *Spectator*, Johnson said, was "a true Whig, arguing against giving charity to beggars, and throwing out other such ungracious sentiments." [32] The opposite of a Whig, in this sense, is a Jacobite, and so we have the amusing scene of Johnson's taking Mr. Langton's young niece by the hand and saying earnestly, "My dear, I hope you are a Jacobite." [33] Boswell records that old Mr. Langton did not see the joke, and it is to be feared that some modern readers still do not see it. But Johnson could, and often did, make fun of himself. He could joke about matters that he took very seriously, and joke about the seriousness with which he took them, and in the midst of joking know that they remained as serious as ever. There is in Johnson (it needs, unfortunately, still to be pointed out) a great deal of the habit of complex irony that one associates with the most sensitive minds.[34]

How seriously Johnson took the label of Tory that his biographers so readily pinned on him is hard to say. Possibly he did not take it very seriously at all. Johnson was not a professional politician nor a hanger-on of politicians. He was a thinker and writer, who fiercely treasured the independence of his pen. There is really no particular reason to believe that he thought of himself as permanently committed to a specific "party line," any more than there is to believe the same of such modern political commentators as Bertrand Russell and George Orwell. It is true that in the writings of these men one may discern a vague general preference for some political philosophy or other, "socialism" or "liberalism" or "conservatism" or whatever it may be. But no one believes that such labelings guarantee the slightest commitment to current party dogma: no more devastating criticism of orthodox socialism was ever produced than Orwell's. Such commentators consider themselves, rightly, "superior to party." It is their job to subject the actions and words of vulgar politicians to philosophical analysis, to scrutinize them in the light of their own knowledge of the world, to expound their consequences and implications.

If this is so in the twentieth century when (thanks largely to Burke) party has become comparatively respectable, it is even harder to believe that Johnson thought of himself as a partisan in the eighteenth, when the depreciation of partisanship was a commonplace; Johnson himself amusingly lampooned the "party-liner" in the *Idler*.[35] When one adds to this tradition the fact that throughout Johnson's lifetime the words "Tory" and "Whig" had become almost devoid of meaning as designations of active political principles, it would appear that modern students generally have tended to think that Johnson used the terms far more seriously and specifically than he actually did. No doubt it was just such literal-minded souls whom it delighted Johnson to confuse with ejaculations like "Where you see a Whig, you see a rascal."

It should be manifest—if for no other reason than that many, perhaps the majority, of Johnson's closest associates and dearest friends were professed Whigs—that in such statements

he is using the word "Whig" anagogically, not literally. There
may also have been at least something of the same spirit of
metaphor in his ready acceptance of the label "Tory." Clearly
he had little in common with the squirearchy who constituted
the nucleus of the only real Tory party of his time. He was a
propertyless intellectual, an artist, a Bohemian; and among
the intellectuals of higher social pretensions with whom he
sometimes associated, the prevailing political atmosphere was
Whig. Why then did he rebel against the political stereotype
of these circles and choose, so far as there was deliberate
choice, the unfashionable appellation of Tory? There may
have been a small residue of boyish partisanship left over
from the Lichfield elections of his youth, in which, as boys
will, he may have vigorously supported the Tory side simply
because it was his father's (though the evidence for this hy-
pothesis, we shall see, is most questionable). But of far more
importance, no doubt, was the simple fact that the label of
Tory *was* unfashionable in intellectual circles, and that Johnson was always a rebel against the tyranny of intellectual
fashion. Insofar as there was a Tory "line" in the political
contests of the century, it was that of rebellion, of protest, of
independence, of refusal to be bound by dogma or by allegiance to the interest of a group of professional politicians. If
it was impossible to avoid having either one of the two current
political labels attached to him, one can see why Johnson, the
independent commentator on men and manners, should have
preferred that of Tory.

   At any rate, in light of the untenability of the old notions
about eighteenth-century British politics, a reassessment of
Johnson's political involvements is overdue. The thesis of
this book is, roughly, that though Johnson may continue to
have a claim to be called a Tory, we are not justified in infer-
ring from that label what nineteenth-century writers inferred
from it: dogmatism, reaction, subservience to authority.

Indeed, so little serious work has been done, so far, in analyzing what, ideologically, eighteenth-century Toryism meant that an examination of Johnson's political attitudes is more likely to contribute something to a definition of eighteenth-century Toryism.

It is not true, as some writers have maintained, that politics played a relatively insignificant part in Johnson's life, thought, and writings, or that he was a mere inept dabbler in the surface of politics, to be dismissed with a patronizing smile. As I shall try to show, there were few long periods in his mature life when he was not intimately involved in either practical or theoretical politics. If one wants to extend the meaning of the word to its legitimate limits, there is a sense in which Johnson is one of the most political of major writers. "No book is genuinely free from political bias," said George Orwell, whose approach to politics, to his calling as a writer, and to life in general is often strikingly similar to Johnson's. Orwell defines political purpose in writing as "desire to push the world in a certain direction, to alter other people's ideas of the kind of society they should strive for. . . . My starting point is always a feeling of partisanship, a sense of injustice. . . . I write . . . because there is some lie that I want to expose, some fact to which I want to draw attention." [36] Johnson would have sympathized with these formulations, which describe so much of his writing, works like the *Rambler* and *Rasselas* as well as his more narrowly political pieces.

Chapter Two

THE MIDLANDS BACKGROUND

1. THE LEGACY OF THE CIVIL WAR

I T is sometimes forgotten that Johnson was not always the Great Londoner. He did not become a Londoner at all until he was nearly thirty. He was also a great Midlander; his childhood, adolescence, and young manhood were spent in Lichfield or near by; and some attention should be given to the possible effect on his political and social thinking of the milieu in which he spent these important years.

What first strikes the visitor to Lichfield is the sight of the three graceful, reddish-sandstone spires of the Cathedral Church of St. Mary and St. Chad, which dominated the small city and the gentle Midlands landscape around it in Johnson's day as they do now—a sight that could hardly fail to leave some lasting impression on the mind of an imaginative boy growing up in their shadow. In the conventional picture of Johnson the orthodox neoclassicist there is little place for such an emotion as a feeling for the old Gothic cathedrals and what they stood for. Yet the evidence is clear. When Johnson, at the age of sixty-four, toured Scotland and was confronted with what was left of the Cathedral of St. Andrews, Boswell tells us, "he was affected with a strong indignation, while he beheld the ruins of religious magnificence. I happened to ask where John Knox was buried. Dr. Johnson burst out, 'I hope in the highway. I have been looking at his reformations.' . . . Dr. Johnson seemed quite wrapt up in the contemplation of the scenes which were now presented to him. He kept his hat off while he was upon any part of the ground where the cathedral had stood." ¹ A little later, after seeing the ruins of the cathedrals of Elgin and Aberdeen, whose leaden roofs had been stripped and sold during the Reformation, Johnson wrote, "Let us not, however, make too much haste to despise our neighbours. There is now, as I have heard, a body of men, not less decent or virtuous than the Scottish council, longing to melt the lead of an English cathedral. What they shall melt, it were just that they should swallow." ² The English cathedral was Lichfield; the body of men not less decent than the Scottish council, its dean and chapter. Johnson later repented of his ferocity: remembering that old Dean Addenbrooke had been kind to him long ago, he substituted for the passages these lines, more decorous but no less powerful: "Our own cathedrals are mouldering by unregarded dilapidation. It seems to be part of the despicable philosophy of the time to despise monuments of sacred magnificence." Thomas Warton recalled that in 1754 he and Johnson "viewed the ruins of the abbies of Oseney and Rewley, near Oxford. After at least half an hour's silence, Johnson said, 'I viewed them with indignation!' We had then a long conversation on Gothick buildings; and in talking of the form of old halls, he said, 'In these halls, the fire place was anciently always in the middle of the room, till the Whigs removed it on one side.' " ³

Of the incident at St. Andrews, Boswell, casting Johnson in the familiar role of "staunch High Churchman," explains, "Dr. Johnson's veneration for the hierarchy is well known. There is no wonder, then, that he was affected." The explanation seems inadequate; one feels reasonably certain that Johnson, contemplating the "monuments of sacred magnificence," did not keep his hat off merely out of shocked respect to a group of corporeal bishops. Johnson's own account of still another and greater ruined shrine, Iona, sheds greater light on his psychology: 'We were now treading that illustrious

island . . . whence savage clans and roving barbarians derived the benefits of knowledge, and the blessings of religion.
. . . Whatever withdraws us from the power of the senses;
whatever makes the past, the distant, or the future predomi-
nate over the present, advances us in the dignity of thinking
beings." [4] Perhaps he was also thinking of Lichfield Cathedral,
whose history stretched far back into ages more dark and dimly
apprehended in Johnson's time than they are now, to the time
when the pagan Offa ruled over the tribes of Mercia and when
Lichfield, under the half-legendary Chad, was a small island
of civilization in a vast sea of what to Johnson was mere bar-
barism and cruelty.

If to Johnson's poetic mind the old Cathedral of Lichfield
was venerable as a symbol of the hard-won victory of light over
darkness, of the continuity of the present with a vaguely apprehended past, to the ordinary citizen of the town in the
eighteenth century it was of more concrete significance. It was
the nucleus of the ecclesiastical, social, and cultural life of a
large area in the heart of the Midlands, so that young Sam
Johnson was able to come into contact with a more polished
and intellectual group of people than he might had he grown
up in some other English communities of the same size. It was
important to the economic life of the town, enabling Michael
Johnson to carry on his trade of bookselling there, and even
to combine with it a small amount of ecclesiastical publishing.
Most important of all, its presence conveyed to the citizens of
Lichfield a great amount of direct historical and political sym-
bolism.

For it was a permanent reminder of the Civil War, that
great dichotomy of the English people, of which it has been
said, not too paradoxically, that it has not even yet ended.[5] In
1642, the Cathedral and the Close, fortified by Royalist troops,
were attacked by the Parliamentarian forces under Robert
Greville, Lord Brooke. Much damage was done by a piece of

artillery trained on the Cathedral, and the great central spire was eventually destroyed. At the height of the siege (significantly, the devout remarked, on March 2, the day of St. Chad, founder and patron of the Cathedral) a bullet aimed from a spire by one "Dumb Dyott" struck and killed Lord Brooke as he directed operations. But his successor continued the assault, and at last the garrison capitulated.

Now occupied by the Parliamentarians, the Cathedral suffered at the hands of those who, like John Knox, regarded "sacred magnificence" as idolatrous. "The army exercised the like barbarisms as were done at Worcester," a contemporary indignantly reports, "in demolishing all the monuments, pulling down the curious carved work," stabling their horses in the building, hunting a cat with hounds in the nave, and so on. Later, as the war surged back and forth across the Midlands, the Cathedral suffered other sieges and further destruction. At the time of the Restoration of Charles II in 1660, it was a battered ruin. During the next twenty years it was repaired, through the vigorous activity of Bishop Hackett; as a young man, Michael Johnson, Samuel's father, would have vividly remembered the process of reconstruction. But the marks of the Civil War are visible on the Cathedral even today.

Not only on the fabric of the Cathedral, but on the loyal families of Lichfield and the surrounding neighborhood did the blows of civil strife fall. The lists of "sequestrations compounded" for cash with the Parliamentarian governing committee at Stafford include such names as those of Sir Richard Leveson of Trentham (£6,000), Walter Wrottesley (£1,332), Lord Paget of Beaudesert (£500), Sir Harvey Bagot (£1,004). Something of the atmosphere of the time can be gathered from a few of the hundreds of such entries in the minutes of the committee as the following:

Mrs. Sneyd, wife of Ralph Sneyd esq. of Keel, to pay to the Committee at Stafford four hundred pounds

That Keel house be forthwith demolished by Capt. Barbor's souldiers and that Mr. Fitzherbert's house of Swinnerton be forthwith demolished by Captaine Stone's souldiers.

Ordered, that Mr. Berry, Parson of Morby, for preaching malicious doctrine against the Parliament, calling them usurpers, be committed to prison.

That no Papist be permitted to come within four miles of Stafford.

Ordered, that the gunner which did commit fornication shall be set upon the great gun, his back scourged by the garrison, and then disgracefully expulsed.

That whosoever [in the army] shall sweare, for the first offence shall forfeit 4d.; for the second offence to ride the horse, with a paper on his backe declaring his offence; and, for the third, to be bored through the tongue and casheard.[6]

The years of the Great Rebellion were not quickly forgotten in Staffordshire. No other part of England suffered longer or more intensely the violence of the contending armies and the regime of repression that followed. The names of the Staffordshire Royalist families who suffered in battle and through sequestration occur again and again in the political history of the shire in the eighteenth century: Wrottesleys, Dyotts, Pagets, Bagots, Sneyds all sat in Parliament for Staffordshire seats—invariably, for several decades after the Restoration at least, on the Tory side among those intransigent "Midland Tories" of whom it has been said that by comparison with Tories from other parts of England they were "genuine reactionaries, heirs to the Counter-Reformation, to the authoritarian High Church, and the Jacobites." [7] Reading the history of Staffordshire in the 1640's, one can understand why this should be so. To grow up in Lichfield in the early years of the eighteenth century, as Johnson did, would be a little like growing up, to use an American analogy, in Atlanta during the later decades of the nineteenth century.

Certainly it would have been a much less alert and curious youth than Samuel Johnson whose political sensibilities would not have been awakened and stimulated by such a heritage of memory and tradition.

At the bottom of Johnson's political thinking, then, there would always have been a vivid awareness of the events of 1640 to 1660. Yet the problem must not be oversimplified. It would be temptingly easy to think of Johnson as being reared in a tight little island of exclusively Tory sentiment, looking back nostalgically to the good old days before Cromwell and his hordes disturbed the "old constitution" of England. But this is not so. Not all the inhabitants of the Midlands were Royalist nor all the citizens of Lichfield Tories. A vigorous Puritan and Parliamentarian tradition flourished at Lichfield from pre-Civil War times well into the eighteenth century. Even before the outbreak of fighting, the Cathedral had been the symbol, to one group of people, of a spiritual regime that they abhorred. In January 1638 "Lady Eleanor Davies, Maria, wife of Michael Noble, town clerk of Lichfield, and Susan Walker, wife to John Walker, clerk, brawled in the Cathedral, and with 'water, tar, and other filthy things, most profanely defiled the hangings at the altar of the Cathedral . . .' and on being remonstrated with by Lady Weston, wife of Sir Simon Weston, replied that 'they had but done their conscience.' " [8] On the morning when Lord Brooke met his death at the hands of "Dumb Dyott," he had set out from the house of one Michael Biddulph, which he had made his headquarters at Lichfield and where he was brought back to die. For several decades in the late seventeenth century, the Biddulphs, as leaders of the Lichfield Whigs, shared the representation of the borough in Parliament with the Dyotts, who led the Tories. On many of the punitive decrees of the Staffordshire Parliamentary governing committee appears the signature of John Swynfen, "the great Parliament man," member for the borough of Stafford in the Long Parliament. Nor did his activities cease with the Restoration: he continued to sit as member for Tamworth for many years, and was one of the framers of the Exclusion bill in 1678. His grandson Richard Swynfen also sat for Tamworth as a Whig. The strong Whig tradition of the Swynfens did not prevent Michael Johnson from taking Samuel Swynfen, Richard's brother and his successor as head of the family, into his house as a lodger, or asking him to be godfather to his elder son: it is not ironic but significant that "the great Tory" Samuel Johnson was named after the grandson and heir of a persecutor of Royalists. Nor did it prevent Samuel Johnson from providing a home, for many years, for Samuel Swynfen's daughter, Elizabeth Desmoulins. The Walmesleys we shall presently meet; and other Staffordshire Whig families could be mentioned, some of them connected with Johnson, who by no means let the political representation of the county go to the Tories by default. When Boswell quipped that Mr. Eld was "a *Staffordshire Whig*, a being which I did not believe had existed," Johnson knew better.[9]

It may be useful at this point to collect what we can of Johnson's ideas about the Civil War and its aftermath. Significantly, his concern seems to center not, as would presumably have been the case with the stereotype of a "blind Tory," on the indignity to King Charles the Martyr and Archbishop Laud,[10] about whom Johnson has little to say, but rather on the Parliamentarian-Puritan regime that followed them. His fullest statement on that regime is to be found among his remarks on *Hudibras:*

Much . . . of the humour which transported the last century with merriment is lost to us, who do not know the sour solemnity, the sullen superstition, the gloomy moroseness, and the stubborn scruples of the ancient Puritans; or, if we know them, derive our information only from books or from tradition. . . .

Our grandfathers knew the picture from life; we judge of the life by contemplating the picture.

Johnson's fairness in emphasizing that his generation's idea of the days of the Puritan ascendancy is only from hearsay is worth noting. With this caveat, he continues,

It is scarcely possible, in the regularity and composure of the present time, to image the tumult of absurdity and clamour of contradiction which perplexed doctrine, disordered practice, and disturbed both publick and private quiet in that age, when subordination was broken and awe was hissed away; when any unsettled innovator who could hatch a half-formed notion produced it to the publick; when every man might become a preacher, and almost every preacher could collect a congregation.[11]

"In the regularity and composure of the present time": the *Life of Butler* was published in the spring of 1779 and composed not long before. The war with the American colonies was reaching its climax; France had just declared war on Britain, and Spain was soon to follow; an invasion was seriously expected.[12] And yet to Johnson it seemed a time of "regularity and composure" by comparison with the memory of the 1640's and 50's. It is perhaps easier for us than for our Victorian ancestors to understand Johnson's horror of the revolutionary state, where the only alternative to anarchy is dictatorship. In Johnson's eyes, the days of Cromwell appeared not, as some writers in the comparative calm of the nineteenth century seemed to regard them, a prelude to Victorian liberal democracy, but rather an adumbration of something not far removed from Orwell's *1984*. Johnson records, in his account of *Hudibras*, an incident that seems to come straight out of that novel: "In one of the parliaments summoned by Cromwell it was seriously proposed that all the records in the Tower should be burnt, that all memory of things past should be effaced, and that the whole system of life should commence anew." It is the premium placed by totalitarian regimes on falsification and suppression of fact, the subjection of the rational intelligence to canting propaganda, that disturbs Johnson as it does Orwell—a milder form of nonsense, in Puritan England than in Orwell's Oceania, but tending in the same direction: "We [in 1779] have never been witnesses of animosities excited by the use of minced pies and plumb porridge, nor seen with what abhorrence those who could eat them at all other times of the year would shrink from them in December." Johnson tells the story of "an old Puritan, who was alive in my childhood," who would allow a neighbor to "treat him at an alehouse with beer, brewed for all times and seasons," but "would have none of his superstitious meats and drinks" when offered on a Church festival.[13]

The errors and dangers of Puritanism are the result of the Puritan or "Whig" temperament, the temperament of opposition, which Johnson feels is the product of a cold-hearted, envious egocentricity, a diseased psychology. This is how he diagnoses Milton: he notes "the want of human interest" in *Paradise Lost,* and says of *Lycidas,* "He who thus grieves will excite no sympathy . . . it is not to be considered as the effusion of real passion." Johnson asserts that the only rational objection Milton offers to monarchy is its expensiveness, and comments, "It is surely very shallow policy that supposes money to be the chief good." "Milton's republicanism," he says, in a well-known passage, "was, I am afraid, founded in an envious hatred of greatness, and a sullen desire of independence; in petulance impatient of controul, and pride disdainful of superiority. . . . He felt not so much the love of liberty as repugnance to authority." "It has been observed," Johnson continues, quoting his own earlier dictum on the slave-owning Americans, "that they who most loudly clamour for liberty do not most liberally grant it." [14]

Another striking description by Johnson of the Puritan temperament is his *Life of Cheynel* (1751), the Parliamentary "reformer" of Oxford University. The portrait is informed with a cold contempt of the man, relieved by flashes of dry and deadly irony:

No one that reads his works can doubt that he was turbulent, obstinate, and petulant. . . . Whatever he believed (and the warmth of his imagination naturally made him precipitate in forming his opinions) he thought himself obliged to profess; and what he professed he was ready to defend. . . . A temper of this kind is generally inconvenient and offensive in any society, but in a place of education is least to be tolerated; for, as authority is necessary to instruction, whoever endeavours to destroy subordination . . . defeats at once the institution; and may be justly driven from a society, by which he thinks himself too wise to be governed, and in which he is too young to teach, and too opinionative to learn.[15]

Not that Johnson's own career at Oxford was always marked by "modesty of temper"; and one wonders whether Johnson's recommendations of the spirit of subordination were not sometimes the product of an uneasy feeling that he himself might have used more of it.

Johnson's account of Puritanism was much denounced during his lifetime, especially by Miltonolaters like Thomas Hollis and Joseph Towers, who were shocked when Johnson declined to participate in the current adulation of their hero. Yet Johnson's attitude toward the Puritans cannot be justly described as wholly blind partisanship. It may be possible to rebut his case against the Puritans by citing other historical evidence that he ignores; but he is obviously trying to give a fair and thoughtful interpretation of the historical evidence that he is aware of. He concedes, we have noticed, that when he discusses Puritanism he is not necessarily dealing with historical reality, but with a traditional and hence fallible picture. He gives a highly rational account of his objection to what he believes to be the dangerous implications of the events of the 1640's, best summed up perhaps in one sentence from the *Life of Milton,* "Nothing can be more just than that rebellion should end in slavery." Discussing the *Areopagitica,* he advances against government licensing of printing an argument perhaps more powerful and subtle than any even Milton uses: "If nothing may be published but what civil authority shall have previously approved, *power must always be the standard of truth.*" [16] He does "justice to the humanity of Cheynel," in his treatment of Chillingworth, who had been committed to Cheynel's custody, and applauds Cheynel's constancy at the end of his life, when he "gave proof that he could suffer as well as act in a cause which he believed just." [17]

It is rather what Johnson does not say about the Puritans than what he does that may be found surprising. In the *Life of Cheynel,* there are no outbursts of indignation at the subversion of the old order at Oxford. In the *Life of Blake* (1740), he praises the great Parliamentarian admiral, rejoices in the glory that Blake added to English arms, and does not once animadvert against the government that gave him his orders. Indeed, the one indignant passage in the *Life* is directed against the Royalists of the Restoration who exhumed and desecrated Blake's corpse: "Had he been guilty of the murder of Charles I, to insult his body [as the bodies of Cromwell and the other regicides were insulted] had been a mean revenge." [18] Tracing the ambiguous political career of Waller, although Johnson directs numerous barbed remarks against the Parliamentarians, he can also comment, "Political truth is equally in danger from the praises of courtiers and the exclamations of patriots," and his severest condemnation of Waller is not for his cooperation with Cromwell and his party, but for his joining in the persecution of Clarendon after the Restoration. [19]

To repeat, Johnson's attitude toward the Puritans, whether mistaken or not, rests not on blind prejudice but on a highly rational foundation. To be sure, the memories of the Civil

War might awaken in someone with Johnson's strong imagination a good deal of conservative feeling—an indignation at wanton destruction by narrow-minded doctrinaires of memorials of the continuity of the human intellect, a healthy fear of the cruelty, anarchy, and eventually despotism entailed by violent subversion of the civil order. Yet these things never become to Johnson as they do to, say, Thomas Hearne and Thomas Carte, Shebbeare and Smollett (to whose writings one may turn for examples of genuine Tory prejudice) matters calling for direct personal resentment. The Civil War and the Puritan regime were after all things of the past, and Johnson, as he freely admits, had no direct contact with them. They remain for him abstractions, illustrations of what he believes to be an element in human nature that, if not corrected, can be ultimately destructive of the basis of civilized society—but historical, not contemporary, illustrations.

And it is even possible to trace at times a certain sympathy in Johnson for aspects of the Puritan movement, culminating in his admiration for Cromwell's ability as exceeding that of "our lawful kings." He once planned to write Cromwell's life, "saying that he thought it must be highly curious to trace his extraordinary rise to the supreme power, from so obscure a beginning." [20] Johnson believed whole-heartedly in *la carrière ouverte aux talents* ("Slow rises worth by poverty depressed"), and if such a belief is anticonservative, then to that extent Johnson is anticonservative. There is a rational case to be made for tradition and stability, Johnson also firmly believes—"All change is of itself an evil, which ought not to be hazarded but for evident advantage" [21]—and he finds much in the history of the Civil War to document that case. But where there *is* evident advantage, as in the genius of a Cromwell as against the stultification of a monarchical education, Johnson is ready to accept change; when a tradition ceases to be rational, he is willing to abandon it. Johnson's rationalism, that is to say, is prior to his traditionalism; and if a recognition of the priority of rationality is to be taken (as some insist) as the distinguishing mark of the liberal or radical political temperament, then Johnson must be classed as such a liberal or radical.

2. THE POLITICS OF STAFFORDSHIRE

As might be expected with such a history, Lichfield in the early eighteenth-century was very much a politically minded town. It is not, like some other cathedral cities, the political capital of the county in which it is situated: the county town of Staffordshire is Stafford, and there, at least once every three years between 1694 and 1716 and every seven years thereafter, were held the elections for the two knights of the shire, who represented the county as a whole in the House of Commons. These were invariably members of the old landed families, Bagots, Pagets, Leveson Gowers, and until the middle of the eighteenth century regularly counted as Tories. Only once in the century was there enough opposition at a Staffordshire county election for it to go to a poll—the famous election of 1747.

But though Lichfield missed the excitement of the county elections, it could provide a good deal of its own. Of the four parliamentary boroughs in Staffordshire (the others were Stafford, Newcastle-under-Lyme, and Tamworth) its electorate was one of the largest and most subject to influence. Those eligible to vote, under a resolution of the House of Commons in 1718, were the "bailiffs, freeholders of forty shillings per annum, and all that hold by burgage tenure, and such freemen only of the said city as are enrolled, paying scot and lot [i.e. local taxes] there." [22] In 1831, the last year before the Reform Act, the total electorate was 861, of whom 420 were freemen.[23] The freemen, the permanent residents of Lichfield, may be said to represent the genuine popular vote of the city. But the franchise of forty-shilling freeholders and "burgage tenants" lent itself easily to manipulation by a politician rich enough to buy up the property involved, split it into parcels large enough to qualify the owner to vote, and distribute the titles among dependents and friends, thus creating "faggot votes" as they were called.[24]

Before 1747 no concerted effort to control the Lichfield elections by this means seems to have been made, and because of the relatively large size of the city's electorate, its elections may be reasonably regarded as representing the "voice of the people." The returns of members from Lichfield from the Restoration down to 1747 do not reveal, as might have perhaps been thought, a preponderance of Toryism. On the contrary, they mirror fairly accurately the general political tendency of the whole country at the time of the election. From 1661 to 1681 Lichfield impartially returned, without a poll (that is, by prior agreement between the parties), one Whig and one Tory member. To the short-lived "Exclusion Parliament" of 1681 it contributed two Whig members; to the loyal first Parliament of James II, two Tories; to the Convention Parliament of 1689, and to the Parliaments of 1698, 1701, and 1702, one Whig and one Tory. During the heyday of Toryism in Queen Anne's reign, Lichfield was loyally Tory, and to each of the Parliaments of 1705, 1710, and 1713 returned two Tories; to that of 1708, when the Whigs were in precarious ascendancy at Westminster, one Whig and one Tory. With equal loyalty, for the first twenty-one years of Hanoverian rule Lichfield returned two members who were counted as Whigs in each of the elections of 1715, 1722, and 1727. With the growing reaction against Walpole, it returned two Tories in 1734 and 1741.[25]

As was generally the case in a reasonably "open" borough in the eighteenth century—Westminster and Bristol were more notable examples—election contests in Lichfield were accompanied by much turbulence, especially when they coincided with other political events on a larger scale, such as threatened Jacobite invasions. In the summer of 1715, Staffordshire was the scene of concerted destruction of Dissenting meeting houses, those at Lichfield, Leek, Uttoxeter, Newcastle, and Stafford falling victim. "The Lichfield Tory mob of 1718 wore white roses in their hats and barbarously abused their enemies." [26] But the most notorious of all Lichfield elections was that of 1747, which achieved more than local fame. A writer in the *Gentleman's Magazine*, making a facetious survey of the election excitement throughout the country, tells of visiting friends engaged in political calculations; one, he says, he found "perusing a list of killed and wounded; in the battle of Val I imagined, but it was at the Litchfield election." [27] At the Lichfield race-meeting in June an enraged Tory horsewhipped the great Whig Duke of Bedford. On September 26, Thomas Hinton, Lord Anson's political agent, reports on Tory activity before the election:

On Wednesday morning the Party began to draw together, and in the afternoon about 150 of the Burton Mobb, most of 'em in Plaid Waistcoats, Plaid Ribbons about their Hatts, and some with White Cocades enter'd the Town in a body headed by Sr Thomas Griesly, Sr Charles Sidley, a Steward of Lord Uxbridge's [head of the Paget family], and an infamous fellow that struck the Duke of Bedford, one Joul, a Dancing Master.

About the same time came in another party of Birmingham people, most of 'em in the same dress, with Sr Lyster [Holt] and some of the Warwickshire gentlemen. Sr Walter Bagott came in alone. As we had been severely threaten'd, we had reason to apprehend a great deal of mischief from such a Meeting; but having no opposition, they behaved in general peaceably, and did no other damage than breaking the arm of a poor soldier, an Out Pensioner, for crying out "God Bless his Majesty King George. Damn yr Plaids." Many of this Mobb drank the Pretender's Health publickly in the streets, singing treasonable songs, but being brought to the town with a notion of free quarters and

finding themselves deceived, went off again in the evening curs-
ing their Hunt and the Authors of it.[28]

It can be seen that mob violence in Midland politics, as well
as elsewhere in England, was by no means always spontaneous;
it was used by political leaders to further their own designs
and must not be taken naively to represent the inarticulate
political aspirations of the unenfranchised. One of the mob
who pulled down the Dissenting meeting house at Newcastle-under-Lyme in 1715 among shouts of "God damn
King George!" is reported to have said, "We will pull down
the Church too, for the same pay we have for that." The Newcastle incident was instigated by William Sneyd of Keele, Tory
candidate in the Lichfield by-election of 1718; the Staffordshire grand jury brought in a true bill against him and forty
others.[29] It was easy enough, at a time when the illiterate had
fewer sources of "harmless pleasure" than today, to gather together a "Mobb" with a promise of "free quarters" and beer
and some head-smashing. The mobs of Staffordshire were
smaller facsimiles of the mobs of Middlesex, of which Johnson
wrote with such scorn in *The False Alarm*. Against the background of mob violence of the eighteenth century, culminating in the Lord George Gordon riots of 1780, Johnson's
insistence on order as one of the prime requisites of successful
government becomes more easily understandable.

Until the year 1747, it is reasonably accurate to discuss
Staffordshire politics in terms of Whig and Tory, using the
words loosely to describe the heirs of the two sides in the great
conflict of the 1640's—Dyotts, Sneyds, Bagots on the one side,
Biddulphs, Swynfens, Offleys on the other. Any real difference
in political principle had long since disappeared—how little
the plaids and white cockades of the 1747 mob meant, Prince
Charles Edward had bitterly discovered for himself two years
earlier.[30] Its disappearance can be dated as far back as the
compromise of 1689. And by now, the middle of the eight-

eenth century, even the ties of traditional groupings had become tenuous. What happened in Staffordshire in 1747 was typical and illustrative of what was happening elsewhere in England: a shrewd and ambitious political connection, foreseeing no future for itself in the traditional and outmoded frame of political reference, simply broke through it, making use of the hoary political maxim, "If you can't beat them, join them." Johnson's remark that he had wished to insert in the *Dictionary* as a synonym for *renegade* the gloss "as they say, a Gower" has been treated as merely another example of his extravagant and whimsical Tory partisanship, and some wonder has been expressed at his ingratitude, considering that Lord Gower, in 1739, had written (if in a somewhat defeatist tone) to try to secure a Dublin degree for Johnson. But in fact, the Gower affair is an illuminating study in eighteenth-century power politics, and Johnson, as a Staffordshire man, had every reason to take it seriously.

The career of the Leveson Gower family, between 1660 and 1800, is an interesting case-history in the development of political "bossism." Sir William Leveson Gower, Bart., the descendant of Royalist country squires, sat as MP for Newcastle-under-Lyme in the 1680's. His Toryism was not so inflexible as to prevent him from supporting the Exclusion bill in the election of 1679.[31] The Toryism of his son John was made of sterner stuff; and since Sir John's chief political activity took place in a time when stern Toryism was in the ascendant, he was promoted to the peerage, as Baron Gower, in 1703. His son and successor, John, the second Baron, continued his father's profitable Tory line. By 1727 two of his brothers sat in the Commons—not only for Newcastle, long in the pockets of the Gowers, but for one of the county seats as well. Lord Gower himself was one of the acknowledged Tory leaders in the House of Lords, and of course the great Tory magnate of the shire.

But by 1742 Lord Gower was becoming weary of his sterile eminence. It suited many county magnates to remain nothing more, maintaining their local ascendancy, controlling an "independent" vote or two in Parliament for the sake of prestige, but not much interested in politics on the national scale at all. The Gowers, however, had aspirations beyond mere provincial power. By judicious matrimonial alliances with the great political families of the Granvilles and Russells, they had long been qualifying themselves for a place in the national arena. The favorable moment arrived in 1742, when Walpole fell from power and the scene at Westminster dissolved into a bewildering flux of power-seeking politicians. After the dust of battle had died down and a clear picture could again be discerned, the Midland Tories were astounded to behold Lord Gower in the camp of his son-in-law, the Whig Duke of Bedford, with the Privy Seal and the Lord Lieutenancy of Staffordshire in his pocket and presently an Earl's coronet on his head.[32] The rage of the other Staffordshire Tories, whom Gower had suddenly left so far behind, can be imagined.

Their first opportunity for a challenge came in the general election of 1747. "For the first time in a hundred years, and for the last time until the Reform Act of 1832"[33] the county election was contested. Against Lord Gower's brother and his son-in-law, Sir Richard Wrottesley, there were put up a staunch "old Tory," Sir Walter Bagot, and an equally staunch "old Whig," John Offley Crewe. Then, as if to demonstrate to the Staffordshire Tories that he was no man to be trifled with, the new Lord Privy Seal decided to try not merely to maintain his power in the face of the opposition he had aroused, but to extend it. He decided to add Lichfield to the number of his pocket boroughs. In this project he found an ally in the Ansons of Shugborough, another old family of the Lichfield neighborhood. Admiral George Anson, after winning fame as a naval hero and circumnavigator of the globe, had acquired, like many other successful professional men of the time, political ambitions.[34] He, too, attached himself to the Bedford faction and obtained a peerage, an ambitious wife, the daughter of the Whig Lord Chancellor Hardwicke, and eventually the post of First Lord of the Admiralty. Later his family acquired the title of Earl of Lichfield, about the time the Leveson Gowers acquired that of Marquess of Staffordshire, as if to commemorate their victories in these political arenas. One of the young sons of Lord Gower and a brother of Lord Anson were put up as Government candidates for Lichfield, against the old Tory members, Sir Lister Holt and George Venables Vernon. How insolent and galling this must have seemed to the Tories of Lichfield, for their city to be converted overnight into another pocket borough of the Bloomsbury gang!

The unsophisticated methods of the provincial Tories were no match for the Gower-Anson faction, backed by the influence of the Government and enormous wealth. For the first few days of the poll, while the freemen, the actual citizens of Lichfield, cast their votes, it looked like victory for Holt and Vernon. But as the poll continued, there arrived a stream of outsiders, from Trentham and Newcastle and Shugborough— tenants and friends of the Gowers and Ansons, "faggot voters," for whom Gower had bought burgage tenures and split freeholds in Lichfield. It was estimated that the 1747 election cost Gower £30,000, and that, up to 1754, Gower and Anson spent £12,519 for the purchase of burgage tenures in Lichfield alone. At the end of the poll the count was Richard Leveson Gower, 278; Thomas Anson, 272; Sir Lister Holt, 237; George Venables Vernon, 221. The poll-book of the election has survived, and it is interesting to note the acquaintances of Johnson among the voters. Edmund Hector and Sir Watkin Williams Wynn voted for Holt and Vernon; David Garrick, Gilbert Walmesley, and Isaac Hawkins Browne voted for Leveson

Gower and Anson; Dean Addenbrooke split his vote between Vernon and Leveson Gower; Sir Brooke Boothby between Vernon and Anson. In the county election the Gowers retained their one seat, the "old Tory" Sir Walter Bagot heading the poll. But Lichfield was a clear victory for what might be called the forces of progress. There were two slight attempts at rebellion later, when Tory candidates stood, unsuccessfully, for Lichfield in 1753 and 1761. But after 1761, the Gowers and Ansons chose whom they liked to represent Lichfield, unopposed.[35]

In this sketch of Staffordshire politics as practiced in the days of Johnson's youth, the most obvious thing to be noted is that we are dealing with a contest between personalities and power groups, not principles. When the Gowers in 1742 suddenly ceased to be Tories and became Bedford Whigs, there is not a scrap of evidence to suggest that any change whatever took place in their political philosophy, if they had one. The words "Whig" and "Tory" by this time denoted little more than "In" and "Out": "by 1750 everyone at Court, in office, and in the centre arena was a Whig, while the name of Tories, by a process of natural selection, was left to the residuum who did not enter politics in pursuit of office, honours, or profits, that is, to the country gentlemen and to the forerunners of urban radicals." [36]

True, there was the perennial question of Jacobitism, surrounded as it was by much talk about the divine or hereditary right of kings, the rights of Parliament, the rights of the people, the position of the Church, and so on. But as one studies eighteenth-century English politics in practice, one feels certain that if the Gowers before 1742 represented the Jacobite interest, it was because they considered that King James III represented the Gower interest. The various meanings of Jacobitism should be discriminated. There was the theoretical Jacobitism that stemmed from the constitutional crisis of 1689, and involved large questions of the nature of the state and the relations between governors and governed: insofar as Johnson's mind concerned itself at all with Jacobitism, it seems to have been with this. There is the much later romantic Jacobitism of Scott and Queen Victoria, which developed when all actual chance of a Stuart restoration was over; it is toward this that Boswell, with his sighings over the hardships endured by "the grandson of King James II" tends. But to the practical politicians of the middle of the century— the Gowers, the Shippens, the Lovats—Jacobitism was a matter of simple and immediate power politics, the taking of calculated risks in the hope of larger profits. In different degrees and with different people, these various motives may have been combined and interwoven; and underlying all of them was the fading memory of the events of the Great Rebellion, which to the more philosophical, like Johnson, might take the form of mourning for the destruction of an ideal, to others, like the Sneyds of Keele, the form of active and bitter resentment for personal wrongs suffered by their families. But on the whole, when someone involved in eighteenth-century politics talks about "the Jacobite interest," we should probably do well to place the emphasis on the word "interest." [37]

What this sketch of public life in the Midlands during Johnson's youth and early manhood has attempted to do is fill in with some concrete detail the background of practical political activity against which Johnson's own activities and opinions were set. This is not to suggest that Johnson himself, who never visited Lichfield between 1740 and 1761, was a participant in the activities that have been described: he took part, as we shall see, in certain political doings in the central arena at Westminster, but there is no evidence that he "engaged in politicks" in the Midlands at this time. Still, Johnson, with so many acquaintances and even relatives who did engage in them, must have had an intimate knowledge of the mechanism of practical politics at the borough and county level, and of the motives that govern individuals in such dealings. From a knowledge of his acquaintance with this background, one might predict that any theory of government at which Johnson might eventually arrive would be based on the facts of the political power of individuals, not on speculative doctrines of rights, natural or divine; that it would be concerned not with the construction of systems but with the part played by the individual in the working of any system. And a consideration of Johnson's remarks on the subject of government in his mature years will show that this is so.

The facts that emerge from this sketch are, however, mostly negative, warning us against unwarranted assumptions about the nature of Johnson's political attitudes, assumptions that have arisen from regarding them in another frame of reference than that in which they actually subsisted. One must not think of Johnson's Toryism as connoting a reverence for wealth or aristocracy or a desire for a powerful central government—these things, in the eighteenth century, were associated with Bedfords, Newcastles, and Gowers, the Whig magnates. And one must not think of Johnson's Toryism as the result of his upbringing in a closed circle of romantic Jacobites and "high-flying" Tories. There was little of the starry-eyed about eighteenth-century politics in Staffordshire; Lichfield was far from being a Tory stronghold; and from his earliest days Johnson seems to have had at least as many and as opinionated Whig friends, acquaintances, and relations as Tory— very probably more. All this may seem confusing to the student familiar only with modern political categories and with the traditional notion of Johnson: eighteenth-century politics *is* confusing, and Johnson was not a simple person. But we can be sure of at least one thing: that whatever the nature of

Johnson's political opinions, they were not arrived at in ignorance of the realities of practical politics. Indeed, there was probably no better school for either the historical background or the *Realpolitik* of the contemporary political scene than a boyhood in early eighteenth-century Lichfield.

Chapter Three

THE YOUNG JOHNSON (1709-1737)

1. THE JOHNSONS AND THE FORDS

IF more were known of the history of Johnson's immediate family, the task of accounting for his political attitudes might be simpler. Had his ancestors suffered for King Charles and the family property been sequestrated, had his father or grandfather been victimized by the Popish plot or ejected from a living for refusing to take the oaths to William and Mary, it would be easy to explain why he should have grown up to be a "Tory" and "High Churchman." As it is, nothing of the kind seems to have happened. There were many people too little even for the attentions of a Parliamentary foraging party, over whom even a civil war (in those happier days) could pass without much altering their fortunes. It was these people, no doubt the majority of the nation, whom Johnson had in mind when he wrote, "The good or ill success of battles and embassies extends itself to a very small part of domestic life," [1] and

> How small of all that human hearts endure
> The part which laws or kings can cause or cure.

He would hardly have written such lines if there had been anything in the history of his immediate ancestors to disprove them.

Certainly the Johnsons, his father's family, were of these little people. His grandfather, William Johnson, who died in 1672, appears to have been in a very small way of life indeed; after his death, his widow and her three sons had to be assisted by the charitable organizations of Lichfield, even to the extent of a "woman's waistcoat" for Catherine Johnson.[2] The fee for the apprenticeship of the oldest son, Michael, Samuel's father, to a London stationer was paid by such an organization, the Conduit Lands Trust. From such a beginning, Michael did well to raise himself to the status of the county's leading bookseller and the holder, from time to time, of important civic office.

Much has been made of the story that Michael Johnson was a Jacobite. This is, however, one of the least satisfactorily documented points in Johnsonian biography. The relevant passages are this from Hawkins,

It may here be proper, as it will account for some particulars respecting the character of his son Samuel, to mention that his political principles led him to favour the pretensions of the exiled family, and that though a very honest and sensible man, he, like many others inhabiting the county of Stafford, was a Jacobite,[3]

and this from Boswell (deriving no doubt partly from Hawkins),

He was a zealous high-churchman and royalist, and retained his attachment to the unfortunate house of Stuart, though he reconciled himself, by casuistical arguments of expediency and necessity, to take the oaths imposed by the prevailing power.[4]

These two statements seem to be absolutely all the evidence there is for Michael Johnson's Jacobitism; we do not know on what authority Hawkins and Boswell made them; and exhaustive researches into the meager documents of Michael's career have uncovered nothing to substantiate them. The city records show that at various times he duly took the required oaths of allegiance to Anne and George I, and of abjuration of Popery and the Pretender; but as to how much "humiliation" these caused him, and how "wryly" and with what "casuistical arguments" and "inward reservations" (to quote the speculations of biographers) he took them, we know nothing at all. Moreover, there is a countertradition: Tom Tyers asserted that Michael Johnson was "a Whig in principle," and Anna Seward that he "had very loyal principles." [5] Until clearer evidence is forthcoming, it is useless to erect large structures of conjecture about the effect of Samuel Johnson of his father's hypothetical and undefined Jacobitism.

It may be more profitable to consider the effect on Johnson of the actual circumstances of his father's life. Until the time of Samuel's birth, it reads like a tale of brilliant "success" out of Defoe or Horatio Alger—the industrious, ambitious, and pious apprentice rising from charity boy to prosperous tradesman, marrying above his station, his business career culminating in his purchase of the Earl of Derby's library, his social career culminating in the spectacular occasion, on the day after Samuel's birth, when, as Sheriff of Lichfield, he invited "all the town *now*" to the ceremony of riding the bounds of the old city. "He feasted all the citizens with uncommon magnificence," his son recorded, "and was the last but one that maintained the splendour of the Riding." [6] The obvious pride with which Johnson recalls this climax of his father's career seems to indicate that he himself was by no means immune to the eternal appeal of the capitalist success story.

Unfortunately, Michael Johnson's career did not stop there, as in the story books. Life went on to add an ironic postscript showing the other side of the same story—the small entrepreneur with too large ideas, unable to cope with the intricacies of the higher levels of business. With the purchase of the Knowsley library, Michael seems to have overreached his capital or his business acumen, both already strained by his branching out into the manufacture of parchment and vellum. Not that free enterprise can be blamed entirely for his failure: when, to make his manufacture of parchment economically feasible, he took to having his waste leather

tanned, he found himself hemmed in with the strict governmental controls of a mercantilist economy. In 1718 he was
indicted, under Elizabethan labor legislation, for practicing
the trade of tanner without having been apprenticed to it. In
1725, he ran afoul of the excise commissioners, leather being
a dutiable article.[7]

With his father's experience of both the grandeurs and
miseries of trade in his memory, Johnson's attitude toward
trade is understandably ambiguous. His remarks are often
derogatory: "We see no qualities in trade that should entitle
a man to superiority. . . . There is nothing in trade connected with an enlarged mind." [8] Johnson is unlikely to be
found, then, supporting a course of action in which the prosperity of trade is made the mainspring of British public policy.[9] At the same time, the Johnson who prided himself on his
skill as a bookbinder, and praised the booksellers of London
as "generous, liberal-minded men," reprobated the romantic
and aristocratic contempt of trade as much as he reprobated
the exaltation of it by political doctrinaires and interested
parties. One of the most satisfying of Johnsonian anecdotes
is that which tells how he shocked a stylish gathering by remarking loudly to Reynolds, "How much do you think you
and I could get in a week, if we were to work as hard as we
could?" "There are few ways in which a man can be more
innocently employed than in getting money," [10] he once com-
mented, anticipating Bernard Shaw's Undershaft.

In Michael Johnson, certain essential lineaments of his
son's character are easily traced: a constitutional melancholy
self-distrust, combined with an awareness of his intellectual
powers; resentment of poverty and low social status; a burning
ambition to "make good." It is a combination that has gone to
make up many revolutionaries, and the affinity of Johnson's
Toryism with the revolutionary spirit has been frequently remarked.[11] The strenuousness of his revolt was reinforced no

doubt by the memory of Michael *agonistes*. It has been questioned whether Johnson himself ever suffered privation enough to account for the terrible force of his refutation of the theological justification of poverty: "The poor indeed are insensible of many little vexations which sometimes embitter the possessions and pollute the enjoyments of the rich. They are not pained by casual incivility, or mortified by the mutilation of a compliment; but this happiness is like that of a malefactor, who ceases to feel the cords that bind him when the pincers are tearing his flesh." [12] The bitterness of such a passage was distilled, perhaps, not only from the unhappiness of the son's early years, but also from the father's ironic progress, from the charity waistcoat to the Shrievalty, and then to the pitiful entry, shortly before the old man's death, in the books of the Conduit Lands Trust, "Pd. Mr. Johnson, a decaid Traidsman 10. 10. 0." [13] In a sense, Samuel Johnson's life is a reliving and a vindication of his father's. Significantly, though he could have claimed prosperous and respectable relatives on his mother's side, he generally identified himself with his father's plebeian stock. "I have great merit in being zealous for subordination and the honours of birth," he said, whimsically yet proudly; "for I can hardly tell who was my grandfather." [14]

The grandfather whom Johnson in this passage chose to ignore was his mother's father, Cornelius Ford, "an independent gentleman of small means," and some slight claim to pedigree. We know more of the Fords than of the Johnsons: they were small landowners or tradesmen or professional people, running the gamut of the middle class from the fairly high (the Reverend Cornelius Ford was an intimate of Lord Chesterfield's) to the fairly low (like Humphrey Heely, tap-keeper at Ranelagh, and Phoebe Ford, housekeeper to Gibbon). What evidence there is of the political and sectarian tendencies of the Fords indicates distinct leanings toward what would now be called the Low Church and its political counterpart, Whiggism. Johnson's grandfather left a library well stocked with books of Puritan tendency. "Aunt Nathanael" Ford, who objected to young Sam's eating too much of a leg of mutton, was a Hickman, of the family of the great Puritan controversialist, Henry Hickman. The younger Cornelius, as a client of Chesterfield, was presumably a Whig. Of the well-to-do Mrs. Harriots of Trysull, whose money sent Sam as a baby to an oculist at Worcester and (probably) as a young man to Oxford, Johnson recounted an amusing story: "My father and Mrs. Harriots, I think, never had much kindness for each other. She was my mother's relation; and he had none so high to whom he could send any of his family. He saw her seldom himself, and willingly disgusted her, by sending his horses from home on Sunday; which she considered, and with reason, as a breach of duty." [15] The point seems to be that Mrs. Harriots, with Puritanical and hence Sabbatarian leanings, regarded Sunday travel as an infraction of religious obligation, a prejudice which Michael, as a "High Churchman," delighted to flout.

The interesting thing about the story is Johnson's judgment that Mrs. Harriots' objections were "with reason"; as between his father's "High Churchmanship" and his cousin's Puritanism, he adjudicates against his father. Students of Johnson have not always given full weight to that element in the complex of his religious attitudes (an element that has certain political implications) which toward the end of the century came to be called Evangelicalism. Evangelicalism derives from the Puritan concern with the individual's responsibility for his own salvation. On the one hand, although skeptical of mere religious formalism, it stresses the value, for the individual, of regularity in religious observance (hence the popular derivation of the word "Methodist"); on the other hand, it insists on the importance of the individual's private religious experience, though attempting to avoid the danger of falling into incomprehensible mysticism or "enthusiasm." And it sees no reason why these attitudes may not exist within the framework of Anglicanism. Early Evangelicals indeed looked on the order, rites, and tradition of the Established Church as of the utmost value to the individual in attaining desired religious ends, though never to be regarded as ends in themselves. The two great figures in the inchoate stage of the movement, William Law and John Wesley, considered themselves High Churchmen, proud of their calling as priests of the Church of England and zealous in maintaining its dignity.

Many of Johnson's characteristic modes of behavior fall into the Evangelical pattern. The frequent reviews, in Johnson's diaries, of the conduct of his life, the resolutions to rise at eight, to fast on Good Friday, to read 160 verses of the Greek Testament every Sunday, which are attributed by Macaulay (who as a child of Evangelicalism ought to have known better) to morbid superstition and by modern students to various interesting neuroses, are in this tradition.

"The short of the matter is," wrote the great Nonjuror [Law], "either reason and religion prescribe rules and ends to all the ordinary actions of life, or they do not; if they do, then it is necessary to govern all our activities by those rules, as it is necessary to worship God." Nowhere did he find more eager disciples than around Wesley's table. This was the problem they discussed night after night—by what rules a Christian ought to regulate his life.[16]

The Johnsonian is interested to learn that "The first Evangelicals always laid great stress on early rising; to them it was a necessary part of a methodical Christian life," and that the Clapham sect, "like all the Evangelicals in those days, were very early risers. . . . Some of Wilberforce's time tables were discovered after his death—so many hours for prayer, so many for study, so many for business, so many for rest, and a column at the end in which to enter all the time that had been squandered." [17] Johnson's resolutions to rise early, his agonies over wasted time, his frequent practice of introspection and self-examination, are not then to be construed merely as idiosyncrasy. Nor is his "fear of death" (or rather of what follows death), terribly intense as it was, the aberration it is often said to be, when one considers the heavy Calvinist content of Evangelical theology.

A complete list of Johnson's Evangelical associations would take long to rehearse. It will suffice to mention the great respect that he always expressed for Wesley (who worshiped Johnson), and his intimacy with the queen of the Evangelicals, Hannah More. As to the political implications of such associations, two points may be made. The first is that in the eighteenth century and the early nineteenth, Evangelicalism and social reform went hand in hand. The Evangelicals were pioneers in the fight for the suppression of the slave trade, and the efforts of Wilberforce and others finally brought about its abolition. The Sunday School movement, led by Hannah More, sought to remedy the illiteracy of the poor. The work of Shaftesbury in the movement for the abolition of child labor and the introduction of more humane working conditions in the factories was an outgrowth of his Evangelicalism. To discover the extent and fervency of Johnson's humanitarianism, one need only glance through the *Rambler* and the *Idler*, with their pleas for the mitigation of the criminal law, for charity toward the lot of the prostitute, their attacks on capital punishment, the imprisonment of debtors, the barbarity of war, the tyranny of brutal country squires over their tenants and neighbors, the experimental mutilation of animals. These attitudes, together with Johnson's hatred of Negro slavery, are not to be regarded as unexpected or anomalous in him. On the contrary, they form the very heart of his political thinking.

Second, the political tradition of the Evangelical movement was distinctly conservative. Of its two leading political figures, Wilberforce was one of the younger Pitt's most active and useful supporters in the House of Commons; and Shaftesbury, though less active, held office under Peel and voted against the Reform Act of 1832.[18] The association, in the eighteenth-century Evangelicals, of humanitarian ethics and conservative politics, is an interesting phenomenon, too complex to be analyzed here in the detail it deserves. One obvious point, at least, may be made: if those in authority are regarded as having a strong responsibility to alleviate human suffering, they must be given the power to interfere with the social and economic conditions that seem to produce such suffering. To early Victorian "liberals," then, like Macaulay and James Mill, whose liberalism implied laissez faire, Johnson and the Evangelical reformers were anti-liberals (and, of course, behind the times, unprogressive, reactionary). Curiously, the word "liberal" has in the twentieth century (especially in the United States) frequently come to mean the precise opposite of a Victorian laissez-faire liberal; and it is one of the many paradoxes of political semantics that a large element, perhaps the controlling one, of Johnson's Toryism is what some people today would regard as admirably modern liberalism.

If important aspects, praiseworthy or deplorable as the reader may find them, of Johnson's religious, moral, and political thinking are consistent with the Evangelical temper, we may ask what incidents in his life could have caused him to fall in with it. For one such, we have Johnson's testimony that his reading of Law's *Serious Call* when he was at Pembroke (at the same time as John Wesley and his friends, a short distance away at Lincoln College, were reading it) was "the first occasion of my thinking in earnest of religion, after I became capable of rational inquiry." [19] Another was his association, beginning in the 1730's, with the Fitzherberts and Hill Boothby, whose amiable Evangelicalism is described (and contrasted with the Whitefieldian "enthusiasm" of Geoffrey

Wildgoose) in some of the pleasantest chapters of Richard Graves' *The Spiritual Quixote*. A third, perhaps the most important of the three, was no doubt the simple religious instruction that the young boy received from his mother in Lichfield. "I remember, that being in bed with my mother one morning, I was told by her of the two places to which the inhabitants of this world were received after death; one a fine place filled with happiness, called Heaven; the other a *sad* place, called Hell." [20] On the evidence, it seems likely that the Puritanism of the Fords had at least as much influence on Samuel Johnson's thinking as did that almost unknown quantity, the "High Churchmanship" of Michael Johnson. But there should be no difficulty, in view of the "High Churchmanship" of the Wesleys and William Law, in regarding Johnson's religious attitudes—which are inextricably combined with his political attitudes—as a harmonious and even logical blending of the two.

2. THE EARLY YEARS

It may be useful at this point to review Johnson's early life, up to the time, in his late twenties, when he moved to London. Samuel Johnson was born in 1709, the first child of the fifty-two-year-old Michael Johnson, and of the forty-year-old Sarah Ford. Johnson left a few brief but illuminating comments on his childhood. His parents were ill-matched intellectually: the strong-minded, plebeian Michael wished to talk about books and ideas, and could not bear to discuss the minutiae of his confused business life; the good-natured, pious, bourgeoise Sarah wished to talk about business and not about the books of which she knew little. Johnson often referred to his childhood in somewhat resentful terms; but the unhappy childhood is the intellectual's privilege. Both parents lavished affection on the child of their age, and encouraged him to make use of his fine mind, of which they were so proud that young Sam used to hide in the branches of a tree to escape being shown off to visitors. Such an upbringing was certainly partly responsible for his deep and permanent confidence in his intellectual ability and his power of thinking independently and, on occasion, perversely. "This now is such stuff as I used to talk to my mother," he said, "when I first began to think myself a clever fellow; and she ought to have whipt me for it." [21] Mrs. Johnson's platitudes were useful in providing something for the boy's keen mind to exercise its edge on, and in developing in him the habit of attacking accepted cant. Credit must be given to Mrs. Johnson for her affectionate patience in submitting to such treatment.

It has been generally taken for granted, following Hawkins and Boswell, that Johnson's political tendencies were initially absorbed from his father, with some reinforcement from his stay at Oxford. What makes this theory hard to accept is the difficulty of imagining Johnson docilely agreeing with authority about anything. One cannot see why young Sam, who disagreed with his father on every other subject, including the way to bring up children, the way to run a business, and the necessity of Sam's attending the market at Uttoxeter, should meekly become a Tory simply because Michael was one—if Michael *was* one. One remembers Johnson's brutally frank remark to Mrs. Thrale: "Poor people's children, dear lady, never respect them." [22] Two early incidents mentioned by Boswell as if they had some relevance to Johnson's political development are not really very helpful. Boswell finds "curiously characteristic" of "the infant Hercules of Toryism" the story that Michael brought the child, perched on his shoulder, to the Cathedral when Sacheverell preached, and observed that it was "impossible to keep him at home; for, young as he was, he believed he had caught the publick spirit and zeal for Sacheverel." [23] Since the only known visit of Sacheverell to Lichfield took place in June 1710, when the infant Hercules was nine months old, the story is hard to take seriously. In 1712, the boy's mother took him to London to be touched for "the Evil" by Queen Anne. Again, this incident cannot be regarded, as Boswell perhaps only humorously suggests, as a touchstone of Jacobitism; the treatment was prescribed, after all, by the eminent physician, Sir John Floyer.

The same observation regarding Michael Johnson's possible influence on Samuel's political convictions may be made about the influence of the instruction at the Lichfield Grammar School, where he attended from his eighth to his sixteenth year. Anna Seward contended that not Michael Johnson (who, according to her, was "very loyal" to the Hanoverians) but her grandfather, the Reverend John Hunter, master of the school, was responsible for Samuel's Jacobitism. But Johnson, though he later developed an intellectual respect for Hunter's learning, was at the time resentful of his discipline and rebellious against it. Hunter, Johnson reported, "was very severe, and wrong-headedly severe. He used to beat us unmercifully; and he did not distinguish between ignorance and negligence." [24] It is hard to see young Sam imbibing an "absurd zeal for the forfeit rights of the house of Stuart" from one whom he regarded thus.

Perhaps of more real importance in forming Johnson's social and political attitudes than Hunter's exhortations were the traditions of the school and the composition of the student body. From Lichfield Grammar School had come many men who attained to distinction in literature and the state from relatively humble beginnings. The example of its most famous alumnus, Joseph Addison, must have often been before the mind of the boy, who was just removing from the lower to the upper school at the time of Addison's early death—Addison who, through his learning, both classical and modern, his skill as poet, dramatist, and journalist, and his conspicuously high moral character, rose to the great office of Secretary of State.

The list of other distinguished pupils before Johnson's time is long: Ashmole, the antiquary; Gregory King, pioneer statistician; Wollaston, the philosopher; there were divines, and above all, there were lawyers, including a chief justice and a puisne judge of the Common Pleas, and a chief baron of the Exchequer. The strong legal tradition of the school was no doubt responsible for awakening Johnson's life-long interest in the law.[25] His own schoolmates seem to have come up to the level of distinction that had been established. One of them was John Eardley Wilmot, later Chief Justice of the Common Pleas; and it is easy to understand why, when Lord Stowell suggested to Johnson, late in life, that if he had gone into the law, he might have become Lord Chancellor, with the title of Lord Lichfield, Johnson was not amused but "in an angry tone, exclaimed, 'Why will you vex me by suggesting this, when it is too late?' " [26]

Of his other schoolmates, the most memorable to Johnsonians are Isaac Hawkins Browne, minor poet and politician; "Tom" Newton, Bishop of Bristol; Dr. Robert James, inventor of the famous "fever powder"; Charles and Richard Congreve; and Johnson's special rival in school, Theophilus Lowe. Johnson's two most intimate friends, at school and in later life, were John Taylor of Ashbourne, and Edmund Hector, the surgeon. They were mostly sons of middle-class families of varying degrees of prosperity, and were all more or less ambitious, and successful in their ambition, to rise in their various professions. It is noteworthy that among all the associates of Johnson mentioned, only one, and he the humblest of the group, can be unequivocally classed as a Tory in later life—Edmund Hector. Dr. James' politics are an unknown quantity—as a popular London physician he perhaps could not afford to have any. But John Taylor, a client of the Dukes of Devonshire, was a strong Whig. Browne was for a time Whig member of parliament for Wenlock. Newton became chaplain to George II in 1756 and was one of Newcastle's last appointments to the episcopal bench; his monumental edition of Milton is perhaps further testimony to his Whiggism. Eardley Wilmot's appointment to the bench was made by Newcastle's administration, and to the chief justiceship by Rockingham's. Although Theophilus Lowe obtained no greater preferment in the Church than that of Canon of Windsor, his post as tutor in the great Whig family of Townshend shows where his political lines were laid. Charles Congreve became chaplain to the Whig Archbishop Boulter, and Archdeacon of Armagh under him.

This preponderance of Whiggism among the most successful of Johnson's schoolmates is not to be wondered at; for throughout the century a career in the public service or the receipt of patronage from those who had patronage to bestow was almost synonymous with Whiggism. Whiggism virtually *meant* being "in." Conversely, Toryism meant being "out." For the young Johnson it meant denial of access to the scholarships and livings and sinecures and tutorships to noble families that were available to Lowe and Congreve. The feelings of the "decayed tradesman's" awkward and unsightly son, left behind in obscurity and neglect while youths whose intellectual prowess he had easily overmatched in school advanced on the smooth road toward success and security, must have played a certain part in forming his attitude toward the world and those who ran it.

In October 1725, at the age of sixteen, Johnson left the Lichfield school. For a year he lived in Worcestershire, first with his cousin Parson Cornelius Ford at Pedmore, and then, presumably, with the boarders at Stourbridge Grammar School, where he seems to have acted as a kind of pupil-teacher. Then came two years of "idleness" back at Lichfield—years that were not lost, however, for in them he apparently devoured most of the contents of his father's bookshop. In October 1728 he was admitted to Pembroke College, Oxford, where he stayed for a brief thirteen months.

It is commonly assumed that Johnson's association at this time with "that magnificent and venerable seat of Learning, Orthodoxy, and Toryism," as Boswell insists on describing it, had the effect of reinforcing the political attitudes already inculcated in him by Michael Johnson or John Hunter. But again one wonders. In later life he concurred in the veneration of Oxford's orthodoxy, and clapped his hands till they were sore at a Jacobitish speech by Dr. William King. But that was in 1759, when Johnson was famous and the holder of an honorary degree from the University. For his attitude toward Oxford when he was nineteen, poor, and unknown, we have his own account: "Ah, Sir, I was rude and violent. It was bitterness which they mistook for frolic. I was miserably poor, and I thought to fight my way by my literature and my wit; so I disregarded all power and all authority." [27] Bishop Percy recorded: "The pleasure he took in vexing the tutors and fellows has often been mentioned. . . . I have heard from some of his contemporaries that he was generally seen lounging at the College gate, with a circle of young students round him, whom he was entertaining with wit, and keeping from their studies, if not spiriting them up to rebellion against the College discipline, which in his maturer years he so much extolled." [28]

Although Johnson in later life demonstrated much respect for Pembroke, this admiration (like that for Hunter) was probably an intellectual process rather than the outgrowth of a deep personal affection for a place where he received, so far as the evidence shows, no material assistance (apart from the "eleemosynary supply" of shoes that he threw away), little encouragement, and not much intellectual profit. Of his tutor Jorden he said, "He was a very worthy man, but a heavy man, and I did not profit much by his instructions. Indeed, I did not attend him much." He admired Dr. Panting, the Master, "a

fine Jacobite fellow"; he began his life-long friendship with
Dr. Adams, the future Master. But his contemporaries—
"Phil" Jones, John Fludyer, Oliver Edwards—seem to have
been an undistinguished lot by comparison with his schoolfellows at Lichfield. He read desultorily in Greek, and wrote
a few "exercises" for Jorden, including his first published
piece, the Latin translation of Pope's *Messiah*. Of this piece
he reported: "I wrote it rather to show the tutors what I could
do, than what I was willing should be done. It answered my
purpose; for it convinced those who were well enough inclined
to punish me, that I could wield a scholar's weapon as often as
I was menaced with arbitrary inflictions. Before the frequency
of personal satire had weakened its effect, the petty Tyrants
of Colleges stood in awe of a pointed remark, or a vindictive
epigram." [29] It does not sound like a relationship in which
Toryism would be acquired through intellectual osmosis.
Johnson's small supply of money ran out in a year—so, at least,
we suppose; yet even if the money had been available, one
may wonder whether the angry young man of Pembroke
would have long continued his association with its petty tyrants and arbitrary inflictions.

"And now," Boswell reports, "(I had almost said *poor*)
Samuel Johnson returned to his native city, destitute, and not
knowing how he should gain even a decent livelihood." [30]
The next eight years, comprising almost the whole of Johnson's twenties, are briefly summarized, for, important as they
must have been in his intellectual development, we know little
about them. He managed to obtain two teaching positions.
One was only temporary. The other, at Market Bosworth, he
abandoned after a few months, quarreling violently with the
brutal country squire, Sir Wolstan Dixie, who was patron of
the school. He applied for others, unsuccessfully: he had no
degree; for one position he was rejected on the frank ground

that his "convulsive movements" might make him "an object of imitation, and possibly of ridicule, with his pupils." He spent more than a year at Birmingham, at the invitation of his friend Hector. Little is known of the society he frequented there; it was probably at the level of small tradesmen like Harry Porter, the mercer, and Thomas Warren, the bookseller, with whom he boarded and for whom he wrote, painfully, his first published book, the translation of *A Voyage to Abyssinia*. Porter died in 1734; nine months later, Johnson married his widow, and with her inheritance of a few hundred pounds, set up a private school at Edial, perhaps the most unsuccessful private school in the history of education. At last, every attempt to make a living in the Midlands having failed, he and his young friend David Garrick, armed with a letter of recommendation from Gilbert Walmesley, left Lichfield, on the second of March 1737, to seek their fortunes in London.

To repeat, the main thing that emerges from this review of Johnson's early life is the scarcity and ineffectiveness of the evidence for attributing much influence on his political thinking to the three traditional sources—his father, his Lichfield schoolmaster, and Oxford. A rebel by nature, he rebelled at the time against the authority of all three, whatever belated amends he subsequently made to their memories. He seems not to have received even a negative intellectual stimulus from them. "A very worthy man, but a heavy man"—the description of his Pembroke tutor probably applies also to Michael Johnson and John Hunter as intellectual influences. Johnson reports numerous childhood conversations with his mother on matters of morals and religion and even literature; he left hardly a single memorial of any intercourse between father and son. Michael was not even often at home, and when he was, he apparently spoke little.

What then, apart from books, *were* the sources of mental

stimulation for the young Johnson? They seem to have been, so far as one can gather from the records, various groups of what may be called Whig intellectuals.

First, there was the circle of Lichfield Close, with Gilbert Walmesley at its center. The Bishops of Lichfield, during Johnson's lifetime, did not reside at Lichfield. Their resident agents for temporal matters were the Chancellors of the diocese. They were, in the nature of things, Whigs. At the time of Johnson's birth, the office was held by one William Walmesley. Walmesley had been member for Lichfield in the short Parliament of 1701, unseating a Whig rival, Sir Michael Biddulph, on petition. Walmesley again contested the seat in the hard-fought "Sacheverell election" of 1710; but in the Tory landslide of that year Lichfield returned two Tory members, and both Walmesley and Biddulph were defeated at the poll.[31] The chief political issue of the time was whether William III's and Marlborough's anti-French policy should be pursued. Walmesley, as a Whig, supported this policy; and when the Tory-negotiated Peace of Utrecht with France was concluded in June 1713, it is understandable that "when the Sheriff and Magistrates went into the Close to proclaim the peace there (as customary on the like occasions) the Chancellor came out of his house and told them they had nothing to do there; and his son, the Register, went out of town that morning, as 'tis supposed, disturb'd with the musick of the bells on the occasion of peace." [32]

It was this son, Gilbert Walmesley, educated at Oxford and the Inner Temple, Register of the Ecclesiastical Court of the diocese from 1707 until his death in 1751, who was so important a figure in Johnson's adolescence: "Such was his amplitude of learning and such his copiousness of communication that it may be doubted whether a day now passes in which I have not some advantage from his friendship. At this man's table I enjoyed many cheerful and instructive hours, with companions such as are not often found." Walmesley was a vigorous, erudite, strong-minded individual, who "had mingled with the gay world without exemption from its vices or its follies, but had never neglected the cultivation of the mind; his belief of Revelation was unshaken; his learning preserved his principles: he grew first regular, and then pious." [33] The man of the world who combines a knowledge of humanity with a love for things of the mind and a concern for things of the spirit: it was an ideal which Johnson admired all his life, and one on which he tried to model himself.

Walmesley, one feels, would have made an excellent "Johnsonian Tory"—except for the fact that he was "a violent Whig, with all the malevolence of his party." When he was nearly seventy he was still active in Whig politics: writing to Lord Anson at the Admiralty in 1747 (the Ansons and Gowers were now in charge of the "Government interest" at Lichfield), Anson's agent reports on a turbulent pre-election meeting of Tory stalwarts, and concludes, "I have inclos'd a list of the principal persons of this meeting, a copy of which is sent to Lord Gower by Mr. Walmesley, who desires his compliments to Yr Lordship and would have written himself but was prevented by some symptoms of the gout in his right hand." [34] Not even age and gout could hinder the stout old Whig from keeping a sharp eye on the Tory dogs. Yet for all Walmesley's "violence," Johnson insists, "difference of opinion did not keep us apart. I honoured him and he endured me." Perhaps Johnson, by printing this tribute to Walmesley a few years before his own death, including it almost irrelevantly in his life of "Rag" Smith, is hinting to his readers that party labels are not so important to him as they have been taught to think.

Later Johnson was introduced by John Taylor to the Ashbourne circle—the Fitzherberts, Astons, Meynells, and Boothbys, well-to-do rural gentry with intellectual tastes. The two circles eventually merged, with Walmesley's marriage to Magdalen Aston, and widened to take in one of Johnson's most important friends of his early years in London, Harry Hervey, of the great Whig family of the Earls of Bristol. To these groups may be added a third, the Stourbridge-Pcdmore-Hagley circle, with whom Johnson spent a year at the impressionable age of sixteen, living with his brilliant cousin Cornelius Ford, whose "conversations" with Johnson so impressed him that he wished to "review" them forty-five years later. It is likely, we have seen, that the whole Ford-Hickman connection at Stourbridge was Whiggishly inclined. There is no doubt, at least, of the Whiggism of young George Lyttelton of Hagley; Bishop Percy conjectured that Johnson, "having some colloquial disputes" with Lyttelton when they met as boys, "is supposed to have conceived that prejudice which so improperly influenced him in the Life of that worthy nobleman" [35]—though few would now concern themselves to rescue "poor Lyttelton" from the impropriety of Johnson's mild contempt.

If anything is needed further to refute the charge of Johnson's blind Toryism, it can be found in his obvious attraction throughout his life to people like these—fairly well-to-do, fairly well read, mildly fashionable, intelligent, sensitive, dilettantish, kind—and Whig. They correspond very well to certain familiar types of the modern intellectual. A good idea of their benevolent, slightly sentimental, more than slightly unrealistic outlook on life can be obtained by reading the works of Lyttelton and Shenstone, and, in particular, from the picture of the Ashbourne circle in *The Spiritual Quixote*. They, in turn, were intrigued by the gauche, brilliant, difficult young Sam Johnson, and were kind and hospitable to him: "Although little better than a schoolboy," Percy says of him at Stourbridge, "he was admitted into the best company of the place, and had no common attention paid to his conversation; of which remarkable instances were long remembered there." [36] Johnson badly needed attention and admiration and kindness, and he was grateful for it. He reciprocated by falling in love with at least three young ladies of these coteries, none of whom one would expect *prima facie* to be the choice of an intransigent Tory High Churchman—Olivia Lloyd, the Quaker; Hill Boothby, the "Methodist"; and Molly Aston, the Whig, to whom Johnson quipped about politics and love,

> Liber ut esse velim suasisti, pulchra Maria,
> Ut maneam liber, pulchra Maria, vale.[37]

The society of these people stimulated him to write, and his earliest serious compositions—verse translations of Horace and Virgil and Addison, an epilogue to Ambrose Philips' *The Distrest Mother*, a remarkable poem "Upon the Feast of St. Simon and St. Jude"—stem from the time of his association with the Stourbridge and Lichfield Close circles.

If one were seeking a psychological explanation of Johnson's Toryism to substitute for the simple one that he dutifully absorbed it from his father and the Oxford dons, one might speculate about his reaction to the society of these "Whig intellectuals." They seem to have fascinated and stimulated the young man, and he delighted in their admiration of his growing intellectual and artistic powers. Had he been a lesser person, he might have succumbed to their attraction and to the comfortable security of a ready-made intellectual pattern, accustoming himself to mouth their facile clichés, ending perhaps as a kind of superior Soame Jenyns. Something like this is, after all, what does happen to the majority of "bright young men." But as it was, Johnson could never stifle the acute awareness that he was not as they were, and never could be. He knew poverty and deprivation, and depths of misery, physical and spiritual, that would always be beyond the limited world of these pleasant people. "Neither from such relations [with 'intellectuals' generally]," Herman Liebert writes of the later Johnson, "nor from the sly satisfaction he took in playing 'Dr. Johnson' could he draw the deeper strength he needed most. This he could only gain, Antæus-like, in the world from which he sprang" [38]—the world of small, ordinary, suffering, inarticulate people, of Michael and Sarah and Nathanael Johnson, of his fantastic, tippling, painted old Tetty, of blind old Miss Williams and cantankerous old Mrs. Desmoulins and crude old Dr. Levet and ungrateful young Frank the Negro and Bet Flint the prostitute. Perhaps Johnson's Toryism was in large part the product of such a revulsion from the high-flown idealizing of Hagley and Ashbourne to the realities of a life about which he had no romantic illusions, but which was unalterably part of him. Perhaps it was an instinctive defensive reaction to preserve his intellectual integrity, his identity even, from the too insidious attraction of this new-found world. Perhaps there is more seriousness than one might at first think in the line "Ut maneam liber, pulchra Maria, vale."

3. TWO EARLY WORKS: *A Voyage to Abyssinia* AND *Irene*

In the dismal years of his mid-twenties, as he migrated fruitlessly about the Midlands, Johnson projected three major pieces of writing. One, an edition and life of Politian, with a history of Renaissance Latin poetry, remained only a project; one, *Irene,* was at least partly written by the time of the move to London; the third, a translation of *A Voyage to Abyssinia,* actually achieved print in 1735. They all contribute something to our knowledge of Johnson's conception of man as a social and political being: even the abortive Politian points to his significant admiration of the Renaissance.

Johnson's first book, the translation of Lobo as it is somewhat inaccurately called, is of more interest than the scant amount of attention given to it indicates. At first glance it

seems a curious choice for a fledgling author, this abridg-
ment [39] and translation into English of a French version of a
Portuguese Jesuit's account of his experiences in Abyssinia in
the early seventeenth century. But the vast range of Johnson's
interests is perpetually astonishing. "A generous and elevated
mind," he says in the dedication of the *Voyage*, "is distinguished by nothing more certainly than an eminent degree of
curiosity; nor is that curiosity ever more agreeably or usefully
employed than in examining the laws and customs of foreign
nations."

Nihil humanum a me alienum—if Johnson's dedication
paraphrases this manifesto of Renaissance humanism, the
opening paragraphs of his preface are in the spirit of the great
motto of scientific skepticism, the motto of the Royal Society,
the motto which Johnson prefixed to the *Rambler—nullius
addictus jurare in verba magistri.*

The Portuguese traveller, contrary to the general vein of his
countrymen, has amused his readers with no romantick absurdities or incredible fictions. . . . He appears by his modest and un-
affected narrative to have described things as he saw them, to
have copied nature from the life, and to have consulted his senses
not his imagination.[40]

Intimately connected with Johnson's empiricism is his refusal
to believe that human nature varies greatly from one part of
the world to another. His preface continues:

The reader will here find no regions cursed with irremediable
barrenness, or blessed with spontaneous fecundity, no perpetual
gloom, or unceasing sunshine; nor are the nations here described
either devoid of all sense of humanity, or consummate in all private and social virtues; here are no Hottentots without religion,
polity, or articulate language, no Chinese perfectly polite, and
compleatly skill'd in all sciences: he will discover what will always be discover'd by a diligent and impartial enquirer, that
wherever human nature is to be found, there is a mixture of vice
and virtue, a contest of passion and reason [p. viii].

The importance to Johnson's political thinking of this belief
in the essential homogeneity of human motivation—a radical
egalitarianism, one is justified in calling it—can hardly be
stressed too much. It is significant that Johnson's earliest
recorded independent pronouncement on the human situation should be to this effect. It *is* independent, for Lobo in his
account makes little effort to mitigate the barbarity of the
Abyssinians, the Gallas, and the Turks. Indeed, his picture of
the Gallas is remarkably like that picture of the Hottentots
which Johnson rejects:

They neither sow their lands, nor improve them by any kind of
culture. . . . They practice no rites of worship, though they believe that in the regions above there dwells a Being that governs
the world. . . . In other matters they are yet more ignorant, and
have some customs so contrary even to the laws of nature as
might almost afford reason to doubt whether they are endowed
with reason [p. 47].

Having translated this, Johnson proceeds, in his preface, to
ignore it firmly. The customs contrary to the laws of nature,
which shock the Jesuit, Johnson is prepared to subsume under
the normal human "mixture of vice and virtue." It is a remarkably liberal attitude, closer to that of the modern scientific anthropologist than to those of either the seventeenth-
century missionary or the eighteenth-century Rousseauist.

The *Voyage to Abyssinia* illustrates another attitude which
the student of Johnson's social and political thinking cannot
ignore. His preface goes on to a tremendous denunciation of
the Jesuit missionaries in Abyssinia and of the Roman Catholic church generally:

It is not easy to forbear reflecting with how little reason these
men profess themselves the followers of JESUS, who left this great
characteristick to his disciples, that they should be known by
loving one another, by universal and unbounded charity and
benevolence.
   Let us suppose an inhabitant of some remote and superior

region, yet unskill'd in the ways of men, having read and considered the precepts of the Gospel, and the example of our Saviour, to come down in search of the True Church: If he would not enquire after it among the cruel, the insolent, and the oppressive; among those who are continually grasping at dominion over souls as well as bodies, among those who are employed in procuring to themselves impunity for the most enormous villainies and studying methods of destroying their fellow-creatures, not for their crimes but their errors; if he would not expect to meet benevolence engaged in massacre, or to find mercy in a court of inquisition, he would not look for the True Church in the Church of Rome [p. ix].

Le Grand's book is, in fact, a highly controversial one, a document of some importance in the study of the relations between politics and religion. The Catholic missionary effort in Abyssinia, of which Lobo's expedition was the final melancholy chapter, lasted over a century, and was from the first linked with Portuguese imperial and commercial ambition.[41] The ancient Christian state church of Abyssinia was subject to the Coptic Patriarchate of Alexandria, which existed under the protection of the Turkish rulers of Egypt. It was thus greatly to the advantage of the expanding Portuguese empire in the East, whose chief rivals were the Turks, to detach the allegiance of the Abyssinian rulers from the native church and bring them under the control of Rome. For a time the attempt succeeded; but in the end the native hierarchy proved too strong, and to this day the church of Ethiopia remains independent of the West. How well Lobo himself was aware of the political and commercial aspects of his mission appears in his own report of the plea he makes to the Portuguese Viceroy of the Indies, after his expulsion from Abyssinia, for a military invasion of the country:

I made it appear with how much ease the Turks might be driven out of the Red-sea, and the Portuguese enjoy all the trade of those countries. . . . I cannot deny that some degree of resent-

ment might appear in my discourse; for though revenge be pro-
hibited to Christians, I should not have been displeased to have
had the Bassa of Suaquem and his brother in my hands, that I
might have reproached them with the ill-treatment we had met
from them [p. 142].

Lobo is much more than a simple missionary "zealous for
his faith, happy in the setting forth of its doctrines and practice" as he has been described.[42] He is shrewd, bold, and
secular-minded. The passages quoted show him to us at his
worst, and his proposal that the propagation of Catholicism
be expedited by a military operation, to the greater glory of
Portuguese commerce and for motives of personal resentment,
is sufficiently shocking to justify Johnson's invective. Lobo is
cast in the same mold as his predecessor, the Patriarch André
Oviedo, whose "sanguinary zeal" Johnson scathingly reprobates—"who was continually importuning the Portuguese to
beat up their drums for missionaries who might preach the
gospel with swords in their hands and propagate by desolation
and slaughter the true worship of the God of Peace" (p. ix)—
and of Lobo's own immediate superior, the Patriarch Alfonso
Mendez, who, Le Grand comments, carried his authority "to
the same height in Abyssinia, as in a country subject to the
Inquisition; turning by these violent measures the whole
world against the missionaries, and raising such a detestation
of the Jesuits as continues in the country to this day" (p. 327).

Le Grand, a French Oratorian, is unsympathetic to the
Jesuits; in his commentary, as in Johnson's, there is a strong
feeling that the methods of the Jesuits, stemming from an
earlier age, are no longer appropriate to the more enlightened
atmosphere of the eighteenth century. Forty years after Le
Grand's book was published, the Society was expelled from
France, and five years later was suppressed by Pope Clement
XIV. But meanwhile, under the regime of Cardinal Fleury,
Jesuit power in France was in the ascendant, and Johnson

notes that Le Grand "is to be esteemed for having dared so
freely in the midst of France to declare his disapprobation of
the Patriarch Oviedo's sanguinary zeal" (p. ix). Johnson
would have been aware, as he wrote this, that friendship with
Fleury's France was the keystone of Walpole's structure of
foreign relations, and that the Portuguese alliance, created by
the Methuen treaty of 1703, was one of the showpieces of
Whig diplomacy. It may be only a coincidence to find Johnson, at this early date, turning into English a book that is on
the whole derogatory of Jesuit and Portuguese colonial activity; but in light of the vigorous opinions he was to express a
few years later on the subjects of both Walpole and colonialism, it is an interesting one.

A Voyage to Abyssinia is much more than the travel book
it is sometimes thought to be. There was widespread interest
throughout Europe in the Portuguese adventure in Africa,
and the ramifications of political and theological controversy
arising out of it were many. The scholar Hiob Ludolf (1624–
1700), a German Lutheran, had attempted, late in the seventeenth century, to break the Roman Catholic monopoly on
Ethiopian scholarship, and in his History of Abyssinia vigorously combated the Catholic contention that the Abyssinian
Church represented a debased, Judaized form of Christianity.
Ludolf, on the contrary, finds striking parallels between the
Abyssinian practices, admittedly going back to very ancient
times, and modern Protestantism, thus supporting the Protestant position that the reformed churches were a return to the
Christianity of the apostolic age before the abuses introduced
by Rome. It is the main purpose of Le Grand, in the "Dissertations" which make up more than half the volume translated
by Johnson, to rebut Ludolf, and he does so, as Johnson says,
with a considerable display of "industry and erudition." In
England, following on Ludolf, Michael Geddes, a protégé of
Bishop Burnet, had entered the battle on the Protestant side,

giving a highly damning account of Jesuit missionary activity in Abyssinia. Ludolf's *History of Abyssinia* was among the books in Johnson's library left for sale after his death,[43] and in his preface to the *Voyage* he recommends a reading of Geddes' book, "in which he will find the actions and sufferings of the missionaries placed in a different light [from Lobo's], though the same in which Mr. Le Grand, with all his zeal for the Roman Church, appears to have seen them." Johnson moderates among the disputants with an appearance of judicious detachment, and concludes with the staunchly Evangelical declaration, "Upon the whole, the controversy [between Le Grand and Ludolf] seems of no great importance to those who believe the Holy Scriptures sufficient to teach the way of salvation, but of whatever moment it may be thought, there are not proofs sufficient to decide it" (p. viii).

There is no hint in the *Voyage* of "Tory" views of government. Abyssinia was a primitive feudal despotism, fraught with dynastic struggles; Lobo describes it dispassionately as it is, and Johnson makes no further comment. The work does, however, testify strongly to Johnson's catholic interest in humanity; the strong bias of his mind toward empiricism and skepticism; his firm conviction that under the skin all human beings are pretty much alike; a fear of "determining on the side of cruelty and envy"; and a strong suspicion that projects of colonization and proselytization often cloak motives of aggrandizement and commercial gain. Altogether, *A Voyage to Abyssinia* was not a bad choice for the apprenticeship of an independent commentator on political and social questions in the eighteenth century.

Irene was not produced or published until 1749. It appears, however, that it was begun at the Edial school, in 1736. Before Johnson left for London in 1737, according to Boswell, "a great part" of the play had been written, and much at least

of the remainder in the early part of 1737. A long early draft
of the play has been dated in the pre-London period.[44]

Two passages in *Irene* have obvious political reference. The
play opens with the Greek nobles Demetrius and Leontius la-
menting the overthrow of their country by the Turks and discussing the causes of it. The Byzantine Greeks loved their
money too much to lay it out for public defense:

Demetrius:
    That Wealth, too sacred for their Country's Use!
    That Wealth, too pleasing to be lost for Freedom!
    That Wealth, which granted to their weeping Prince,
    Had rang'd embattled Nations at our Gates:
    But thus reserv'd to lure the Wolves of Turkey,
    Adds Shame to Grief, and Infamy to Ruin. . . .

Leontius:
    Reproach not Misery.—The Sons of Greece,
    Ill-fated Race! So oft besieg'd in vain,
    With false Security beheld Invasion. . . .
    And not one Prodigy foretold our Fate.

Demetrius:
    A thousand horrid Prodigies foretold it.
    A feeble Government, eluded Laws,
    A factious Populace, luxurious Nobles,
    And all the Maladies of sinking States.
    When publick Villainy, too strong for Justice,
    Shows his bold Front, the Harbinger of Ruin,
    Can brave Leontius call for airy Wonders? . . .
    'Twas Vice that shook our Nerves, 'twas Vice, Leontius,
    That froze our Veins, and wither'd all our Powers [I, i, 20–57].

This passage has been interpreted as anti-Walpolian propaganda; as one student puts it, "Johnson's other writings of the
same period—his *London, Marmor Norfolciense,* and the
ironic *Vindication of the Licensers*—make it evident that in
him it was no display of *ad hoc* patriotic rant to denounce the
avarice, vice, and self-interest that he saw rampant in the gov-

ernment of the late thirties. At this time he was a 'patriot'—
that is, an enemy to Walpole—and there is plenty of conviction in his jeremiad." [45] But there are difficulties in this reading, even if we ignore the difference of two years between the
assumed date of the "first draft" of *Irene* (in which the substance of the passage quoted is found) and the date of the
publication of *London,* the earliest of the other works cited.
The great issue of the time was Walpole's pacific policy toward
Spain, which, according to the opposition, was plundering the
wealth of Britain on the high seas. The opposition can hardly
be imagined conceiving of George II as a "weeping Prince,"
vainly begging his recalcitrant subjects to spend their money
for the defense of their country against the threat of Spanish
aggression. To be sure, the opposition acted with sublime inconsistency throughout this debate: while urging a warlike
policy against Spain, they relentlessly opposed any attempt of
Walpole's to increase the size of the regular army or to "range
embattled nations" at the gate of Britain by means of subsidies
to potential allies.[46] The normal charge made against Walpole's government was not that it was "feeble," but that it was
too high-handed and arbitrary. It is not "avarice, vice, and
self-interest" in "the *government* of the late thirties" but in
the whole "factious populace" that is reprobated in the play.
The Grecian parallel mentions no guilty head of the state on
which its fall can be blamed: the "weeping Prince" is obviously on the right side of politics. It might be part of opposition tactics in the thirties to blame Walpole for corrupting the
people, but it would be extraordinary for them to insist on the
corruption of the people without mentioning Walpole.

Indeed, the picture is so little one of the specific political
scene of the late thirties that the epilogue to the play was contributed by, of all people, Sir William Yonge, Walpole's own
Secretary at War in the late 1730's, the member of his ministry
most closely concerned with questions of expenditure on de-

fense.[47] Since it was, after all, the opposition who obstructed such expenditure throughout the thirties, one might even argue that the opening passage of the play can be read as a piece of *government* propaganda.[48] But the safest conclusion is probably that the historical parallel is at least as vague as that in Addison's *Cato*, which each party found it possible to apply to its own advantage, and that *Irene* provides no real evidence for dating Johnson's "patriotism" earlier than his arrival in London.

The other important political passage of the play occurs in Act I, Scene 2, when Cali Bassa, the "First Visier" of the Emperor Mahomet, discloses to Demetrius and Leontius the woes of a Prime Minister's lot and his determination to help them overthrow his master. Cali then delivers this interesting dissertation:

> Such are the Woes when arbitrary Pow'r,
> And lawless Passion, hold the Sword of Justice.
> If there be any Land, as Fame reports,
> Where common Laws restrain the Prince and Subject,
> A happy Land, where circulating Pow'r
> Flows through each Member of th' embodied State,
> Sure, not unconscious of the mighty Blessing,
> Her grateful Sons shine bright with ev'ry Virtue;
> Untainted with the Lust of Innovation,
> Sure all unite to hold her League of Rule
> Unbroken as the sacred Chain of Nature,
> That links the jarring Elements in Peace [I, ii, 53–64].

The "first draft" contains significant variants:

> Cali Bassa . . . launches into the misery of absolute Governments, where if a Man serves his Country counterfeit Plots and false Suspicions, then breaks out into the Praises of that Country (after having blam'd the Eastern Tryanny) which he has heard of in the North
> Where King and People own one common Law
> one common Interest, mutual duties
> And feel one happiness and one Misfortune.

Where Swain smiles over his little fields, his rising harvest his feeding flocks, and says these are mine, and gathers his children about him and portions out to them the acquisitions of his Industry.[49]

Of the passage beginning "If there be any land . . ." Bronson says that it depicts "the contrasted ideal [to that of Walpole's England], the England of his [Johnson's] dream." [50] Nichol Smith and McAdam comment, "This is a good statement of Johnson's Tory creed, and none the worse for the implied satire on the Whigs. It is the only passage in *Irene* in which the political allusion is specific; and it is introduced cautiously, with the responsibility for the anachronism thrown on the broad shoulders of Fame, for it was not the English constitution in the days of the Wars of the Roses that Johnson had in mind to praise." [51]

The passage is an important one. But it is at least as much a statement of a Whig creed as of a Tory. It is, I think, pure Locke. Significantly, in the draft, the passage on government, "Where King and People own one common Law," is immediately followed by a passage on the virtues of security of property—"Where Swain smiles over his little fields . . . and says *these are mine,* and gathers his children about him and portions to them *the acquisitions of his Industry.*" [52] Property is the basis of the Lockean system, and property is created by the individual's industry: "Though the earth and all inferior creatures be common to all men, yet every man has a property in his own person. . . . The labor of his body and the work of his hands we may say are properly his." The end of government, for Locke, is the preservation of a state in which every man can enjoy his own; for "God gave the world . . . to the use of the industrious and rational (and labor was to be his title to it), not to the fancy or covetousness of the quarrelsome and contentious." [53] According to Locke, "civil government" —that is, government by "the rule of law," not by arbitrary power—developed from such a state of pastoral life as Johnson depicts; and the essence of it is that "The legislative, or supreme authority, cannot assume to itself a power to rule by extemporary arbitrary decrees, but is bound to dispense justice, and decide the rights of the subject by promulgating standing laws, and known authorized judges." If not, men's "peace, quiet, and property, will still be at the same uncertainty as it was in the state of nature."

For Locke's system is profoundly conservative. Locke is at great pains to explain that it is under arbitrary despotism, under dictatorships, that "the Lust of Innovation" prevails, that it is in a totalitarian state (as we should call it) where one cannot be sure from one day to the next what is to happen to one's life or property. Democracy, or government by popular consent, is much more propitious to stability and security: "To this perhaps it will be said that, the people being ignorant and always discontented, to lay the foundation of government in the unsteady opinion and uncertain humor of the people is to expose it to certain ruin; and no government will be able long to subsist if the people may set up a new legislative whenever they take offense at the old one. To this I answer: Quite the contrary. People are not so easily got out of their old forms as some are apt to suggest." And he goes on to argue from the stability of the English constitution, which "still kept us to, or after some interval of fruitless attempts still brought us back again to, our old legislative of King, Lords, and Commons." [54]

That the seat of this tradition of government is to be found "in the North," as Johnson's draft has it, refers obviously to the doctrine that government "by popular consent" was the special heritage of the Teutonic cultures, and that to them the English constitution owes its characteristic features. The notion, which had its origin in Tacitus, was a commonplace of English political theory from the sixteenth to the nineteenth centuries.[55] Although in later years it became the peculiar property and pride of Whigs and "liberals," eighteenth-century Tories apparently accepted it with equal complacency. No Whig historian could have stated the doctrine more emphatically than Hume:

Kingly government, even when established among the Germans (for it was not universal) possessed a very limited authority; and though the sovereign was usually chosen from among the royal family, he was directed in every measure by the common consent of the nation over whom he presided. . . . The free constitutions then established [at the time of the Northern invasions], however impaired by the encroachments of succeeding princes, still preserve an air of independence and legal administration, which distinguish the European nations; and if that part of the globe maintain sentiments of liberty, honour, equity, and valour superior to the rest of mankind, it owes these advantages chiefly to the seeds implanted by those generous barbarians.[56]

It is interesting that Locke equates the end of "civil government," the quiet enjoyment of the fruits of man's industry, with "rationality"; that he finds the rule of law—"politic society"—necessary " 'to furnish ourselves with competent store of things needful for such a life as our nature doth desire—a life fit for the dignity of man' " (the words, quoted approvingly by Locke, are Hooker's); that under arbitrary government, man "as if he were degraded from the common state of rational creatures . . . is exposed to all the misery and inconveniences that a man can fear from one who, being in the unrestrained state of nature, is yet corrupted with flattery, and armed with power." Locke goes on in a passage curiously Johnsonian in style:

For he that thinks absolute power purifies man's blood, and corrects the baseness of human nature, need but read the history of this or any other age, to be convinced of the contrary. He that would have been insolent and injurious in the woods of America, would not probably be much better in a throne; where, perhaps, learning and religion shall be found out to justify all that he shall do to his subjects, and the sword presently silence all those that dare question it. For what the protection of absolute monarchy is, what kind of fathers of their countries it makes princes to be, and to what a degree of happiness and security it carries civil society, where this sort of government is grown to perfection, he that will look into the late relation of Ceylon may easily see.[57]

Or, perhaps, he that looks into Knolles' *General History of the Turks*. To say of *Irene* that its theme is the effect of power on character—that absolute power corrupts absolutely—would be an oversimplification of this not too coherently organized or sharply pointed early work of Johnson. Yet the statement is a valid commentary on the fate of Mahomet and the two most nearly connected with him, Irene and Cali. The play demonstrates, what was already demonstrated in the *Voyage to Abyssinia* and was often to be demonstrated in his later writings, that Johnson had a deep-seated aversion to an excess of the power of one rational human being over another.

It must be insisted that the expression of this aversion is not something anomalous and unexpected in Johnson. It would be wrong to summarize the political tendencies of these two early works by saying that "they reveal no evidence of Johnson's later Toryism," or some such question-begging formulation. We are trying to determine, from the evidence, what the nature of Johnson's Toryism was, and we must avoid being seduced by Whig propaganda into prejudging the question and assuming that, by definition, Whiggism has a monopoly on the regard for individual liberty. It is clear that the Toryism of Johnson and Hume accepted as wholeheartedly as any species of Whiggism Locke's principle of the rule of law, sanctioned by popular consent, as the only possible basis for a satisfactory system of government. Conversely, it is clear that Locke, no less than Johnson and Hume, derived much of his concern to foster the "rule of law" from the memory of the events of 1640–60, of such examples of arbitrary government, of "the Lust of Innovation," as the Staffordshire Parliamentary governing committee provided. "A wise Tory and a wise Whig, I believe, will agree," wrote Johnson, in all seriousness. "Their principles are the same." The political references in *Irene* and *A Voyage to Abyssinia* are important in defining those common principles; and they should be thought of not as something opposed to later expressions of "authoritarianism" by Johnson, but as something fundamental to them.

Chapter Four

LONDON AND WALPOLE (1737–1739)

1. GRUB STREET AND WESTMINSTER

WHEN JOHNSON set out from Lichfield for London in 1737, he was twenty-eight years old, and a failure. A career in the University, the Church, the learned professions had been denied to him by his poverty, or the unavailability of a patron, or the unlikelihood of his being willing to cultivate one if one had appeared. Even in the poor makeshift of elementary schoolmastering, he must have come to see that his deficiencies of personality were almost impassable barriers to even a minimum of success. There was only one further alternative means of earning a living by the use of his brains—that of writing for money; and so Johnson went to London as the most likely place to earn it.

The sociological implications of Johnson's decision have often been canvassed. It is hardly necessary to describe once again the low social status of Grub Street, to point out how Johnson's stubborn refusal to feel himself degraded by his occupation raised the estate of his fellow writers and "dealt the death blow to patronage," or to comment on the irony with which, if Johnson were the opponent of "levelling tendencies" and subversion of the social order he is said to have been, the example of his own career should have contributed greatly to just these things. It may be, as Sir Sydney Roberts suggests, that the circumstances which thrust him into Grub Street to sink or swim were on the whole a good thing both for us and for Johnson.[1] Perhaps. Yet men do not always feel kindly toward what in the long run turns out to be "good for them."

If Johnson could at times stridently assert the dignity of the trade of letters and offend the aesthetes by proclaiming that "no man but a blockhead ever wrote except for money," [2] no one was better acquainted with the agony that extended composition affords to an acutely critical, self-distrustful mind. The decision forced on him to abandon hope of an easier and more respectable path to security must have produced in him, as he first surveyed the squalor of Grub Street existence, the culmination of all his bitterness. Though flashes of emotional violence had occurred in his earlier writings and were to occur sporadically in the writings of his later life, this violence is nowhere so concentrated as in the productions of his early years in London—the poem *London* itself, the *Marmor Norfolciense,* the *Vindication of the Licensers of the Stage.*

These early works, so highly political in their content, are obviously important for understanding the development of Johnson's political thought, and one wishes that more were known about the circumstances that led to their writing. One can at least say that the political atmosphere in which Johnson lived and worked during this time was certainly not predominantly Tory, and insofar as it was Tory at all the Toryism of the hard-working, impecunious journalists of St. John's Gate would have been a very different thing from the high-flying, fashionable, and slightly precious Toryism of the Dawley-Twickenham coterie of Bolingbroke, Pope, Swift, Gay, and Arbuthnot. William Guthrie, Johnson's close associate on the staff of the *Gentleman's Magazine,* was, according to Boswell, "an adherent of the unfortunate house of Stuart" [3]—whatever that may have meant—and was pensioned by the Pelham government in 1745 to keep him quiet. But a Jacobitism so easily quieted could not have been particularly vigorous. Cave, Johnson tells us, had been a Tory in the years immediately after his apprenticeship, when he wrote for *Mist's Journal.* But when he obtained "a small place in the Post-Office" through his wife's influence, "as interest is powerful, and conversation, however mean, in time persuasive, he by degrees inclined to another party; in which, however, he was always moderate, though steady and determined." [4] Birch, a client of Lord Chancellor Hardwicke, was a Whig. Hawkins was an admirer of Walpole. Harry Hervey Aston, although continually squabbling with his staunchly Whig family, was certainly no Tory, and during Johnson's first year in London sought to ingratiate himself with his brother and the Court by turning into English (perhaps with Johnson's assistance) Lord Hervey's Latin eulogy of his late friend Queen Caroline.[5] Although Elizabeth Carter, as became so moral and learned a young lady, seems to have had no particular politics, she was at various times the protégée of the Whig Archbishop Secker and the great Pulteney, Earl of Bath.

But of all Johnson's friends of his early days in London, one was pre-eminent in the fascination that he exercised on Johnson; and if a spark of bitterness was smoldering in Johnson's breast when he arrived in London, Richard Savage was the one person above all others suited to fan it into flame. Temperamentally, the two men had much in common: the affair of the boots at Oxford is a disturbing parallel to the anecdote that Johnson relates of Savage's rejecting a suit of clothes that had been offered to him "with some neglect of ceremonies." If there was one time in Johnson's life more than another when he was susceptible to the contagion of self-pity, it was in the years 1737 to 1740, after he had uprooted himself from whatever suggestion of security the Midlands may have afforded him and before he had any assurance that he would be able to survive in London.

Not only did Savage provide Johnson with reinforcement for Johnson's own latent "injustice-collecting" tendencies; he also provided him with a perfect object for "unconscious aggression" [6]—Sir Robert Walpole. The two crowded centuries that have passed since Walpole's death, and the careers of the various men, many of them complex and interesting figures, who succeeded him in the office of Prime Minister, have not rendered him the less fascinating and enigmatic. It is difficult even today to regard him without a feeling of partisanship for or against him. No man, certainly no politician, seems to have cared less what people in general, and his enemies in particular, thought about him, or sought less to appease them. Yet his admirers were extravagant in their admiration, and included persons so diverse and little given to facile hero-worshiping as his son Horace, Queen Caroline, Edmund Burke, and Sir John Hawkins. The two most detailed studies of Walpole, one of the eighteenth and one of the twentieth century—both small classics of biography, in spite of their obvious faults—present Walpole as virtually flawless in his personal character and in the conduct of his public life. To F. S. Oliver, for whom "politics is . . . the noblest career that any man can choose," Walpole appears as the type of every political virtue.[7] Coxe thinks so highly of Walpole as to be able to pass off his notorious sexual laxity, which the Archdeacon candidly admits "in his latter years was totally incompatible with his age and figure," as "this foible" which he "shared in common with many able men, and particularly with cardinal Richelieu." [8]

As remarkable as the enthusiasm that Walpole aroused among his admirers was the extent and virulence of the opposition that pursued him unceasingly for the twenty years that he held the office of First Lord of the Treasury. When he came into power in 1721, the leader of a small group of rebellious Whigs, after the official Whig leadership of Stanhope and Sunderland had become hopelessly lost in the debacle of the South Sea Bubble, the opposition arrayed against him included "the Sunderland faction in the cabinet, the Hanoverian courtiers around the King, the press, the City of London, the writers and the wits in Parliament, the self-styled Tories, the opposition

Whigs, and the Jacobites." [9] Later, though some of these opposition groups disappeared, others were added when Walpole
alienated his own most able supporters, Townshend, Carteret,
and Pulteney; when Frederick, Prince of Wales, set up his
political standard; and when Walpole, with almost contemptuous carelessness, permitted the attainted Bolingbroke to return to England and lend his strident aid to the opposition.
Walpole's supporters, who consisted of Queen Caroline (dutifully seconded by the king), a few obedient and unimpressive
politicians like the Pelhams and Sir William Yonge, and a few
second-rate writers and journalists, seem by comparison hopelessly outmatched.

Nevertheless Walpole did remain in power, commanding a
majority in Parliament, for a length of time never since
equaled in the history of Great Britain. Since his conduct
enters so frequently into the literary history of the time, it is
of some importance that the literary scholar should try to regard him with a view, if possible, undistorted by the propaganda of the time. It is understandable that students of English literature, spending the bulk of their time with opposition
writers of the period, of one political shade or another, Pope,
Swift, Gay, Thomson, Fielding, and, most influential of all,
Smollett—for it was in Smollett's, for many decades the standard "popular" English history, that the stereotype was given
its accepted form and passed on to succeeding generations—
should frequently encounter the myth of Walpole as the cynical corrupter of all that was good in English political life, and
even life in general. But of all species of myth, the political is
the last that should be received uncritically.

There is much to be said for Walpole. As valid a presenta-
tion of it as any can be found in Savage's own *Epistle to Walpole* (1732),[10] like much of Savage's work an uneven, derivative, confusedly organized, but always intelligent piece of writing. Savage begins by reprobating the "zeal" of other regimes.

He mentions the persecution of the Jews in the guise of religion, and the suppression of knowledge and general uncertainty of life under a religious despotism. Not only are there domestic inconveniences in such a state, but the zealot "sends red Massacre abroad . . . to please with zeal, wild zeal! the God of Peace." "No less abuse," he continues, "had scourged the civil state / When a king's will became a nation's fate." He reviews the miseries of absolutism—the most obvious reference is to France under Louis XIV—with

> . . . commerce flying to some safer shore
> And property reduc'd, to pow'r a prey,
> And Sense and Learning chas'd by Zeal away.

Under the liberty fostered by Queen Elizabeth and William III, by Walpole and George II, Savage contemplates an idyllic England where security of property, freedom of investigation under which "genius now from want to fortune climbs"— all the Lockean virtues—are cherished and encouraged. Throughout the poem, the emphasis is on the individual's right to security as the basis of satisfactory government, and his insecurity under a totalitarian regime. The parallels are obvious between Savage's denunciation of religious proselytization by means of the sword and Johnson's similar denunciation in the preface to *A Voyage to Abyssinia,* and between Savage's Lockeanism and the passage in *Irene* beginning "Such are the woes when arbitrary pow'r."

Savage is supposed to have begun life as a Jacobite (whatever that may mean, one must again interject), and later, after his temporary aberration into Walpolianism, was found in the opposition camp of the Prince of Wales, along with Thomson and Aaron Hill. But how little those labels tell us can be illustrated by comparing the ideas of the *Epistle to Walpole* with those in *Of Public Spirit in Regard to Public Works,* published by Savage in 1737 and subtitled *An Epistle to His Royal*

Highness, Frederick, Prince of Wales,[11] Walpole's deadliest enemy. There is no difference between the political principles enunciated in the one poem and in the other. Frederick is substituted for Walpole as their patron, but the change involves no more alteration in the philosophy asserted than occurred in the *Dunciad* when Cibber was substituted for Theobald as the hero. In Savage's later poem, the basic Lockeanism is found again—the importance of property and trade, the security afforded them by a popular system of government, the increase of knowledge under such a system. There is—a rather novel idea at the time—a vigorous statement of the virtues of an educated middle class; there is a long rhapsody on the benefits of colonization, ending with a humanitarian plea for the proper treatment of natives and against slavery. And this system is traditional and conservative, based on precedent:

> Some [scholars] call from history past time to view,
> And others trace old laws, and sketch out new;
> Thence saving rights by legislators planned,
> And guardian patriots thence inspire the land.

The value of Savage to the student of the history of ideas is not that he was a distinguished or original thinker, but rather the opposite—that his opinions represent those of the average "enlightened" intellectual of the time. The fundamental Lockean assumptions of this complex of political ideas—"the rule of law"; the virtuousness of industry; the natural equality of all men, whatever the color of their skin; the conception of the middle class as the vehicle of a majority of the virtues; a distrust of institutionalized religion; the subjection of the various interacting branches of government to a stable, conservative constitution based on historical precedent; a general aura of humanitarianism—all were certainly accepted, after 1688, by the great bulk of Englishmen capable of thought about such matters, whether they called themselves Whigs or

Tories; and indeed they are basic to much liberal thinking today. That Johnson was not prepared to subscribe to Savage's political opinions *in toto* is evident in his life of his friend, where he treats some of them, such as his notions about colonization, with considerable acidity. Nevertheless, it is clear that, on the whole, this complex of political ideas and attitudes, whether it be called liberal or some other name, was the matrix in which the specific political attitudes of Johnson and some other eighteenth-century Tories were formed.

2. *London*

At just what time Johnson and Savage met and began to walk "round Grosvenor-square till four in the morning, in the course of their conversation reforming the world, dethroning princes, establishing new forms of government, and giving laws to the several states of Europe" [12] is not certain. But some stimulus caused Johnson to plunge into the midst of current politics with *London: A Poem in Imitation of the Third Satire of Juvenal,* which appeared on May 13, 1738. Hawkins tells the story of how George Lyttelton, now one of the rising hopes of the opposition Whigs, came running with a copy of it to Pope, little knowing that his praise was bestowed on his boyhood antagonist of Hagley.[13] That Lyttelton, whose *Henry II* Johnson characterized as "vulgar Whiggism," [14] should have admired the poem is understandable, for it rehearses all the commonplaces of contemporary opposition propaganda against the Walpole regime. It is a haphazard list of the various things connected with London that Johnson dislikes. Many of these have no particular connection with politics: probably not even the most virulent of the *Craftsman's* writers would have gone so far as to blame Walpole for the prevalence of female atheists, falling houses, and castrati. The matter about which Johnson writes with most feeling, "SLOW RISES WORTH

BY POVERTY DEPRESSED," he does not relate very specifically to politics. But there is still left a considerable amount of pure political propaganda. The great issue of the moment was the alleged oppression inflicted by the Spanish on British commerce. The session of Parliament that had opened on January 24, 1738, was given over to excited inquiry into stories of Spanish depredations, and in March Captain Jenkins produced his famous ear before an investigating committee of the House of Commons. By way of contrast to this state of things, Johnson recalls the golden days of Elizabeth—a favorite myth of the opposition—when the English flag was

> The guard of commerce, and the dread of Spain,
> Ere masquerades debauch'd, excise oppress'd,
> Or English honour grew a standing jest.

It must be remembered, when considering modern assertions (chiefly by literary students) that Walpole and his Whigs were the representatives of the commercial and moneyed interests and that the opposition stood for the good old English pastoral virtues, that one of the opposition's main charges against Walpole was that he was neglecting commerce and subverting the interests of the trading community.[15] The Spanish war was as clearly motivated as any war has ever been by the desire for commercial gain, the desire of the London and Bristol trading interests to break Spain's long monopoly of South American and Pacific trade. The most vociferous advocates of the war in the House of Commons were Aldermen Perry and Willimot and Sir John Barnard, members for the City of London, ably assisted by young William Pitt, whose family had made its fortune in the East India trade and who was just beginning his career as the great proponent of British expansion. It is on their side that Johnson is undeniably found in *London:*

> Here let those reign, whom pensions can incite
> To vote a patriot black, a courtier white;
> Explain their country's dear-bought rights away,
> And plead for pirates * in the face of day.

Along with hatred of Spain is inculcated hatred of France—"I cannot bear a French metropolis." One of the chief elements of Walpole's foreign policy was his alliance with France under the Regent Orleans and Cardinal Fleury. The themes of the corruption, decadence, subservience, susceptibility to bribery, and loss of public spirit of the British nation, on which all the opposition writers played endless variations, are again re-hearsed.[16] References are made to the great days of Queen Elizabeth, who beat the Spanish, of Henry V and Edward III, who beat the French, of King Alfred, when "no spies were paid"—Walpole and Newcastle were alleged to use the secret-service funds for their own political ends—and "no special juries known." [17] There is a slap at the memory of Marl-borough, and at Lord Hervey,[18] the Court's tame intellectual. Sneering mention is made of the "licens'd stage" [19]—the Stage Licensing Act of 1737 became the subject of another of John-son's satires just a year later. The excise and the government propagandist organ, the *Daily Gazetteer*, are lampooned. A final attack is made on George II for his annual trips to his mistress in Hanover:

> Propose your schemes, ye Senatorian band,
> Whose ways and means support the sinking land:
> Lest ropes be wanting in the tempting spring,
> To rig another convoy for the k——g.

All these things are the merest commonplaces of opposition propaganda. Even when one exercises the willing suspension of disbelief and accepts the myth of Walpolian diabolism,

* [Johnson's note:] The invasions of the Spaniards were defended in the Houses of Parliament.

London, as a poetic version of political emotion, is far below Pope's great *Epilogue to the Satires,* published on the same day. To be sure, there is an exuberant vigor about it that makes it far from negligible as poetry; and obviously Johnson is being very serious indeed—the fine textuie of the poetry supports the judgment—in the passages where he illustrates the pain of *res angusta domi.* But on the whole, the work, as serious political criticism, is jejune.

Some explanation of Johnson's sudden incursion into violent partisan politics seems called for. If one attempts a psychological reconstruction of the way his political writings of 1738 and 1739 came into being, one must imagine the young Johnson newly arrived in London, sore at the neglect of the world, repelled by the ugliness of city life, and homesick for the gentler scenes of the Midlands. Through the instrumentality of Savage, or Hervey, or Guthrie, or the *Craftsman,* there is revealed to Johnson the appalling wickedness of Walpole's regime, which is responsible for the sad state of a world in which "slow rises worth." The young man's eyes are opened. He eagerly seizes on the Walpolian iniquities and uses them as pegs on which to hang his own griefs: bribery and castrati and masquerades become projections and symbols of the Johnsonian dissatisfaction with the world (as, in his maturer poems, the death of Charles XII or of old Levet becomes the vehicle for Johnson's sense of the *lachrymæ rerum*). This is to make out Johnson to be a rather naive young man; yet, after all, until he arrived in London he had lived on the whole a bookish and academic life, and there is little evidence of his having had close contact with the realities of current national politics. True, there had been the discussions around Walmesley's hospitable table; but it may be imagined that they had chiefly to do with a repetition of the great battles of the days of Queen Anne or the *minutiæ* of the operations of the Lichfield party machines rather than with the scene at Westminster. There would have been nothing in his earlier experience to cause Johnson to doubt, *prima facie,* the horrendous picture of a vast Walpolian conspiracy to subvert the liberties and virtues of England.

3. *The State of Affairs in Lilliput*

Another anti-Walpole tract evidently by Johnson appeared the next month after *London.* This is the piece in the *Gentleman's Magazine* for June 1738 entitled "Appendix to Capt. Lemuel Gulliver's Account of the Famous Empire of Lilliput" and in the running heads of the pages "State of Affairs in Lilliput." [20] To introduce the famous series of "Debates in the Senate of Lilliput" which the magazine ran from 1738 to 1746, in which Johnson was at first concerned as helper and reviser to Guthrie, and later as sole writer, a narrative was invented of how Captain Gulliver's grandson returned to Lilliput; discovered that the cloud under which his grandfather had left the island had dissipated, and was received hospitably; was told that Lilliput had undergone a revolution and the constitution of the island been resettled on precisely the same basis as that of Great Britain; and learned further that the Lilliputians of his grandfather's time had scandalously deceived him about the geography of the Lilliputian universe—far from consisting only of Lilliput and Blefuscu, it was a microcosmic duplicate of the world of the eighteenth century. After three years' stay, young Gulliver returned to England with a cargo of "Histories, Memoirs, Tracts, Speeches, Treaties, Debates, Letters, and Instructions," of which the *Gentleman's Magazine* now proposes to favor its readers with regular instalments.

In order that they may properly understand the first instalment of the Lilliputian papers (i.e. the current debates in Parliament), the author proposes to bring them up to date in Lilliputian affairs; and this proposal affords him a fine opportunity for editorial comment on recent British politics. Since the main topic of debate at the moment is the imminent war with Spain over trade with her overseas possessions, the commentary is mostly a discussion of colonial policy, a favorite topic of Johnson's. Indeed, the piece provides as clear a statement as any we have of Johnson's very decided views on the matter of colonies:

> The people of Degulia, or the Lilliputian Europe . . . have made conquests, and settled colonies in very distant regions, the inhabitants of which they look upon as barbarous, tho' in simplicity of manners, probity and temperance superior to themselves; and seem to think that they have a right to treat them as passion, interest or caprice shall direct, without much regard to the rules of justice or humanity; they have carried this imaginary sovereignty so far, that they have sometimes proceeded to rapine, bloodshed, and desolation. . . .
>
> It is observable that their conquests and acquisitions in Columbia (which is the Lilliputian name for the country that answers our America) have very little contributed to the power of those nations which have, to obtain them, broke thro' all the ties of human nature. They have indeed added extent to their territories, and procured new titles for their princes, but at the same time have exhausted their mother country of its inhabitants, and subjected themselves to a thousand insults, by possessing vast tracts of land which are too spacious to be constantly garrison'd, and too remote to be occasionally and duly supply'd.[21]

All this is greatly relevant to Johnson's later pronouncements, in *Taxation No Tyranny* and elsewhere, on the subject of colonialism. The writer goes on to say that the Spanish acquisitions in America have only wasted the power of Spain, although "It must be observed to the honour of the Lilliputians [the British], who have in all ages been famous for their politicks, that they have the art of civilizing their remote dominions without doing much injury to their native country" (a beautifully ironic remark), and speaks in equally ironic praise of the British system of penal transportation.

From here a transition is made to the rise of the current quarrel with Spain. The usual jingoistic opposition view is expressed—"The Lilliputians, contrary to the ancient genius of that martial people, made very liberal conccssions, such as rather drew upon them the imputation of cowardice than procured them the praise of moderation; but the Iberians, insatiable in their ambition, resolved to insist on nothing less than the absolute uninterrupted possession of that whole quarter of the world"—and the usual reports of Spanish atrocities against British seamen are rehearsed. Gulliver Junior now turns to an account of the great revolution of Lilliput: at the end of his grandfather's visit,

the People, who had been irritated against him by false reports, finding the same evil measures that were imputed to his advice still pursued . . . surrounded the royal palace, and demanded the heads of the Man-Mountain's accusers. The Ministers, according to custom, ran for shelter to the royal authority; but far from appeasing the people by that artifice, they involved their master in the common destruction. The people . . . set fire to the palace, and buried the whole royal family in its ruins.

The sedition implied in this is hair-raising.

After a new king is chosen and the constitution "new-modelled" after the British, things begin to go to the bad again: the House of Clinabs (Commons) "were at first elected every moon, but now continue in office seven moons; to which alteration many attribute the present venality and dependency discovered in their assemblies. They were likewise anciently paid by the people they represented for their attendance on the public business; but of late it is more common for the Clinabs to pay the people for admitting them to attend." The Septennial Act of 1716, extending the life of Parliament to seven years, was a constant object of attack by the opposition, especially the Tory section of it.[22] There follows a scathing denunciation of the moral character of contemporary mem-

bers of Parliament. The narrative then states the purpose that
"incited Mr. Gulliver to pursue his search into their laws, customs, and history," and that inspires the *Gentleman's Magazine* to reprint the Lilliputian documents—"if haply he might
discover, since human nature generally operated alike in all
parts of the world [a truly Johnsonian sentiment], by what
means the government of Lilliput, which had been once
established on so excellent a plan, became so miserably degen-
erate; while the government of Britain, its original, maintained inviolate the purity and vigour of its primitive constitution." On this nicely ironic note, Gulliver Junior's narrative
concludes.

As political criticism, the *State of Affairs in Lilliput* is more
mature than *London*. A kind of (negative) theory of colonies
is worked out, which leads to a very different conclusion from
the view expressed in *London* of colonies as the refuge of the
innocent victims of oppression—

> Has Heaven reserv'd, in pity to the poor,
> No pathless waste, or undiscover'd shore. . . .
> No peaceful desart yet unclaim'd by SPAIN?
> Quick let us rise, the happy seats explore. . . .

Here, colonies are, with Spain, the excuse for massacres and a
radical source of weakness to Spain herself; with Britain, a
dumping ground for criminals. It is a retreat from the Rous-
seauistic notions of Savage and a return to the realism of the
preface to *A Voyage to Abyssinia*, to Johnson's normal distrust
of colonialism, for both humanitarian and economic reasons,
which will be found consistently in his writings over the next
forty years, and which is basic to Johnson's whole interpretation of British policy in that age of Britain's expansion. For
the rest, the remarks about septennial parliaments, the vituperation against the Walpolian House of Commons, and the
cry of "degeneration" from the good old times, are standard
opposition polemics.

4. *Marmor Norfolciense*

Johnson returned to the attack in the spring of 1739, with the publication of *Marmor Norfolciense; or, An Essay on an Ancient Prophetical Inscription in Monkish Rhyme Lately Discovered near Lynn; by Probus Britanicus* [23]—a tract so virulent that, according to Hawkins, it roused the government, used as it was to invective, to issue a warrant for Johnson's arrest, which he avoided by "going underground" for a time in Lambeth. A stone is dug up in a Norfolk field, Norfolk being the home of the Walpoles and Townshends; indeed, Robert Walpole was member of Parliament for King's Lynn, mentioned in the subtitle. The stone bears a cryptic prophecy, which the writer, donning the mask of a judicious and pedantic scholar, well-affected to the administration, purports to interpret.

> Whene'er this stone, now hid beneath the lake,
> The horse shall trample, or the plough shall break,
> Then, O my country! shalt thou groan distrest,
> Grief swell thine eyes, and terror chill thy breast.

So the inscription begins, and it goes on to enumerate in detail the usual "woes" under which the opposition asserted the country was groaning. "Scarlet reptiles" swarm over the land and devour its substance: that standing armies were a Whig invention, designed to oppress and enslave the people, had been an article of the Tory credo since the days of Cromwell. At the same time, France triumphs over England:

> The lilies o'er the vales triumphant spread;
> Nor shall the lion, wont of old to reign
> Despotic o'er the desolated plain,
> Henceforth th' inviolable bloom invade.

Captain Jenkins and his ear appear again:

> His tortured sons shall die before his face
> While he lies melting in a lewd embrace—

while George II visits his mistress:

> And yet more strange! his veins a horse shall drain
> Nor shall the passive coward once complain.

The white horse appears on the Hanoverian arms: that the king's subordination of British to Hanoverian interests is draining Britain of her wealth and power is another opposition commonplace.

Thus the doggerel ends, and the bumbling commentator adds to the fun by professing to find it all very obscure and refusing to accept the obvious meaning. The exposition of the prophecy is interrupted by a number of digressions which are perhaps more revealing of Johnson's own particular prejudices than the hackneyed party line put forward in the prophecy itself. As well as the specific reference to George II, there is a sarcastic account of kings in general: "Those whom I have consulted on this occasion [says the loyal commentator] . . . have almost unanimously determined that it [the prophecy] was written by a king. For where else, said they, are we to expect that greatness of mind, and that dignity of expression, so eminently conspicuous in this inscription? . . . Every excellence is inherent in a king." But the commentator disagrees: "For after a laborious and attentive perusal of histories, memoirs, chronicles, lives, characters, vindications, panegyrics and epitaphs, I could find no sufficient authority for ascribing to any of our *English* monarchs, however gracious or glorious, any prophetical knowledge or prescience of futurity . . . nor is it easy to find in the lives of our monarchs many instances of that regard for posterity which seems to have been the prevailing temper of this venerable man." "*Any* of our English monarchs": we are a long way from the golden days of Eliza and Alfred and Henry and Edward.

I have seldom in any of the gracious speeches delivered from the throne . . . discovered any other concern than for the current year, for which supplies are generally demanded in very pressing terms, and sometimes such as imply no remarkable solicitude for posterity. Nothing indeed can be more unreasonable and absurd, than to require that a monarch, distracted with cares and surrounded with enemies, should involve himself in superfluous anxieties, by an unnecessary concern about future generations. . . . That this has been the conduct of most princes is evident from the accounts of all ages and nations.

"Most kings is rascals," Johnson seems to be agreeing with Huckleberry Finn's Jim. The student who has taken his notions of Johnson from the standard textbooks may be surprised to hear the accents of a mayor of Chicago in the mouth of the great Tory.[24]

Another digression concerns the incompetence and subservience of the *Daily Gazetteer*. The satire culminates in the proposal that a Society of Commentators be chosen to provide a definitive interpretation of the inscription. Half of these are to be from the Inns of Court and half from the regular army— Walpole had recently been making much use of the legal profession in prosecutions for seditious libel, and a distrust of the army (and an exaltation of the navy) were part of the Tory creed. The commentators are to be housed in Greenwich Hospital, a charitable institution for disabled sailors, "by the expulsion of such of the seamen as have no pretensions to the settlement there but fractured limbs, loss of eyes, or decayed constitutions." The question of how the commentators are to be paid gives Johnson an opportunity for a final pillorying of various fiscal institutions that were butts of the opposition— including Johnson's own *bête noire:* "The salary to be allowed each professor cannot be less than 2000 l. a year, which is indeed more than the regular stipend of a commissioner of excise . . . [but] a commissioner (unless he imprudently allows himself to be carried away by a whimsical tenderness for his country) has an establishment for life." Altogether the Society will cost the country no more than £650,000 a year, "which may be paid out of the sinking fund; [25] or if it be not thought proper to violate that sacred treasure by converting any part of it into uses not primarily intended, may be easily raised by a general poll-tax or excise upon bread."

5. *A Compleat Vindication of the Licensers of the Stage*

In the same Swiftian vein, but more suavely done, is *A Compleat Vindication of the Licensers of the Stage from the Malicious and Scandalous Aspersions of Mr. Brooke, Author of Gustavus Vasa, with a Proposal for Making the Office of Licenser more Extensive and Effectual; by an Impartial Hand,*[26] which was also published in May 1739, only two weeks after *Marmor.* The Stage Licensing Act of 1737,[27] it is pointed out by Coxe, who says for it what can be said for it, was a codification of loosely defined powers that had long been exercised by the Lord Chamberlain and before him the Master of the Revels; it was passed by Parliament speedily and without objection, except from Chesterfield. Its provisions are still in force in England, and there seems to have been not too much overt opposition to it between the times of its two most bitter assailants, Samuel Johnson and Bernard Shaw.

But the first case in which the Lord Chamberlain's examiners denied a license to a play under the new legislation provided the opposition with a fine piece of political capital. The play was *Gustavus Vasa,* the first production of young Henry Brooke. A reading of it demonstrates two things. One is that despite Brooke's denial, in his preface, that he had any thought of reflecting upon the contemporary political scene, the Walpolians cannot be blamed for wanting to ban it; for the situation in the play is a barefaced allegory of the state of England as portrayed in opposition propaganda. A Danish king, with the interests of his own country ever at heart, reigns over Sweden. The Swedes have a long tradition of political

liberty, but their baser passions, worked upon by the usurper
Cristiern, have betrayed their heritage. Cristiern and his despicable prime minister, Trollio, take a cynical view of human
nature and believe that every Swede has his price. But the
patriotic Gustavus returns from exile and conquers the corrupters, restoring their birthright of freedom to the Swedes.
Cristiern vents his wrath on Trollio, "who taught the throne
of pow'r to fix on fear." Trollio perishes in an agony of re-
pentance, and with the utmost melodrama departs (literally)
to hell. All this reproduces so exactly the myth of Walpole as
presented by the *Craftsman,* and presents it with such dema-
gogic violence, that the government might very well have had
a riot on its hands if the play had been produced in London.
With two active candidates available for the role of Gustavus
—Frederick Louis and James Edward—there is a good case
to be made out for the charge of sedition against it.

The second point is that it is easy to detect in the rhapsodic
language of the play many of the elements that commentators
have seen in the later Brooke—an adumbration of the views
of Rousseau, Godwin, Paine, the publicists of the American
and French Revolutions.[28] Liberty and virtue are to be found
in the state of nature, among *sans culottes* and *descamisados.*
Liberty is one of the "rights of man," inherent in Nature
and Reason, and an object for profound, lively, and continuous emotion. Kings are naturally bad, and when in the course
of human events it seems expedient to do so, the people have
the right, indeed the duty, to revolt. Toward the end of the
play the monster Trollio suddenly remembers that in addition
to his other duties he is Archbishop of Upsala, and calls down
the Church's anathema on Gustavus. This gives Gustavus an
opportunity for a long tirade against the Church. It is basically
the same complex of political attitudes as that found in Savage's poem *On Public Spirit,* but much farther advanced in
the direction of the last king hanged with the entrails of the

last priest. And with all this—or at least with Brooke's right to say it—Johnson vigorously concurs.

The *Vindication* is, in fact, a fiery defense of the right of free public discussion of public questions, an expression of withering scorn for official obscurantism, worthy of comparison with *Areopagitica*. If the technique is cruder than that of Milton's tract or some of Swift's great pieces of irony, its faults arise from an excess of emotion, from the exuberance with which the scornful innuendoes come tumbling out one after another. The "vindicator" is a masterpiece of contemptuous caricature, into which Johnson puts all the force of his hatred of intellectual hypocrisy. The spokesman for the government begins by marveling at the opposition's "reference to futurity," a sentiment which he is unable to comprehend:

We have no name for it *at court;* but among themselves they term it by a kind of *cant-phrase,* A REGARD FOR POSTERITY. . . . So strong is their infatuation, that they seem to have forgotten even the primary law of self-preservation . . . and appear in every step to consult not so much their own advantage, as that of *posterity.* Strange delusion! that can confine all their thoughts to a race of men whom they neither know, nor can know; from whom nothing is to be feared, nor any thing to be expected.

It was once prevalent in ancient Rome—this must be the one time on record when Johnson gives currency to the eighteenth-century libertarian myth of republican Rome—but "in England it never prevailed to any such degree: some few of the ancient Barons seem indeed to have been disordered by it" (the reference is no doubt to Magna Carta; it is worth noting that the picture of the English nobility as the ancient guardians of liberty is pure Whiggism). The worst offenders are poets, "who have laid out their lives upon the composition of poems, for the sake of being applauded by this imaginary generation." The Quixotic regard for posterity, the vindicator complains, is almost always complicated with ideas of the high prerogatives of human nature, of a sacred unalienable birthright, which no man has conferred on us, and which neither kings can take, nor senates give away. . . . The natural consequences of these chimeras is contempt for authority, and an irreverence for any superiority but what is founded upon merit; and their notions of merit are very peculiar, for it is among them no great proof of merit to be wealthy and powerful.

But Brooke will find little support from the public, "since the opinions of the sect in which he is enlisted are exposed, and shewn to be evidently and demonstrably opposite to that system of subordination and dependence, to which we are indebted for the present tranquillity of the nation, and that chearfulness and readiness with which the two Houses concur in all our designs."

The satire continues with a "vindication" of the arbitrary actions of the licensers—"What is power but the liberty of acting without being accountable?" That is why the Licensing Act was passed, to empower the Lord Chamberlain "to do that *without* reason, which *with* reason he could do before. We have found by long experience, that to lie under a necessity of assigning reasons is very troublesome." And the vindicator exemplifies his point by showing that none of the reasons the government gives for maintaining a standing army satisfies its critics.

At last he comes to the play itself, and in horror quotes some of the more subversive passages:

> Great Nature's law, the law within the breast,
>   . . . stamp'd by Heav'n upon th' unletter'd mind.

By which he evidently intends to insinuate a maxim which is, I hope, as false as it is pernicious, that men are naturally fond of liberty till those unborn ideas and desires are effaced by literature. . . .

The tatters of Gustavus, the usual dress of the assertors of these doctrines, are of more divinity, because they are sacred to freedom, than the sumptuous and magnificent robes of regality itself. Such sentiments are truly detestable.

The vindicator concludes by recommending that the censorship of the stage be extended to include all intellectual pursuits. The most effective way of combating insubordination is by closing all grammar schools, "in which the lower ranks of the people, and the youngest sons of our nobility and gentry are taught, from their earliest infancy, the pernicious arts of spelling and reading." "It may be made felony to teach to read without a license from the Lord Chamberlain . . . and the nation will rest at length in ignorance and peace."

It is crude, it is obvious, but its vigor is very fine. It is also Whiggism of the first water. There are only two suggestions in it of attitudes that would have been inconsistent with its having been written by a disciple of Paine or Rousseau. One is Johnson's avoidance of anything resembling the anticlericalism found in Savage and Brooke. There is nowhere in any of Johnson's most violent writings of this period any criticism of the Anglican episcopacy who supported Walpole and came in for much abuse by the opposition writers. On the contrary, in the *Vindication* Johnson is careful to make it seem that the enemies of the Church are on the side of the government— "Are we to suspect," his vindicator cries, "our placemen, our pensioners, our generals, our lawyers, our best friends in both houses, *all our adherents among the atheists and infidels,* and our very Gazetteers, clerks, and court pages, as friends to independency?" This is certainly straining the facts, when the most notorious infidel of them all, Bolingbroke, was one of the chief figures of the opposition, and when the villainous prime minister of Brooke's play is represented as Archbishop of Upsala; but it shows where Johnson's real allegiance lay. Again, in his exposition of Brooke's remark that liberty is "stamp'd by Heav'n upon th' unletter'd mind," Johnson avoids the obvious course of treating the passage in the primitivistic spirit in which it was certainly written, of suggesting that true wisdom lies in illiteracy ("I'd smile with the simple and feed with the poor"), but ingeniously twists it so that the government's spokesman is made to retort that "the unlettered have been our warmest and most constant defenders." This is hardly what Brooke had in mind, but it is a tribute both to Johnson's powers of casuistry and to his profound distrust of ignorance.

It is also notable that in this pamphlet Johnson seems to be distinctly allying himself not with the Tories, but with the Whigs, of the opposition, especially the younger and more intransigent Whigs—"the boys," as Walpole called them. Two members of the opposition are mentioned by name, or rather by initial, the Whigs Lyttelton and Pitt. Lyttelton's pamphlet, *Considerations on the Present State of Affairs* (1739), is favorably referred to, and "Enquiries into the Conduct of the Administration" might mean Pulteney's *Enquiry into the Conduct of Our Domestic Affairs* (1734). No Tories are mentioned at all. It must be kept in mind that the real Tories of the House of Commons never allied themselves completely with the agitation against Walpole. In February 1737, for instance, Pulteney introduced in the House a resolution requesting the king to settle an annual income of £100,000 on the Prince of Wales. The measure was designed to embarrass Walpole, and it nearly accomplished its purpose, being defeated by a vote of only 234 to 204. "This small majority of 30," Coxe reports, "would have been reduced to a minority, had Sir William Wyndham been able to fulfil the promise of support which he made to the prince in the name of his party. But forty-five Tories considered the interference of parliament as hostile to the principles of the British constitution, highly democratic, and such a dangerous innovation that they quitted the house in a body before the division." [29] The Tories supported Walpole on other critical occasions, and did so more frequently after Wyndham's death in 1740 dissolved the uneasy connection that Bolingbroke had with them. It must be said, then, that if a label has to be given to the politics manifested in Johnson's *Vindication* of 1739, it cannot legitimately be that of Tory; it must be opposition Whig, and "left-wing" opposition Whig at that.

These pieces, *London, Marmor Norfolciense,* and the *Compleat Vindication* (together with the "State of Affairs in Lilliput"), have always been a difficult problem for those who wish to store Johnson's political philosophy away in a neat pigeonhole marked "Tory reactionary." Too much of what Johnson condemns in them, especially in the *Vindication,* sounds like a malicious travesty of the later Johnson as Boswell has taught us to see him. Perhaps it is all insincere. So Joseph Wood Krutch seems to think:

Since Johnson himself was probably not greatly concerned over the question of the rightness or wrongness of the lord chamberlain in the exercise of his new duties as licenser of the stage [why not, with *Irene* in his pocket?] . . . both pamphlets [*Marmor* and the *Vindication*] were probably pure hack work. . . . It is hardly too much to say that most of the themes of [*London*], from the sad fate of those condemned to suffer under a corrupt and tyrannical government to the felicities of rural retirement, come under the head of the cant which he so impatiently urged Boswell to "clear his mind of." [30]

Conceivably so. Yet it is hard to read through the *Vindication* and not catch some warmth from the white heat in which Johnson forges his shafts against the "petty Tyrants" of vested bureaucracy, types of anti-intellectualism of all ages and places. "Incendiary" and "sulphurous" are the adjectives one student uses to describe the *Marmor* and the *Vindication,* and they are well chosen.[31]

It is easy enough to find "explanations" of Johnson's political extremism during these two years, 1738 and 1739—for instance, the suggestion made above that, embittered at his failures in the Midlands and still unsure of himself in Grub Street, he was easily persuaded by the irresponsible and attractive Savage, perhaps with help from Harry Hervey and Guthrie, to find an outlet for his emotional violence in the opposition cause. Certainly, greater experience and maturity modified this violence. It is wrong, however, to view this episode, as Krutch and others have done, as an aberration from Johnson's "real" political attitudes. For one thing, we do not know that Johnson, up until this time, had formulated any very definite opinions about politics at the national level. Second, and more important, there is no reason for believing that the political principles underlying these early pamphlets are in fact essentially different from those underlying his later political writings. There is no evidence, in his later works, that he ever retracted his affirmation, implicit in the *Marmor* and the *Vindication,* that the only satisfactory basis for a political system must be the enlightened minds of free and responsible individuals. There is no evidence that he ever came to regard as "cant" "the sad fate of those condemned to suffer under a corrupt and tyrannical government": Johnson himself places the word "cant" in the mouth of his contemptible "vindicator." "A regard for posterity," "liberty,'" "tyranny," and "slavery" are not in themselves cant: they represent very real and serious concepts. Their *use* by polemicists in situations where there is no sufficient basis for them in fact, no valid referent, is cant.

We may disagree with Johnson in his interpretation of the facts, his reading of the implications of some situations; but we have no reason to assert that his *principles* changed. It is not paradoxical that Johnson in the 1730's should speak vigorously for the liberty of the stage, whereas in the 1770's he should condemn the "cant" of those who spoke for the "liberty" of the Americans. He himself, in the 1770's, used in regard to Negro slavery the same libertarian vocabulary that in the mouths of American and Whig "patriots" he called cant. There is no contradiction of principles necessarily involved in this: the slavery in which the Americans held their Negroes was, in concrete terms, a very different thing from the "slavery" in which the same Americans protested they were held by George III. Johnson's hatred of cant about liberty is evidence of his high, not low, esteem for the thing itself: it appalled him that words like "freedom" and "slavery," which stood for hard and important facts of existence, should be degraded to the claptrap of opportunistic politicians. If one considers the similar degradation in the twentieth century of words like "democracy" and "fascism," one can better understand Johnson's opposition to the "cant" use of "liberty" and "tyranny" and "patriotism"—words which have, in fact, now become virtually meaningless in political discussion. The debasement and perversion of the vocabulary of morals and politics is filled with the gravest potential danger; and Johnson, like Orwell after him, was properly concerned about a future in which "Freedom is slavery" might become a viable slogan. That Johnson deplored cant about "liberty" no more means that he deplored liberty than a modern writer's disapproval of, say, Stalinist cant about "democracy" means that he disapproves of democracy.

True, Johnson came to see before very long that his interpretation of the political scene in the late 1730's had been naive, and he retracted that interpretation. He came to the conclusion that the liberty of the individual was not, on the whole, in danger under Walpole, just as he concluded that it was not in danger at the time of Wilkes and the Middlesex election. But we have no justification for thinking that had a real threat arisen, Johnson would not have opposed it as vigorously as he opposed the Stage Licensing Act. Perhaps the best

word to describe what is common to his pamphlets of the
1730's and the 1770's is "radical," in that he always insists on
getting to the root of the matter, on going behind the façade
of vague and impressive words and slogans and trying to see
what they meant in actual practice. To view the freedom of
the stage and the "freedom" of the Americans as two cognate
and inseparable articles of faith, to be accepted without question by all who profess themselves "liberals," is precisely the
sort of uncritical attitude toward politics—the worship of
words, not things—that Johnson consistently attacked. To
him, they were two separate propositions, that must be reduced to concrete terms, thoroughly analyzed, and their consequences reviewed, before judgment could be passed on
them. What annoyed some of his contemporaries about Johnson, and still annoys some of his readers, is just this insistence
that all propositions involving human conduct are subject to
scrutiny and not to be accepted merely because they have been
subsumed under some fashionable formula. If the most important key to Johnson's thinking is his conviction that the individual has an inalienable responsibility to examine and judge
all human matters for himself, *nullius in verba*—if the meaning of Johnson's "Toryism" is that the label freed him from
the necessity of following any given party line or fashionable
doctrine—then the pamphlets of the 1730's are not so inconsistent with Johnson's later writings as they have sometimes
been asserted to be.

6. THE *Life of Sarpi*

Johnson wrote many other things, of course, during the
years 1738 and 1739. Two of these may be selected as of
special interest to the student of his political opinions. One is
the so-called "Letter on Du Halde's History of China," published in the *Gentleman's Magazine* for July 1738. Its ascrip-
tion to Johnson is far from certain; it is a silly little piece of

propaganda on behalf of Frederick, Prince of Wales, whose greatness of mind is illustrated by his allowing himself to be persuaded of the justice of the Marquess of Carnarvon's claim to act as a proxy godfather at the infant George III's christening, although Frederick had previously chosen someone else for the honor. The introductory paragraphs, containing some ambiguous remarks on the value of studying Chinese history—Cave had recently published a translation of Du Halde—where much more enlightened political manners than those of England can be found, and a quite unambiguous gibe at George II's irascibility, may be by Johnson. Conceivably, the magazine had been requested, by Savage or some other partisan of Frederick's, to publish the anecdote, and Johnson, in the course of his editorial duties, "touched it up."

Of much more importance is Johnson's involvement with the great Venetian historian Paolo Sarpi. Johnson had done a good deal of work on a translation of the *History of the Council of Trent* for Cave, before it was abandoned when a competing translation was discovered to be in progress. None of Johnson's work in connection with this has survived, except a short *Life of Sarpi*, published in the *Gentleman's Magazine* of November 1738,[32] presumably to arouse interest in the forthcoming translation. Like several early "Lives" by Johnson, it is in large part derivative; [33] but the Johnsonian additions are interesting. His account of Sarpi's controversy with the Papacy on the question of the relations between the Roman Catholic Church and the state is heavily weighted against the papal position: "The Venetian writers, whatever might be the abilities of their adversaries, were at least superior to them in the justice of their cause. The propositions maintained on the side of Rome were these: that the Pope is invested with all the authority of heaven and earth. That all princes are his vassals, and that he may annul their laws at pleasure . . . maxims equally shocking, weak, pernicious, and absurd." He quotes approvingly a passage from one of Sarpi's letters: "There is nothing more essential than to ruin the reputation of the Jesuits: by the ruin of the Jesuits, Rome will be ruined; and if Rome is ruined, religion will reform of itself."

The condemnation of ultramontane political theory and of the Jesuits, here and in the preface to *A Voyage to Abyssinia,* reminds the student that Johnson was familiar with the great era of politico-theological controversy of the late sixteenth and early seventeenth centuries, of which Sarpi's *History* was itself an important document. The conflict between, on the one hand, the antinationalistic and antimonarchical doctrines set forth by Pope Paul V and ably argued by Cardinals Baronius, Bellarmine, and Du Perron, and the Jesuits Suarez and Mariana,[34] and, on the other, the nationalist and secularist views put forward by the liberal Catholic Sarpi and by many Protestant writers, was of immense importance in forming English political theory and the climate of political opinion in the seventeenth century. To confirm this, it is enough to mention the connection of the Jesuits and of Mariana's justification of regicide with the Gunpowder Plot of 1605. The court of James I became the headquarters for anti-Jesuit polemics; there James, himself a skilled writer, coordinated the work of such Protestant controversialists, continental and native, as Isaac Casaubon and Lancelot Andrewes.[35]

It is clear that a basic source of Johnson's political thinking, as of English Tory thought of the seventeenth and early eighteenth century generally, was the Protestant side in this controversy. Johnson was familiar with the writings of such anti-Papal polemicists as Buchanan (tutor of James I), Joseph Scaliger, and Sarpi himself; and, of course, the greatest of all political writers of the seventeenth century, Grotius. Neville Figgis, whose treatment of the controversy is classic, remarks how in the late seventeenth century Anglican writers iden-

tified Jesuits and Dissenters as opponents of the English constitutional system: "The commonest term for a Dissenter is
Jesuit. . . . All the special tenets of the Society go for nothing beside this one striking fact, that its members deliberately
weaken the bonds of allegiance and argue that under certain
conditions a nation may resist and even depose its sovereign.
Now the Dissenters teach the same doctrine, and therefore
they may without injustice be dubbed Jesuits in disguise." [36]

As another writer puts it, "In itself, and in its origin, the
doctrine [of the divine right of kings] was nothing more than
a necessary assertion of the independence of the state in the
face of the 'Hildebrandism' of Rome and Geneva alike." [37]
Both the Jesuits and the Staffordshire parliamentary governing committee would subject the individual to an ecclesiastical
tyranny, to a civil, moral, and intellectual totalitarianism;
and to such a condition Johnson is always and unwaveringly
opposed. But a full treatment of the influence on Johnson's
thinking of the politico-theological writings of this period
must wait until a careful study of his reading has been made.

Chapter Five

THE PARLIAMENTARY DEBATES
(1740–1743)

THE summer of 1739 was an eventful one for Johnson. In July, Savage left London forever, parting from Johnson, the latter tells us, with tears in his eyes. Soon after, Johnson left London for the Midlands. He was still trying to escape from Grub Street, and engaged in fruitless negotiation for an appointment as headmaster of a school in Leicestershire. As usual, there were financial troubles: when money was needed for medical attention for his wife, Johnson and his mother mortgaged the house in Lichfield. During this time also, Johnson visited his old school friend, John Taylor of Ashbourne, and met the Ashbourne circle of the Fitzherberts, Boothbys, and Meynells. In the spring of 1740, he returned to London and resumed his work for Cave.

The episode seems to mark a dividing line in the development of Johnson's political attitudes: after his return to London, although the tension in national politics continued to increase and the attacks of the Pulteney-Bolingbroke group against Walpole grew even more violent, Johnson published no more pieces of extended vituperation such as those of 1738 and 1739. Possibly this sudden mildness may indicate greater emotional maturity, some kind of reconcilement to his lot. The disturbing presence of Savage was removed. Possibly, too, the death of Sir William Wyndham, on June 17, 1740, has some bearing on the question, since it dissolved the main link between the Parliamentary Tories and the "patriots" of the opposition.

But the most obvious explanation of why Johnson lacked, if not the conviction, the time and energy for full-dress diatribes against the Walpole regime is that he was engaged to preside over its liquidation in another capacity. During three sessions of Parliament,[1] Johnson was the sole reporter of its debates for the *Gentleman's Magazine*.

The precise determination of the canon of the Johnsonian "Debates" is a difficult problem, and the discussion here will be restricted to the traditional group, those published in the magazine between July 1741 and March 1744.[2] A full analysis of even these is manifestly impossible here, since they make up a document of nearly half a million words. But some general observations and a brief sampling of their contents may be useful. Superficially, the Johnsonian "Debates" are not, of course, much like a modern Hansard or Congressional Record. For one thing, the "Debates" were not published immediately after their occurrence; Cave had apparently determined that no debate should be printed during the session of Parliament in which it took place (presumably to lessen the risk of an action against him for breach of privilege), so that Johnson sometimes had months in which to work up a report—to review deliberately the material at his disposal, then to select, organize, and polish at will. The question of how accurately the printed debates represent what actually took place on the floor of the House has often been discussed and is too technical to go into in great detail here,[3] but it seems to be agreed that what Johnson was doing was *composing* speeches, rather than *reporting* them, in the modern sense.[4]

One thing the reader notices about Johnson's "Debates" is that by contrast with the vast panorama of varied activity that a modern set of Parliamentary debates reflects, only a few major topics are dealt with in each session. Of the various individual debates that took place in the Session of 1740–41 (counting a debate in the Lords and one in the Commons on the same bill or resolution as separate debates), Johnson wrote up a total of sixteen, amounting to 301 pages of the *Gentleman's Magazine* in all; [5] of these, four, the debates on the Seamen's Bill, on the raising of new regiments, and on the address to the King for the removal of Walpole (one in the Lords and one in the Commons), account for nearly 200 pages, an average of fifty pages to each debate, while the other twelve debates get on the average only eight or nine pages each. In his reports of the 1741–42 session, omitting two pages on the proceedings for the choice of a speaker, there are only six debates reported, in a total of 151 pages, or an average of 25 pages each. In the session of 1742–43, Johnson reports only four debates, totaling 185 pages; of these, the two earlier run to only eleven and nineteen pages respectively, whereas the last two, those in the Lords on the state of the army and on the "Gin Bill" are respectively 70 and 85 pages long, each requiring five issues of the magazine to print.

Johnson's method, then, is to take one important controversial topic and make of it a set piece, a formal and exhaustive dissertation in dialogue form. And since the same topic, or different aspects of it, might come up for debate more than once in the same session, or in successive sessions, it is possible to combine these dissertations into even larger groups. Indeed, 405 of the 639 pages of the traditional canon, almost two-thirds, are devoted to two subjects, the removal of Walpole (163 pages) and the state of the armed forces (242 pages). Three other subjects, foreign relations, trade and commerce, and the control of alcoholic liquor, account for almost all the rest of the work. To have to deal with a topic at such exhaustive length must have been a magnificent schooling for Johnson in the art of political analysis.

The question of the dramatic verisimilitude of the "Debates" has considerable bearing on our assessment of Johnson's skill as a student of politics. Hawkins (who was contemporary with the events reported and a careful student of them) asserted that the style of the speeches was well adapted to the character of each speaker. Later students, including Boswell and Hill, have denied this. "Of debating he knew nothing," Hill complains. "There is indeed scarcely any examination of an adversary's arguments." [6] But the careful examination of an adversary's arguments is not so frequent in legislative assemblies as Hill seems to think. A distinction is to be made, of course, between the procedure when a House is in formal session, with the Speaker in the chair or the Chancellor on the woolsack, and the procedure when it is meeting as a committee. On the former occasion, each speaker is limited to one speech on the question at issue, and it is likely to be long, formal, and dignified—in fact, prepared in advance without much knowledge of what the preceding orator is going to say, and linked with it only by the perfunctory efforts that appear in Johnson's reports. It is when the House is in committee and there is no limitation on the number of times that a speaker may rise that we find the rough-and-tumble of informal debate. Even here, the generality of politicians being no more addicted to close reasoning than the average human being, much of the debate is likely to consist of wranglings over points of fact and procedure rather than of logical examination and confutation of argument. Johnson is perfectly aware of these facts, and is able to reproduce the confusion of a Commons committee as well as a formal debate on a second reading in the Lords. As practical a method as any, within the limited space of this essay, of giving the reader some idea of what Johnson was doing in the "Debates" will be to describe in some detail two of his debates, one informally conducted, on an unimportant matter, the other formal and extremely important. The serious student of Johnson will not, of course, be satisfied with these samplings, but should read his way thoughtfully through the whole canon. No one who does will find it possible to acquiesce in the notion that Johnson was a mere dabbler in politics.

One of the most amusing of the debates is that in the Commons on March 13, 15, and 16, 1741, when the House takes the annual Mutiny bill through the committee stage.[7] Sir William Yonge, as Secretary at War, is responsible for piloting the bill. He takes up the clauses of the current Act that relate to the billeting of soldiers on innkeepers and the rates which such innkeepers are allowed to charge the soldiers for subsistence. It appears, says Yonge, that the innkeepers of Ledbury and Wakefield, discovering what they think a loophole in the Act, not only refused troops quartered on them "victuals at the accustomed rates, but proceeding from one latitude of interpretation to another, at length denied them not only the privilege of diet, but the use of kitchen utensils, to dress the provisions which they bought for themselves, and at last denied their claim to the fire itself." Yonge has consulted with the law officers of the Crown and ascertained that the Act does not in fact admit of such interpretation. Nevertheless he intends to move an amendment which will make it explicit that innkeepers are required to feed soldiers billeted on them at fixed rates.

This proposal, innocent as it seems, gives the opposition an opportunity for some fine rhetoric. "The burthen, Sir, of a standing army," declares Samuel Sandys, one of the noisiest of the opposition Whigs, "is already too heavy to be much longer supported, nor ought we to add weight to it by new impositions." Times are hard; "the calamity of famine, one of the severest scourges of providence, has filled the whole land with misery and lamentation, and surely nothing can be more inhuman than to choose out this season of horror for new encroachments on their privileges, and new invasions of the rights of nature, the dominion of their own houses, and

the regulation of their own tables." He refuses to "combine
in laying a new tax upon any class of my countrymen, when
they are sinking under an enormous load of imposts, and in
want of the necessaries of life."

Yonge is not impressed. "Sir, nothing is more easy than out-
cry and exaggeration. . . . The most necessary measures may
often admit of very florid exclamations against them, and may
furnish very fruitful topics of invective." He urges that his
proposal will only have the effect of making definite law what
is now customarily received as such, and that "it is safer to
fix the price of provisions, which must sink in their value,
than to raise the pay of the army, which may never afterwards
be reduced."

"The Urg; *Gybnob*"—Phillips Gybbon, member for Rye,
another active opposition Whig—now rises to attack a brutal
and licentious soldiery:

By enacting laws in general terms, as he [Yonge] seems to advise,
we should leave the unhappy inn-keeper wholly at the mercy of
his guests, who might plunder and insult him under the protection of the legislature. . . . These, Sir, are the natural consequences of a military subjection; and if these consequences are
not always speedily produced by it, they must be retarded . . .
by the frequent inculcation of the wickedness of contributing to
the propagation of slavery, and the subversion of the rights of
nature; inculcations which cannot be avoided by men who live
in constant fellowship with their countrymen.

But soldiers shut up in a barrack . . . will lose all sense of
social duty and of social happiness, and think nothing illustrious
but to inslave and destroy.

Henry Pelham, for the Government (as Paymaster-General
to the Forces the bill concerns him also), deprecates Gybbon's
"loud exaggerations and affected expression of tenderness":
"The question before us, Sir, is in its own nature so simple
. . . that . . . I cannot easily conceive by what art it can be
made the subject of long harangues, or how the most fruitful

imagination can expatiate upon it." He goes into the history
of billeting of soldiers on innkeepers, and points out that innkeepers know they are subject to such billeting when they
take out a licence. "With regard to barracks," he says, in an
admission of interest to the historian of British military life,
"I cannot deny that they are justly names of terror to a free
nation, that they tend to make an army seem part of our constitution, and may contribute to infuse into the soldiers a
disregard of their fellow-subjects, and an indifference about
the liberties of their country."

The debate then becomes wide open. Alexander Hume
Campbell, Solicitor General to the Prince of Wales, argues
that "The power of raising money at pleasure has been
hitherto denied to our kings, and surely we ought not to place
that confidence in the lowest that has been refused to the
most exalted of mankind, or invest our soldiers with power
which neither the most warlike of our monarchs could con-
strain us nor the most popular could allure us to grant." Sir
John Barnard sensibly points out that a number of innkeepers
affected by the Act have no real facilities for accommodating
troops, and that an exception should be made in their case.
Old General Wade begins, "Sir, I have been long conversant
with military affairs," and goes on to expound what was the
practice in King William's day. Pulteney, for the opposition,
closes the day's debate with a masterly speech, in which,
though refusing to concede that the previous opposition
speeches have been uncalled for, as the Government speakers
protest, he nevertheless approaches the question in a moderate and sensible way, acutely criticizing Yonge's proposal and
ending by himself suggesting an amendment that gives the
innkeeper the option either of feeding at a fixed rate soldiers
quartered on him, or of furnishing them with "candles, vinegar, and salt, and with either small beer or cyder, not exceeding three quarts for each man a day gratis, and to allow

them the use of fire, and the necessary utensils for dressing
and eating their meat," while the soldiers provide their own
food.

At the next session, Yonge, after duly deprecating the opposition's tactics, nevertheless accepts Pulteney's amendment.
It might seem that this action should bring the discussion to
a harmonious close. But no: one Thomas Carew, a Tory back-
bencher, objects to the amount of beer allowed: "Three
quarts a day are surely more than the demands of nature
make necessary, and I know not why the legislature should
promote, or confirm in the soldiery, a vice to which they are
already too much inclined, the habit of tippling." Another
Tory, Velters Cornewall, MP for Herefordshire, says, with a
display of Parliamentary wit: "Sir, it is not without the greatest diffidence that I rise to oppose the gentleman who offered
the amendment [Yonge], for his abilities are so far superior
to mine . . . I know not whether it may be allowed me to
observe that the difference between our faculties is with regard to strength and quickness the same as between the cyder
of his country and that of mine." It is an insult to Herefordshire cider to suggest that three quarts of it are equivalent to
three quarts of small beer. One bottle of it sells for more than
a soldier's allowance for a whole day's provisions, and it is
"of such strength that I, who am accustomed to the use of it,
never was able to drink three quarts in a single day."

Yonge replies, a little sourly, "I know not why the gentleman has thought this a proper opportunity for displaying his
eloquence in the praise of his own cyder," but springs nevertheless to the defense of that of his own county, Devonshire:
"In my opinion, the cyder of my native country is of equal excellence with that which this gentleman has so liberally extolled." Cornewall rejoins:

The laws of honour, Sir, require this from me, as they oblige
every man to stand forth a vindicator of merit slighted and op-

pressed; and gratitude calls loudly upon me to exert myself in the protection of that to which I have been often indebted for a pleasing suspense of care, and a welcome flow of spirit and gaiety.

The cyder, Sir, which I am now rescuing from contemptuous comparisons, has often exhilarated my social hours, enlivened the freedom of conversation, and improved the tenderness of friendship, and shall not therefore now want a panegyrist. It is one of those few subjects on which an encomiast may expatiate without deviating from the truth.

Johnson was not to forget this passage when he later came to rebut Jonas Hanway's slurs on the character of tea.

Again the debate is wide open. A Mr. Gore intervenes: "Sir, that the allowance of two quarts a day is sufficient, and that to demand more is a wanton indulgence of appetite, is experimentally known, and therefore no more ought to be imposed upon the inn-keepers." He also objects to the requirement that the innkeeper provide vinegar: "Neither reason nor experience will inform us that vinegar ought to be ranked among the necessaries of life." Various other members interject their views of the amount of small beer a day that a soldier should consume. Yonge for a time defends his three quarts: "There are a few members of this House who do not more than once a day drink tea, coffee, chocolate, or some other cooling and diluting infusion; delicacies which the soldier cannot purchase and to which he is entirely a stranger, and of which the place must be supplied by some other cheap and wholesome liquor." Lord Baltimore agrees: "I believe, Sir, every gentleman who examines the expence of his family, will find that each of his servants consumes daily at least three quarts of small beer, and surely it is not to be required that a soldier should live in a perpetual state of war with his constitution, and a constant inability to comply with the calls of nature." General Handasyde stands up for his soldiers: a private's pay is sixpence a day, of which fourpence goes for food and lodging:

There remain then only two pence, Sir, to be disbursed for things
not immediately necessary for the preservation of life, but which
no man can want without being despicable to others and burden-
some to himself. Two pence a day is all that a soldier has to lay
out upon cleanliness and decency, and with which he is likewise
to keep his arms in order, and to supply himself with some part
of his clothing. If, Sir, after these deductions he can from two
pence a day procure himself the means of enjoying a few happy
moments in the year with his companions over a cup of ale, is
not his œconomy much more to be envied than his luxury?

Yonge eventually agrees to a compromise between the Government's proposal of three quarts of small beer and the opposition's of two quarts, and the bill is at last reported out of
committee with the contentious clause reading, to everyone's,
or no one's, satisfaction, "five pints." "A few days afterward,
being read a third time, [it] was passed, and ordered to the
Lords, where it occasioned no debate."

Johnson must have had a great deal of fun with this. Its
very triviality is proof of his ability to convey the realities of
Parliamentary "debate." Irrelevance, digression, absurdity,
the tendency to expatiate on trifles which a speaker is familiar
with from his own experience, and the constant watch for opportunities to make political capital are the characteristics of
Parliamentary, and other, committee meetings, as any observer knows; it is not Johnson's fault if they are not conducted, as Hill seems to think they should be, like a college
debating society. The first lesson any political writer must
learn is with how little wisdom the world is governed, and
Johnson could have found no better place to learn it than at
the heart of government itself.

As to Hill's charge that the speeches "are commonly formed
of general statements which suit any one speaker just as well
as any other" [8] —a charge that would be fatal to any claim of
political acumen for Johnson if it were true—it is clear, in
this debate at least, that the various speakers, under a certain

façade of Johnsonian prose style of course, are discriminated with care. General Wade makes a point of being a "plain soldier," with his reiteration of "In King William's time we did so-and-so." Sandys and Gybbon, two perpetual opposition gadflies, are made to look a little ridiculous: Hawkins' account applies perfectly to them—"When a more popular orator takes up a debate, his eloquence is by him [Johnson] represented in a glare of false rhetoric, specious reasoning, an affectation of wit, and a disposition to trifle with subjects the most interesting." The Tory back-benchers, Carew and Cornewall, act like back-benchers, innocuous country members, generally inarticulate except when some topic comes up about which they have particular knowledge or concern—in this case, the potency of Herefordshire cider. Sir John Barnard injects some of his businessman's common sense into the mass of verbiage. Advocate Hume Campbell is a pettifogging lawyer. Pelham is a solid and respectable mediocrity. Yonge, who as Secretary at War is supposed to be in control of the debate, appears as well-meaning and worthy, but more than a little confused. The hero of the piece is certainly Pulteney, whose speech represents a level of intelligence and polished style far above the others, combined at the same time with a shrewd awareness of the realities of practical politics. These characteristics correspond well with the judgments that history has passed on these men.

Johnson, then, is representing his speakers with considerable dramatic skill and as they appeared to their contemporaries, and there is no clear evidence of distortion or partiality. His famous remark, that he took care that the Whig dogs should not have the best of it, was probably no more than a piece of ordinary jocularity.[9]

The best place to test a charge of partiality is in the great series of debates dealing with the conduct of Walpole as prime minister. After many unsuccessful attempts, lasting over many years, to bring about his downfall, the opposition finally thought themselves strong enough to mount a frontal attack, a formal vote of want of confidence in Walpole personally. The war with Spain was going badly, and with Frederick of Prussia's aggression against the Silesian territories of Maria Theresa, the prospect of England's becoming involved on the losing side of a great continental war was ominous. It was the opposition's great chance; and on February 13, 1741, Carteret in the House of Lords and Sandys in the House of Commons introduced a motion to address the king, requesting him to dismiss Walpole.

It was this great debate, the climax of twenty years of bitter political struggle, that Johnson was first called upon to report, singlehanded, for the *Gentleman's Magazine*. His report still appears as the quasi-official account, in the *Parliamentary History*. It was an important and must have been an exciting duty for the still young and obscure hack writer to create in effect a piece of history for his contemporaries and for posterity. Johnson proved equal to the responsibility.

The Lords debate, as it appeared in the *Gentleman's Magazine* for July and August 1741, is informed with solemnity and even grandeur. There are only eleven speeches reported on the main motion, and the debate moves in stately antiphony between, on the one side, Carteret and Abingdon (the proposer and seconder), Argyle, Carlisle, Halifax, and Bedford, and on the other, Newcastle, Hardwicke, Cholmondeley, the Bishop of Salisbury (Sherlock), and Hervey. Each side begins with its heaviest armament. Carteret's speech moves with a magnificent sweep up to its final climax:

Such is the present unhappy state of this nation, and such is the general discontent of the people, that tranquillity, adherence to the government, and submission to the laws cannot reasonably be hoped, unless the motion I shall now take leave to make your Lordships be complied with: And I move, That an humble ad-

dress be presented to his Majesty, most humbly to advise and be-
seech his Majesty, that he will be most graciously pleased to remove the Right Honourable Sir Robert Walpole, Knight of the
most noble Order of the Garter, First Commissioner of his Majesty's Treasury, and Chancellor of the Exchequer, and one of
his Majesty's most honourable Privy Council, from his Majesty's
presence and councils for ever [July 1741, p. 350].

Newcastle replies at equal length, in a more labored and solid
fashion. All the important questions of foreign and domestic
policy are stated and restated as the debate proceeds, and it
is at last concluded, by Bedford on the one side and Hervey
on the other, with a short, pointed, and vigorous speech. Hervey's peroration for the defense is worthy Carteret's opening:

> To condemn a man unheard is an open and flagrant violation
> of the first law of justice, but it is still a wider deviation from it
> to punish a man unaccused; no crime has been charged upon
> this gentleman proportioned to the penalty proposed by the mo-
> tion, and the charge that has been produced is destitute of proof.
> Let us therefore, my Lords, reverence the great laws of reason
> and justice, let us preserve our high character and prerogative
> of judges, without descending to the low province of accusers
> and executioners, let us so far regard our reputation, our liberty,
> and our posterity, as to reject the motion [August 1741, p. 416].

The whole debate is a magnificently organized piece of
rhetoric. It would be wrong, however, to give Johnson sole
credit for its effect. The House of Lords in the 1740's did,
after all, pride itself on its oratory. The speakers were classi-
cally educated at Eton and Westminster and Oxford and
Cambridge, and men like Carteret and Hervey would be considered fine classical scholars today. They knew their Cicero
and Demosthenes, and were as conscious as Johnson that on
this occasion they were taking part in a scene of history not
unworthy to be reported by a Thucydides or Tacitus. The
order of speakers, and the substance of their utterances, seem
in fact to be very nearly authentic.[10] Nevertheless, if the ma-

terial of a work of art was here at Johnson's disposal, it is apparent, by comparing Johnson's report with that in the *London Magazine,* that he gave it its final shaping.

Johnson's report of the debate in the House of Commons on the same day did not appear until a year and a half after the report of the Lords debate—two years after its actual occurrence. One can only speculate as to the cause of the delay. One possible reason is that some of the speeches in the Commons against Walpole are so incredibly violent that Cave may well have thought it unsafe to publish them while Walpole was in power. For the general tone of debate in the Commons was—and still is—very different from that in the Lords; as Hawkins puts it, "The characteristic of the one assembly we know is Dignity; the privilege of the other Freedom of expression." [11] Of that privilege, the Commons made copious use on February 13, 1741, and Johnson was able to give the speeches of the opposition the full benefit of the training in composing abuse he had acquired in *Marmor Norfolciense* and the *Vindication of the Licensers.* The invective of some passages is magnificent in its violence, in its grand, rolling, baroque rhythms—and utterly vicious in its content:

[Sandys] When this important period shall arrive, when justice shall call out for the corrupters of their country, the deserters of their allies, and the enemies of commerce; when liberty shall punish the crimes of those by whom she has been long ridiculed and oppressed; when the cries of the exasperated people shall be too loud to be repressed, and vengeance shall impend over those heads which have so long been lifted up with confidence, against truth and virtue, then will be the time in which the army must become the refuge of those who have so long supported it.

Then will the corrupter and his associates, the lacqueys of his train, and the slaves of his levee, then will those who have sold their country for opportunities of debauchery, and wasted the rewards of perfidy in the pleasures of the stews of the court, implore the protection of their military friends, and request them to repay those benefits which they have formerly received. What is then to be expected, but that either they will be given up to punishment by those whom they have pampered at the expense of the public, which is most ardently to be hoped, or that the people will have recourse to arms in assertion of their demands, and that the nation will be laid waste with all the devastations of a civil war? [February 1743, p. 70]

[Pitt] The Minister who neglects any just opportunity of promoting the power or increasing the wealth of his country is to be considered as an enemy to his fellow subjects; but what censure is to be passed upon him who betrays that army to a defeat, by which victory might be obtained; impoverishes the nation whose affairs he is intrusted to transact by those expeditions which might enrich it, who levies armies only to be exposed to pestilence, and compels them to perish in sight of their enemies without molesting them?

It cannot surely be denied that such conduct may justly produce a censure more severe than that which is intended by this motion, and that he who has doomed thousands to the grave, who has cooperated with foreign powers against his country, who has protected its enemies and dishonoured its arms, should be deprived not only of his honours but of his life; that he should be at least stripped of those riches which he has amassed during a long series of prosperous wickedness, and not barely be hindered from making new acquisitions, and increasing his wealth by multiplying his crimes [March 1743, p. 133].

This is demagoguery of the highest, or lowest, order—one hears in it the authentic note of the French Revolution. Surely, it will be said, if Johnson gives much of this kind of thing to the opposition—and there are many pages of it—surely this is partiality; surely for once Johnson is deliberately giving the opposition the best of it. One might think that nothing put into the mouths of the Government speakers could efface the impression of this overwhelming torrent of denunciation.

Only one thing could; and Johnson finds it. After the invective has continued for hours, the debate at last draws to its close. All eyes are directed at Walpole, who has been sitting quietly through it all, not opening his lips. He rises and merely asks "That I may know the whole accusation against me before I offer my defence." Pulteney accepts the challenge, and sums up the opposition's case against Walpole in a speech of great force. At last he is finished, and Walpole rises for the last time. He speaks briefly, simply, quietly, and with utter and devastating courtesy: "The gentlemen who have already spoken in my favour have indeed freed me from the necessity of wearying the House with a long defence, since their knowledge and abilities are so great that I can hope to add nothing to their arguments, and their zeal and their friendship so ardent, that I shall speak with less warmth in my own cause." He devotes a few words to the opposition:

If their dream has really produced in them the terrors which they express, if they are really persuaded that the army is annually established by my authority, that I have the sole disposal of posts and honours, and that I employ this power only to the destruction of liberty, and the diminution of commerce, compassion would direct us to awaken them from so painful a delusion, to force their eyes open and stimulate them to a clear view of their own condition and that of the public, to show them that the prerogative has made no incroachments, that every supply is granted by the senate, and every question debated with the utmost freedom, as before that fatal period in which they were seized with this political delirium that has so long harassed them with the loss of trade, the approach of slavery, the power of the Crown, and the influence of the Minister.

He replies briefly and calmly to Pulteney's charges of personal corruption, concluding,

As to myself, I know not how I have given occasion to any charge of rapacity or avarice, or why I should be suspected of making exorbitant demands upon his Majesty's liberality, since, except the places which I am known to possess, I have obtained no grant from the Crown, or fewer at least than perhaps any man who has been supposed to have enjoyed the confidence of his sovereign. All that has been given me is a little house at a small distance from this city, worth about seven hundred pounds, which I obtained that I might enjoy the quiet of retirement without remitting my attendance on my office.

The little ornament upon my shoulder I had indeed forgot, but this surely cannot be mentioned as a proof of avarice; nor, though it may be looked on with envy and indignation in another place, can it be supposed to raise any resentment in this House, where many must be pleased to see those honours which their ancestors have worn restored again to the Commons.[12]

Having now, Sir, with due submission offered my defence, I shall wait the decision of the House without any other solicitude than for the honour of their counsels, which cannot but be impaired if passion should precipitate, or interest pervert them. For my part, that innocence which has supported me against the clamour of the opposition will establish my happiness in obscurity, nor shall I lose by the censure which is now threatened any other pleasure than that of serving my country.

When he had done speaking, the question was put and carry'd in the negative 290 to 106 [April 1743, pp. 180–3].

So the report ends. It is probably the most dramatic thing Johnson ever wrote. What is most striking about it is that the final speech by Walpole, which provides the dramatic shock, seems to be largely a fiction composed by Johnson for the occasion. Coxe, Walpole's more-or-less official biographer, working from the *London Magazine's* report and from private and presumably authentic sources, produces an entirely different speech, in which Walpole defends himself at length, in monotonous detail, and in a tone of haughty and querulous indignation.[13] Since Walpole was a practicing politician rather than an artistic genius, it seems likely that this is how he would in fact have replied. But such a speech as that in Coxe, capable at best only of equaling, not surpassing, the violence of what has gone before, could not have conveyed the impact of the bare, simple, even noble understatement that Johnson puts into Walpole's mouth. Here, on an occasion of the greatest moment, we seem to have caught Johnson doctoring the evidence—but to make Walpole appear greater, not to discredit him.

This may sound at first a little mad; but it is not. Fine as the drama of the scene is, certain hard political realities underlay that final vote of confidence in Walpole. A hint of what was coming revealed itself near the end of the debate. Lyttelton, declaiming against Walpole, had cited the fact, much insisted on by the opposition, that in 1715 Walpole had moved the impeachment of Harley, and hence need look for no mercy when he himself was in danger. "It is reasonable," Lyttelton proclaims, in no very Christian spirit, "that the authors of evil counsels should feel the effects of their own schemes, and that every man should find that treatment which others have received from him." When Lyttelton had finished, the Tory Edward Harley, later third Earl of Oxford, the nephew of the impeached Lord Treasurer, rose and stated that in spite of his dissatisfaction with the Government's conduct of affairs, he would not vote for the motion to remove Walpole. "I am now, Sir, glad of this opportunity to return good for evil, and do that Hon. gentleman and his family that justice which he denied to mine" (April 1743, p. 172). At another point in the debate, William Shippen, the leader of the most extreme Tories, declared that "he looked on this motion as only a scheme for turning out one minister, and bringing in another . . . it was quite indifferent to him who was in or who was out; and he would give himself no concern in the question." [14] He and thirty-four of his followers abstained from voting, and another twenty Tories voted for Walpole and against the motion.

The Tories had again demonstrated that they preferred Walpole to Pulteney, Carteret, Sandys, Pitt, Lyttelton, and the rest.[15] It is important to remember this fact in considering Johnson's political allegiance at this time. What that was he makes explicit. Immediately following the *Gentleman's*

Magazine report of the debate and the vote in the Commons, there occurs the following passage of editorial comment, which has not been mentioned before by Johnsonian students but is certainly by Johnson and is obviously of value in determining his political attitude at the time:

Thus ended this important and memorable Debate, which produced in one Party loud Exultations, by confirming them in their Opinion of their own Strength, and in the other apparent Dejection, and the usual Consequence of ill Success, Discord and Disunion. Some of the *High-heeld* [Tory] Members of the Senate had withdrawn without voting, others had voted against the Motion, and were therefore branded by some who patronised it with the Name of *Sneakers,* and challenged in a celebrated Pamphlet to answer for their Conduct. . . .

This Reproach soon produced a Vindication, in which it was shown, that the *High-heel'd* Party had acted only according to the Principles, which from Age to Age they had been known to maintain, and from which it was Madness to demand that they should depart on particular Occasions; that Compliance upon any other Motive than Conviction was equally criminal and corrupt, whether it was paid to the Crown or to the People. It was proved farther, that the Method of Prosecution in which they were expected to concur was without Precedent. That the Attainder of the Eral of *Straffrod* [Earl of Strafford] had been censured by the Legislature, that the Bill against the Eral of *Clarednon* [Clarendon] was now universally confessed to be unjust in itself, and mischievous in its Consequences, and that the Imprisonment of the Eral of *Odfrox* [Oxford] was always considered as cruel and illegal. That the *High-heel'd* Party had never favoured Accusations without Evidence, or Punishment without Conviction, and that though it had been affirmed that no Punishment was intended by the Motion, it was apparent that to deprive any Man of his Employments by an Address of the House was to fix a Mark of Ignominy upon him, and that to make him incapable of being employed again was to deprive him of his Birthright, and condemn him to languish out the rest of his Life under the Weight of publick Censure. To this Apology no Reply was attempted.[16]

Johnson then would have simply been acting as a consistent Tory in framing Walpole's final speech in such a way as to ensure that the sympathies of the reader remained with him rather than with Sandys, Pitt, and Pulteney.

Walpole had triumphed over his enemies once more. But the end was in sight. The military and diplomatic situations did not improve, and at the general election of April 1741 Walpole's supporters lost ground. The first session of the new Parliament convened on December 1. The first trials of strength came with divisions on petitions regarding disputed elections, and resulted in defeat for the administration or victory by the barest margin. Walpole gave in. On February 9, 1742, he was created Earl of Orford, and on the eleventh resigned all his ministerial offices. His care was now to protect himself from the long postponed vengeance of his opponents; and he found that Pulteney and Carteret were willing to give him a pledge of protection in return for his own cooperation (and that of his followers) with their new Government. But the rank and file of the late opposition were not so willing to relinquish their prey. A committee of the Commons was appointed to investigate Walpole's conduct during the previous ten years; but it immediately found itself thwarted when the witnesses from whom it expected to get evidence of bribery on Walpole's part refused to testify on the grounds that their answers might incriminate themselves. A motion was made to grant immunity from prosecution to these witnesses; it was narrowly defeated, and eventually Walpole was left in peace.

These later debates arising out of the Walpole affair, as reported by Johnson, are of no less intellectual interest, though less dramatic, than the great debates of February 1741. The case of the reluctant witnesses before the Parliamentary investigating committee, involving the complex legal problem of self-incrimination, is particularly interesting, in view of certain precise parallels in the United States in the 1950's; [17] and there is no better introduction to that problem than to read Johnson's report of the debate on the Indemnification Bill of 1742. But space will not permit a full discussion of this and other important items in the Johnsonian "Debates." A full analysis of the whole canon would add a good deal to our knowledge of his acquaintance with legal and political matters, his artistry, and generally of the contents of his mind and the way it worked.

One thing that we learn, if we did not know it before, is that in pursuit of the answer to a political question—as to almost any kind of question except, perhaps, certain religious ones—Johnson was indefatigable in pushing down to fundamental principles and in referring "schemes of political improvement" to the effect they would have on the ordinary man. An immense anthology of general political wisdom could be compiled from the contents of the "Debates":

In all political questions, questions too extensive to be fully comprehended by speculative reason, experience is the guide which a wise man will follow with the least distrust [March 1742, p. 123].

All political measures are in some degree right and wrong at the same time; to benefit some they very frequently bear hard upon others [April 1742, p. 171].

Customs, if they are not bad, are not to be changed, because it is an argument in favour of a practice that the people have experienced it, and approved it, and every change is disagreeable to those who judge only by prejudice, of whom I need not say how great is the number [Supp., 1742, p. 691].

It has been observed that with regard to governors and subjects, power subsists upon opinion [March 1743, p. 118].

In political as in private transactions mutual trust is unavoidable [March 1743, p. 121].

In questions relating to the public affairs, it is rational to suppose those measures wrong which are not proved to be right [April 1743, p. 174].

One could quote endlessly. The greatest merit of the "Debates"—one of many merits of this unjustly neglected piece of literature—is, in the words of their latest student, "that Johnson, by characteristic methods of shaping arguments, and choosing emphases, does unconsciously reveal, not his precise political beliefs, but the dominant concerns of his thoughts: 'the people,' liberty, representative government— large questions of individual and public morality." [18] A comment which has been made on Thucydides is relevant: "To the speeches is due in no small measure the imperishable intellectual interest of the History, since it is chiefly by the speeches that the facts of the Peloponnesian War are so lit up with keen thought as to become illustrations of general laws, and to acquire a permanent suggestiveness for the student of politics." [19] In a sense, Johnson in his "Debates" is the Thucydides of the great political wars of the 1740's in Great Britain.

In later life, Johnson made ample amends to Walpole for his writings of 1738 and 1739. Hawkins reports: "Of Sir Robert Walpole, notwithstanding that he had written against him in the early part of his life, he had a high opinion: he said of him, that he was a fine fellow, and that his very enemies deemed him so before his death: he honoured his memory for having kept this country in peace many years, as also for the goodness and placability of his temper." [20] William Seward records Johnson as saying, "He was the best minister this country ever had; as [and?] if *we* would have let him (he speaks of his own violent faction) he would have kept the country in perpetual peace." [21]

It has sometimes been assumed that the change in Johnson's attitude toward Walpole, from fervent detestation to fervent admiration, took place in his middle life, about 1760 or later, after he had acquired his pension, mellowed, and become generally a reactionary, a supporter of arbitrary government. But clearly Johnson's "conversion" must be dated much earlier than this. There is no evidence that he, speaking for himself, ever wrote or said anything disparaging about Walpole and his administration later than May 1739, when the *Vindication of the Licensers* was published. He composed, of course, as a dramatist, the violent speeches of Sandys, Pitt, Pulteney, and the others in the "Debates"; and the very effort of composing some of this half-wild rhetoric may have sublimated part of the passionate resentment against the world which he had felt during his first two years in London and which had been directed against the image of Walpole. But a closer acquaintance with the facts of political life had taught him no longer to accept patriotism uncritically. The process was no doubt aided, as I have suggested, by the death of Wyndham in 1740 and the consequent shift of many of the real Tories from the position of unenthusiastic opponents to that of unenthusiastic supporters of Walpole. And there was also Savage's removal to Wales in the summer of 1739.

If anything was needed to confirm Johnson's distrust of the professions of the "patriots," it was the course of events that followed Walpole's resignation. Pulteney and Carteret did not have the Parliamentary following to be able to set up an administration of simon-pure patriots, and a compromise was inevitable. A sort of unstable coalition Government was set up (the modern term is not precisely applicable, but it will serve) in which Walpole's principal henchmen, Newcastle, Pelham, Hardwicke, and Yonge, retained office, and had as colleagues Carteret and Sandys, who a short time before had been denouncing them and all their works. The loyal Hervey was turned out, justly indignant, to make room for the ex-

Tory Gower. Pulteney inexplicably took no office at all, but directed operations from the side lines.[22] All this confusion was probably the result of ineptness rather than lack of principle on Pulteney's part, but to the man in the street it bore all the carmaiks of a "deal." And when the paragon Pulteney a little later accepted the Earldom of Bath, any last illusions the public may have had about the disinterestedness of the patriots vanished. If Johnson's later remarks on Pulteney are evidence ("as paltry a fellow as could be; a Whig who pretended to be honest"),[23] he concurred with the man in the street.

Some commentary on Johnson's shifting political views at this time is provided by his *Life of Savage*. Savage died on August 1, 1743, and Johnson at once undertook to write the life of the companion of his old patriot days. It is a strange, though fine, work, with an extremely complex psychological pattern, quite unlike anything else Johnson ever did. He is evidently trying to give an impartial estimate of his friend, but the impartiality is not the detached, intellectual objectivity with which, in the later *Lives of the Poets*, he judiciously sorts out the good from the bad in their lives and works. He is still very much involved emotionally with Savage, and the *Life* seems to be an attempt, not entirely successful, to lay the ghost of that old friendship.

Since politics was one of the chief bonds between them, there is a good deal about politics in the *Life*. I have suggested that the politics of Johnson's pieces of 1738 and 1739 owes much to the politics of such works of Savage as *On Public Spirit*, or at least that they have much in common. But in the *Life*, when Johnson comes to discuss *On Public Spirit*, his praise is very faint indeed, and soon changes into a long denunciation of the view of colonization expressed in Savage's poem (the same view, it will be remembered, which is expressed or implied in *London*):

The settlement of colonies in uninhabited countries, the establishment of those in security whose misfortunes have made their own country no longer pleasing or safe . . . cannot be considered without giving rise to a great number of pleasing ideas . . . and, therefore, whatever speculations they may produce in those who have confined themselves to political studies, naturally fixed the attention and excited the applause of a poet. The politician . . . may very properly enquire why the legislature does not provide a remedy for these miseries, rather than encourage an escape from them.[24]

An instinctive hostility to any solution to a problem that seems to savor of escapism is one of the most consistent traits in Johnson's psychology. The historian, the moralist, and the psychologist may argue among themselves whether to describe this aspect of Johnson as Puritanism, heroism, or masochism. The politician, Johnson continues,

may conclude that the flight of every honest man is a loss to the community . . . that those who have by misconduct forfeited their claim to favour ought rather to be made useful to the society which they have injured, than driven from it. But the poet is employed in a more pleasing undertaking than that of proposing laws, which, however just or expedient, will never be made, or endeavouring to reduce to rational schemes of government societies which were formed by chance, and are conducted by the private passions of those who preside in them.

Johnson now evidently considers himself at least as much a politician as a poet, and with some justification. Few writers have had a better opportunity than the Parliamentary reporter for the *Gentleman's Magazine* to observe the irrationality of societies and the part played in government by private passions. Yet the sneer against poets is a little distasteful: after all, it was not so long before that Johnson himself was engaged in the "more pleasing undertaking" of poetizing about politics. Perhaps that is why the tone of the passage is a little acrimonious: Johnson does not like to be reminded of his own naiveté of four years ago.

Bolingbroke is mentioned: "He [Savage] had taken care to distinguish himself in coffee-houses as an advocate for the ministry of the last years of Queen Anne, and was always ready to justify the conduct and exalt the character of Lord Bolingbroke, whom he mentions with great regard in an *Epistle upon Authors,* which he wrote about that time, but was too wise to publish." [25] Johnson's tone is not that of an enthusiastic admirer either of the Harley ministry or of Bolingbroke.

Walpole enters the narrative several times: he promised a "place" to Savage and did not give it to him. Earlier, such conduct would have drawn from Johnson's pen invective at least equal to that which he bestows on Lady Macclesfield; but now the incident is reported with a dry, half-cynical indifference.

Most significant, however, are the passages in which Johnson describes Savage's behavior as an opposition "patriot," a role which Johnson himself had played for two years. There is a damning comment on Savage's poem in praise of Walpole: as Savage "was one of those who were always zealous in their assertions of the justice of the conduct of the late opposition, jealous of the rights of the people, and alarmed by the long-continued triumph of the court, it was natural to ask him what could induce him to employ his poetry in praise of that man who was, in his opinion, an enemy to liberty, and an oppressor of his country? He alleged that he was then dependent upon the Lord Tyrconnel, who was an implicit follower of the ministry." [26] An important passage refers to a dedication, with which Savage was concerned, dealing with the freedom of the press:

The enumeration of the bad effects of "the uncontrouled freedom of the press," and the assertion that the "liberties taken by the writers of Journals with their superiors were exorbitant and unjustifiable," very ill became men who have themselves not always shewn the exactest regard to the laws of subordination in their writings, and who have often satirised those that at least thought themselves their superiors, as they were eminent for their hereditary rank and employed in the highest offices of the kingdom. But this is only an instance of that partiality which almost every man indulges with regard to himself: the liberty of the press is a blessing when we are inclined to write against others, and a calamity when we find ourselves overborne by the multitude of our assailants; as the power of the crown is always thought too great by those who suffer by its influence, and too little by those in whose favour it is exerted; and a standing army is generally accounted necessary by those who command, and dangerous and oppressive by those who support it.[27]

This is about as close as it is possible to come to a formal retraction by Johnson of the interpretation of the political scene that he had put forward in *Marmor* and the *Vindication of the Licensers;* it is almost a public apology by Johnson to Walpole. In its skepticism and pragmatism, its expression of distrust for fashionable slogans, its insistence on probing beneath them to the real motives of individuals concerned with propagating them, the statement provides a key to Johnson's political attitudes from that time until the end of his life.

And yet, after all this, the *Life* closes with a passionate vindication of Savage, which is at the same time a vindication of the young Samuel Johnson, the Johnson who in bitterness of spirit composed *London* and *Marmor Norfolciense* and walked the streets of London at night with Savage (too poor to obtain a lodging), inveighing against the Minister and resolving that they would stand by their country:

The insolence and resentment of which he is accused were not easily to be avoided by a great mind, irritated by perpetual hardships and constrained hourly to return the spurns of contempt, and repress the insolence of prosperity; and vanity may surely readily be pardoned in him, to whom life afforded no other comforts than barren praises, and the consciousness of deserving them.

Those are no proper judges of his conduct who have slumbered away their time on the down of plenty, nor will any wise man presume to say, "Had I been in Savage's condition, I should have lived or written better than Savage." [28]

The *Life of Savage* seems to represent the final stages of some sort of process of purgation that was going on in Johnson's mind. In Walpole's short speech which concludes the great Commons debate of February 13, 1741, we have seen how Johnson insistently uses the imagery of a dream world to describe the state of mind of the Prime Minister's opponents: "They carry on their fiction which has once heated their imaginations. . . . If their dream has really produced in them the terrors which they express . . . compassion would direct us to awaken them from so painful a delusion . . . to show them that . . . every question is debated with the utmost freedom, as before that fatal period in which they were seized with this political delirium." It is indeed possible for intellectuals like Johnson and Savage, in "the dangerous prevalence of imagination," to lose themselves in a political dream world that bears little relation to reality. There is a certain pleasure in indulging in delusions of persecution, such as the opposition papers had been fostering for years. Johnson and Pope both had tendencies in that direction, and it was perhaps unfortunate for them both that they should have encountered Savage, in whom this was more than a tendency. And it was probably fortunate for Johnson's sanity that he should have immediately thereafter become engaged for three years in an occupation that could have left him no possibility of delusion about the realities of British political life. Yet there is often a reluctance, and it is often painful, to awake from such a dream, to renounce a world in which the political scene is painted in sharply contrasted blacks and whites, in which the questions all have simple, definite answers, and to substitute for it one where there are only varying hues of grey shading into one another, where there are no heroes and villains but only fallible, greedy, passionate human beings, where "all political measures are in some degree right and wrong at the same time." The pain of such a renunciation is part of the pain of growing up, of leaving the generous if often mistaken spontaneity of youth behind one. That pain perhaps accounts for some of the curious ambivalence of the *Life of Savage,* which is an important document in the study of Johnson's political attitudes as well as of his life and art.

Savage died on August 1, 1743; Pope on May 30, 1744; Walpole on March 18, 1745. A few months later, Swift, long insane, followed his old enemy to the place where fierce indignation tears the heart no more. The world moved on into a new political age in which the old clichés had lost their meaning and their charm, and new ones took their place. At some time during this period Johnson gave up his work as Parliamentary writer and turned his mind to other matters. In 1745 there appeared *Proposals for a new Edition of Shakespear;* in 1746 he wrote the first draft of a Plan for an English Dictionary. It was some years before he was again to write extensively on political topics.

Chapter Six

THE SECONDARY LEGISLATOR
(1744–1760)

1. PARTY TRUCE (1744–1755)

IT HAS BEEN for many years lamented," Johnson tells the readers of the *Gentleman's Magazine* at the beginning of 1744, ". . . that the struggles of opposite parties have engrossed the attention of the public and that all subjects of conversation and all kinds of learning have given way to politics," and in future the magazine will emphasize political matters less and nonpolitical more.[1] The announcement perhaps indicates a revulsion on Johnson's own part from his intense preoccupation with politics during the previous six years. It is not until more than a decade later—in 1756—that we find him again extensively engaged in political writing.

There was no great reason for him to do so in the meantime, for after the hectic political strife of the 1730's and early 1740's, a comparative calm descended on British party politics. A certain disillusion had set in when, after Walpole's spectacular fall from office in 1742, he was replaced by a regime whose policies were indistinguishable from Walpole's. Internal strife among the Whigs themselves diminished, especially after 1746, when the Pelham brothers emerged victorious from a trial of strength with Carteret and Pulteney, now Lords Granville and Bath and relegated to the ranks of elder statesmen. True, there were sporadic outbursts of the old spirit, at the Lichfield election of 1747 and the Westminster election of 1749, in jockeyings for position among

minor politicians. But these were limited and local in character. Nor merely Johnson but politically minded citizens
generally seem to have suffered a reaction to the strong political stimulation of the years from 1737 to 1742.

The details of Johnson's life during this time are obscure.
We must imagine him as remaining in London and working
away at various large projects of writing and editing—the
Catalogue of the Harleian Library, the *Harleian Miscellany,*
the *Medicinal Dictionary* of Dr. Robert James, his old schoolfellow; perhaps some abortive work on a new edition of
Shakespeare. On June 18, 1746, he signed a contract with a
group of London booksellers to prepare a dictionary of the
English language; that, together with the *Rambler* (1750–52)
and contributions to the *Adventurer* (1753–54), was to be his
main occupation for the next eight years.

Yet the decade is by no means entirely lacking in interest
for the student of Johnson's political views. He managed to
find time, in the intervals of work on his major projects, for
a considerable number of small pieces of occasional writing,
many of which contain revealing comment on political subjects.

The most interesting of these, perhaps, are several pronouncements in which Johnson insists on the importance of
a public well informed on political matters. In the same preface to the *Gentleman's Magazine* of 1743 where he deprecates the "usurpation of the mind" by politics, he makes an
important concession: "Under a form of government like
ours, which makes almost every man a secondary legislator,
politics may justly claim a more general attention than where
the people have no other duty to practise than obedience and
where to examine the conduct of their superiors would be to
disturb their own quiet." The phrase "a secondary legislator"
pleased Johnson so well that he used it again four years later

in the preface to the *Preceptor*, a compendium of general knowledge the existence of which is itself a sign of the times:

The principles of *laws* and *government* come next to be considered; by which men are taught to whom obedience is due, for what it is paid, and in what degree it may be justly required. This knowledge, by peculiar necessity, constitutes a part of the education of an *Englishman*, who professes to obey his prince according to the law, and who is himself a secondary legislator, as he gives his consent, by his representative, to all the laws by which he is bound, and has a right to petition the great council of the nation, whenever he thinks they are deliberating upon an act detrimental to the interest of the community.[2]

Johnson's most emphatic enunciation of the right and duty of the average Englishman to know what is going on in his government appears in his "Essay on the Origin and Importance of Small Tracts and Fugitive Pieces," which introduces the *Harleian Miscellany* (1744). "There is, perhaps, no nation," Johnson says, "in which it is so necessary as in our own" to collect and reprint political and theological pamphlets; "for . . . our constitution in church and state naturally gives birth to a multitude of performances, which would either not have been written, or could not have been made publick in any other place." Just as in 1739 Johnson had vindicated the right of the English stage to freedom of political discussion, he now vindicates, more calmly but with equal seriousness, the liberty of the English press:

The form of our government, which gives every man that has leisure, or curiosity, or vanity, the right of enquiring into the propriety of publick measures, and by consequence, obliges those who are intrusted with the administration of national affairs to give an account of their conduct to almost every man who demands it, may be reasonably imagined to have occasioned innumerable pamphlets, which would never have appeared under arbitrary governments, where every man lulls himself in in-

dolence under calamities of which he cannot promote the redress, or thinks it prudent to conceal the uneasiness of which he
cannot complain without danger.[3]

This, like the *Vindication of the Licensers,* is not too far
from the *Areopagitica* in spirit. It should not be very surprising that this is so, for Johnson was one of the great pioneer
journalists in the history of the English press. In *Rambler*
145 he wrote an apology for journalists—a little tentative, perhaps, for it was a novel proposition: "The authors whom I am
now endeavouring to recommend have been too long *hacknied
in the ways of men* to indulge the chimerical ambition of im-
mortality; they have seldom any claim to the trade of writing
but that they have tried some other without success; they perceive no particular summons to composition except the sound
of the clock . . . about the opinion of posterity they have
little solicitude." And yet, "These papers of the day, the
Ephemeræ of learning, have uses more adequate to the purposes of common life than more pompous and durable vol-
umes. If it is necessary for every man to be more acquainted
with his contemporaries than with past generations, and to
rather know the events which may immediately affect his fortune and his quiet than the revolutions of ancient kingdoms
. . . the humble author of journals and gazettes must be considered as a liberal dispenser of beneficial knowledge." "The
time is now come," Johnson begins a number of the *Literary
Magazine* in 1756, "in which every Englishman expects to be
informed of the national affairs, and in which he has a right
to have that expectation gratified." [4]

Such statements are important in a consideration of Johnson's political position. If democracy means primarily the
participation of the people in their own government, they
contradict the traditional conception of Johnson's wishing
to "stem the rising tide of democracy," of hankering after
arbitrary government. If, as Herbert Butterfield suggests, not

formal constitutional change but the growing interest and participation in political affairs of the ordinary intelligent citizen is the key to the political development of the eighteenth century,[5] Johnson contributed at least as much as any one writer in the century to awaken such citizens to a serious awareness of their own responsibility in public affairs, to foster a widespread political consciousness—through the Parliamentary "Debates," through the great political essays of 1756 and 1757 in the *Literary Magazine,* and through a multitude of lesser publications. That Johnson could be partisan from time to time, that he could write in single-minded support of a cause, is sufficiently apparent from the anti-Walpole tracts of 1738 and 1739 and from his four pamphlets of the 1770's. But there is much else in the canon of his political writings where his concern is rather to inform the reader of the facts, to point out aspects of an argument that may not be obvious to him, to encourage him to do his own thinking, than to present him with a ready-made answer—where his tone is that of an educator, not a propagandist.

This kind of treatment is illustrated in the earliest of a number of scattered pieces of political commentary which appeared in the 1740's and early 1750's, and which may be conveniently collected here before turning to the important group of political writings of 1756. This (to go back a year or two) is his review, in the *Gentleman's Magazine* of February 1742, of the *Account of the Conduct of the Dowager Duchess of Marlborough.*[6] Sarah Churchill survived her great husband twenty-two years, and shortly before her death arranged for the publication of her memoirs under the supervision of Nathaniel Hooke. Johnson's appreciation of the staunch old Whig's apology is remarkable. He praises its style and documentation. Without being "concerned about the character which it is principally concerned to preserve or retrieve," he declares, the historian may learn from it much about the "progress of great transactions, and discover the secret causes of important events"; the "inquirer into human nature" may find out much about the psychology of the great historical figures whom it treats, and about the psychology of politics generally.

Using the evidence provided in the book, Johnson passes judgment on some of these historical figures. He talks of the folly of estimating statesmen by their outward manner, and his illustrations are not those one would expect of a Tory propagandist. "Charles the Second," he decides, "by his affability and politeness made himself the idol of the nation which he betrayed and sold. William the Third was, for his insolence and brutality, hated by that people which he protected and enriched." Macaulay himself could not have stated the Whig view more emphatically. Of Queen Anne, the Tory saint, Johnson discovers from her letters that she had "a temper timorous . . . helpless dependence on the affection of others . . . there is nothing great, or firm, or regal; nothing that enforces obedience and respect." He takes almost a pleasure (for all that he says he does so "not without pain") in finding out that the common notion of Queen Mary does not correspond with the facts: "What can be charged upon this delight of human kind? . . . Nothing less than that *she wanted bowels,* and was insolent with her power; that she was resentful . . . that she descended to mean acts of revenge."

The whole piece is, in fact, an essay in recommendation of skepticism, of perpetual suspicion of the received view. "Distrust," Johnson says flatly, "is a necessary qualification of a student in history." Yet he makes it clear that a scholarly skepticism is not the same as indiscriminate incredulity, and the first six paragraphs of the review are a carefully reasoned dissertation on the nature of historical evidence. Interest in such memoirs as those of the Duchess, he begins, may be ascribed "to that ardent love of truth, which nature has kindled in the breast of man, and which remains even where every other laudable passion is extinguished." Yet, he reflects, the greater knowledge the writer of memoirs has of contemporary events, and the greater the role he has played in them himself, the greater is his motive for wishing to distort the evidence in his own favor. What then is the reader to do? Dismiss all history as reflecting the writer's own prejudices and therefore untrustworthy? "The man who knows not the truth cannot, and he who knows it will not, tell it; what then remains, to distrust every relation, and live in perpetual negligence of past events, or what is still more disagreeable, in perpetual suspense?" The comment resembles some modern Marxist reasoning on the subject of history. But Johnson finds the proper resolution, that of weighing the probabilities in the spirit of scientific, Humean, not Pyrrhonic, doubt: "Distrust quickens [the student's] discernment of different degrees of probability, animates his search after evidence, and perhaps heightens his pleasure at the discovery of truth; for truth, though not always obvious, is generally discoverable," and he goes on to point out why and to what extent contemporary memoirs may be believed. Only after settling this fundamental question does he proceed to consider the *Memoirs* themselves. This is journalism on a very high level, directed not at persuading the reader of the truth or falsity of a given doctrine, but at educating him to judge for himself of truth and falsity in historical and political questions generally.

The "Essay on the Origin and Importance of Fugitive Pieces" (1744) has been mentioned, in which Johnson insists on the importance, to the common reader as well as to the historian, of compilations of "ephemeral" historical documents. Johnson seems at this time to have been particularly concerned with the problem of historical evidence, perhaps because he was actively engaged in a project of political historiography the identity of which is still a mystery. Writing to

Cave, in a letter ascribed to the autumn of 1743, he speaks at length of "our Historical design." [7] The letter is tantalizingly full of detail about the nature of this: it is to be "the most complete account of Parliamentary proceedings that [can] be contrived"; it is "to partake of the spirit of History, which is contrary to minute exactness, and of the regularity of a Journal, which is inconsistent with spirit"; "the exact dates of the most important events" are to be inserted in the margin; it is apparently to cover the reign of George I; it is to run to thirty-five printed sheets—280 quarto or 560 octavo pages—of which Johnson has already written perhaps five. But exactly what it was is still unknown.

Other desultory passages of political interest from Johnson's writings of the time may be noted here. In the *Miscellaneous Observations on Macbeth* (1745), King James I is treated in no very respectful fashion: "as the ready way to gain King James's favour was to flatter his speculations, the system of *Dæmonologie* was immediately adopted by all who desired either to gain preferment or not to lose it." James' Stuart blood does not exempt him from Johnson's general suspicion of monarchs as a class peculiarly susceptible to flattery. Another familiar theme is the identification of the interest of Jesuits and Dissenters: "The Jesuits and Sectaries took advantage of this universal error [belief in witchcraft] and endeavoured to promote the interest of their parties by pretended cures of persons afflicted by evil spirits, but they were detected and exposed by the clergy of the established church." [8]

An interesting and little-known work of Johnson's of the 1740's is a charity sermon which he composed for his friend the Honourable and Reverend Henry Hervey Aston (formerly Harry Hervey) and delivered by him at St. Paul's on May 2, 1745.[9] In the introductory part of the discourse, Johnson works out a rationale of public charity that inevitably impinges on political theory. There are three passages of particular interest. One is a rejection of narrowly nationalistic patriotism:

Others [who have wrongly limited the practice of charity] have carried their benevolence still farther, and taught, that the general duty of life, is the love of our country; these, likewise, were mistaken, not in asserting that this was a duty, but that it was the only duty; that it was to absorb all other considerations, and that consequently nothing was criminal, by which the greatness of a particular society might be augmented, or its prosperity advanced: This principle was the dictate, not of piety, but ambition; we are to endeavour, indeed, the happiness of our country; but in subordination to the happiness of mankind.

Another expresses Johnson's detestation, found in the preface to *A Voyage to Abyssinia,* the *Life of Drake,* and elsewhere, of overzealous missionary activity: Enthusiasm, he says, has taught

that error, however involuntary, is entitled to no compassion even from fallible beings; and that those, whom GOD hath cursed with ignorance, are to be excluded from the general charter of humanity, to be persecuted as beasts of prey, and swept away, as too prophane to enjoy the same sun, or to tread on the same earth, with the favourites of their maker. But far different are the doctrines inculcated by the precepts, and enforced by the example, of our blessed Saviour, who . . . when He commanded his Apostles to preach the Gospel, authoriz'd them to use no other methods, than those of lenity, meekness, and beneficence.

Perhaps the most interesting passage for the political student is this:

Among Christians, some sects have attempted to recommend themselves by an ardour of benevolence, well adapted to dazzle the weak and to ensnare the needy; but which was never commanded by the author of our religion, and is not practicable without confusion. They have introduced an absolute community of possessions, and asserted, that distinction of property is inconsistent with that love, which we are commanded to exercise towards one another.

Communism, with the idea that *la propriété c'est le vol,* has had a long and persistent history among Christian sects. It was, and is, regarded as heretical by the major churches, including the Church of England.[10] Johnson goes on to put the Church's doctrine on a Lockean basis: "The absurdity of this notion, it is not difficult to shew. Every man must easily discern that difference of property is necessary to subordination, and subordination essential to government; that where there is no property, there can be no motive to industry, but virtue; and that the bad must then always be supported by those, whose generosity inclines them to provide for them." [11]

Johnson's characterization, in the preface to the *Preceptor* (1748), of political science as peculiarly the study of the "secondary legislator," the ordinary intelligent citizen, of England has been noted. Also of interest is its listing of political works which Johnson recommends the student to read, "that he may obtain such knowledge as may qualify him to act and judge as one of a free people." [12] Such a list is obviously an important clue to the nature and sources of Johnson's own political thought; and if the believer in Johnson's High Toryism expects to find Filmer or Sacheverell or *Eikon Basilike* in the list, he will be disappointed. It does not contain the work of a single writer who can be properly called a Tory, though it contains the writings of several who were distinctly Whigs —Locke *On Government;* Sir William Temple's *Introduction to the History of England;* the *Plato Redivivus* of Henry Neville (1620–94), whom the *DNB* calls "a strong doctrinaire republican"; the *Historical Discourse on the Laws and Government of England,* by Nathaniel Bacon, published in 1647 as a piece of Parliamentarian polemics; and Harrington's *Oceana.* On second thought, Johnson evidently found Harrington too strong, and in the second edition (1754) he expunged the *Oceana* and substituted Richard Zouche's *Elementa Juris Civilis,* like Thornhaugh Gurdon's *History of*

Parliaments a piece of straightforward exposition. Sir John Fortescue's *Treatises* and Hooker's *Ecclesiastical Polity* conclude the list. If all these can be said to have one thesis in common, from old Fortescue down to Gurdon (1731), it is that England is not an absolute but a limited and constitutional monarchy. The two most important items in the list are evidently Hooker and Locke, who owed so much to Hooker.

The *Rambler* (1750–52), Johnson's great work of the period before the publication of the *Dictionary*, though it contains fine statements of the moral and philosophical attitudes underlying his politics—such things as "The common voice of the multitude, uninstructed by precept and unprejudiced by authority . . . in questions that relate to the heart of man, is, in my opinion, more decisive than the learning of Lipsius" (No. 52), and "The great law of social beings, by which every individual is commanded to consult the happiness of others" (No. 148)—and though it contains many expressions of Johnson's comprehensive humanitarianism, is remarkably free of direct expressions of specifically political opinion. So too are his contributions to the *Adventurer* (1753–54), where almost the only politically interesting passage is that in No. 99, where Johnson, in his best Brownean style, expresses his revulsion from hero worship:

I am far from intending to vindicate the sanguinary projects of heroes and conquerors, and would wish rather to diminish the reputation of their success, than the infamy of their miscarriages: for I cannot conceive why he that has burned cities, wasted nations, and filled the world with horror and desolation, should be more kindly regarded by mankind than he who died in the rudiments of wickedness; why he that accomplished wickedness should be glorious, and he that only endeavoured it should be criminal. I would wish Cæsar and Catiline, Xerxes and Alexander, Charles and Peter, huddled together in obscurity or detestation.

Johnson goes on to explain that although he disdains such "projectors" in politics, he admires projectors in technology, "whose ends are generally laudable, and whose labours are innocent; who are searching out new powers of nature, or contriving new works of art. . . . That the attempts of such men will often miscarry, we may reasonably expect; yet from such men, and such only, are we to hope for the cultivation of those parts of nature which lie yet waste, and the invention of those arts which are yet wanting to the felicity of life." All this is very much in the spirit of Bacon and the Royal Society, and of Victorian liberalism and meliorism.

In the *Life of Roscommon* (1748) there is a notable passage in which Johnson speaks of Swift's and Roscommon's advocacy of the founding of a literary academy. Johnson's contempt for such a project is well known, but one of his reasons for predicting its failure is worth remarking here:

Suppose the philological decree made and promulgated, what would be its authority? In absolute governments, there is sometimes a general reverence paid to all that has the sanction of power and the countenance of greatness. How little this is the state of our country needs not to be told. We live in an age in which it is a kind of publick sport to refuse all respect that cannot be enforced. The edicts of an English academy would probably be read by many, only that they might be sure to disobey them. . . . The present manners of the nation would deride authority; and therefore nothing is left but that every writer should criticize himself.[13]

The tone is one of regret that such is the case; and yet nothing is more certain than that Johnson himself would have been the first to "refuse all respect" to such authority.

The reference to a "philological" academy to "fix the language" reminds one that Johnson was at this time in the midst of his work on the *Dictionary*. The *Plan* (1747) and the *Preface* (1755) of Johnson's dictionary seem unlikely places to find comment of a political nature; but Johnson was constantly aware that language is a social phenomenon. Linguistic change, he thinks, is more rapid in a civilized country, "in a people polished by arts, and classed by subordination, where one part of the community is sustained and accommodated by the labour of the other," than in a primitive and pastoral society like that of "some of the Mahometan countries." [14] (It is noteworthy that Johnson here makes "subordination" equivalent merely to the principle of division of labor, the distinguishing characteristic of the economy of a civilized society.) Although "total and sudden transformations" of a language, due to "conquests and migrations," now seldom occur, the modern world provides other more gradual but nevertheless powerful causes of linguistic change: "Commerce, however necessary, however lucrative, as it depraves the manners, corrupts the language." It is axiomatic that "all change is of itself an evil, which ought not to be hazarded but for evident advantage. . . . 'Change,' says Hooker, 'is not made without inconvenience, even from worse to better.' There is in constancy and stability a general and lasting advantage, which will always overbalance the slow improvements of gradual correction." [15] It is necessary to "acquiesce with silence, as in the other insurmountable distresses of humanity" in linguistic change; yet it may be possible, by the construction of dictionaries, to postpone it: "We have long preserved our constitution, let us make some struggles for our language." This gloomy proposal of a rear-guard action against linguistic change might convince us of Johnson's complete reactionism if it were not that in the paragraph preceding this sentiment he fires up again at the suggestion of an academy for precisely the purpose that he desiderates; an academy, he exclaims, "which I, *who can never wish to see dependence multiplied,* hope *the spirit of English liberty* will hinder or destroy." [16] There is no denying that Johnson can be difficult at times.

As for the *Dictionary* itself, the student who sets out to assess its value as a source of evidence for Johnson's political opinions must avoid falling into the trap of regarding its definitions as deliberate expressions of Johnson's own political, theological, and philosophical creeds. This bad habit has been properly criticized in recent studies showing to what a large extent he was merely following accepted lexicographical tradition.[17] Even some of the examples cited by Boswell as most clearly expressing Johnson's own prejudices are arguable. It has been shown that his remark, in his definition of "oats," that in Scotland this grain "supports the people," has a long and respectable history, going back through Miller's *Gardener's Dictionary,* Johnson's immediate source, to Pliny and Galen.[18] The blast against "excise," though it undoubtedly expresses Johnson's personal feelings in the matter, also expresses that of many other thoughtful Englishmen of the time; and it is perhaps no more surprising to find such editorializing in Johnson's dictionary than it is to find it in the *Commentaries* of the judicious Blackstone, who, after enumerating the articles on which excise is paid, exclaims, "A list, which no friend to his country would wish to see farther increased." [19] The famous definitions of "Whig" and "Tory" have been mentioned above.[20] There still remain a number of little gems, such as the entry under "irony": "A mode of speech in which the meaning is contrary to the words: as, *Bolingbroke was a holy man.*" [21] But it is certain that the *Dictionary* as a whole is not to be considered, as it has sometimes been in the past, a significant vehicle for the expression of Johnson's political attitudes.

2. THE *Literary Magazine* AND THE GREAT WAR (1756–1757)

Valuable as such passages in Johnson's writings of the decade or so before 1755 are for an understanding of the bases of his political thinking, they have little direct bearing on the contemporary political scene; and indeed, in the years of the making of the *Rambler* and the *Dictionary* there was little in that scene to tempt his pen. The end of these halcyon days was signaled by the death, in March 1754, of the colorless but competent Henry Pelham. Strife at once broke out between his brother Newcastle, the heir to his prime ministership, and Henry Fox and William Pitt, who up to this time had been satisfied with minor positions in the Government, but now aspired to higher things. More ominous, however, than the struggle for power at Westminster was the news from India and North America, where the increasing frequency and violence of border clashes between French and British made it apparent that the great struggle to determine the destinies of these nations as world powers had begun. The British declaration of war against France on May 18, 1756, was an event which even the most short-sighted could see was pregnant with great consequences. It was perhaps not entirely a coincidence that in the same month as the declaration of war, Samuel Johnson, now at last finished with the harmless drudgery of a lexicographer, should bring out the first number of a new periodical which, in spite of its name, was dedicated throughout the period of Johnson's editorship chiefly to politics: "The time is now come," he proclaimed, "in which every Englishman expects to be informed of the national affairs, and in which he has a right to have that expectation gratified." The words "*every* Englishman" and "has a *right*" are surely indicative of the growing spirit of democracy of the eighteenth century, which Johnson was concerned to foster and to cater to.

Little is known of the circumstances of the origin and conduct of the *Literary Magazine, or Universal Review*. Boswell says that Johnson "engaged . . . to superintend and contribute largely to it," and an examination of the contents of the first volume (May to December 1756) shows that Boswell's account of Johnson's function is probably correct for this period.[22] The quality of the magazine as a vehicle of information for a thoughtful reading public is, during the time of Johnson's editorship, high. Its three main interests are politics, science, and history, in that order of importance. In Johnson's preface to the *Magazine* [23] he makes it clear where the emphasis is going to be. After paying a pleasant tribute to the *Gentleman's,* as the prototype of the magazine, and disclaiming any intention of competing with it, he states his design to "give the history, political and literary, of every month," and then makes it clear that the word "political" precedes "literary" intentionally: "The chief political object of an Englishman's attention," he begins, "must be the great council of the nation, and we shall therefore register all public proceedings with particular care." But "we shall not attempt to give any regular series of debates, or to amuse our readers with senatorial rhetoric"; and then follows an amusing recantation of his work for the *Gentleman's Magazine* fifteen years earlier—"The speeches inserted in other papers have been long known to be fictitious, and produced sometimes by men who never heard the debate, nor had any authentic information." In fact, accounts of Parliamentary proceedings occupy little of the space of the *Literary Magazine:* Johnson's heart is obviously more in the part of the work which is next proposed—"As the proceedings in parliament are unintelligible without a knowledge of the facts to which they relate . . . we shall exhibit monthly a view, though contracted yet distinct, of foreign affairs." Only after he has discussed in some detail his proposed treatment of political history, foreign and domestic, does he pass on to explain how he will treat "the labours of the learned," "the productions of science," "the elegant trifles of literature," and "inquiries into the history of nature, which has hitherto been treated as if mankind were afraid of exhausting it."

For anyone wishing to begin a study of the Seven Years' War, there is no better introduction than to read the first volume of the *Literary Magazine*. Not only is the monthly "Historical Memoirs" of events abroad and at home remarkably complete and clear, but the *Magazine* adopts a policy, not too frequent even in modern journals, of printing the full texts of important documents of the time as they appeared— declarations of war, diplomatic exchanges, official dispatches from the theaters of war, proceedings of courts martial, the text of important bills introduced in Parliament. This policy, of course, is in keeping with Johnson's empirical habit of mind, of presenting the facts and letting his reader draw his own conclusions from them.

Two of Johnson's known contributions to the *Magazine* are the detailed commentaries on two such sets of documents. One is the Militia Bill [24] introduced in March 1756 in the House of Commons; it had the approval of Pitt, then in opposition, and was passed by the House of Commons, but was opposed in the Lords by Newcastle and Hardwicke, and defeated. Johnson criticizes it clause by clause, and concludes, "It seems to be a good bill in the fundamental parts, to contain the rudiments of a military establishment which may be of great use in this kingdom, by enabling us to defend ourselves against any insult or invasion and by placing the sword in the hands of the people." This last "democratic" sentiment represents the traditional Tory position of favoring the home-grown (if incompetent) militia, of which the country gentlemen formed the corps of officers and their tenants and dependents the body of troops, and which was theoretically directly responsible to Parliament, as against the innovation of a regular or standing professional army, directly under the control of the Crown. Johnson approves of the provision of a property qualification for officers: "The regulation of military rank in the national army by the gradations of property is rational and just. The man who hazards most has most right to be trusted, and men willingly obey in the field those whom they are accustomed to respect in all other places." What most concerns him, however, is the number of provisions for the administration of oaths: all militiamen are required to take the oath of allegiance, and in disciplinary cases witnesses are required to give testimony under oath.

Surely nothing has more tendency to make bad subjects than irreligion, and nothing will sooner make men irreligious than the frequency of oaths. . . . When the obligation of an oath is weakened, the security of property, and of life, is at an end; and oaths will be reverenced less, as they are oftener repeated. . . . The reverence of an oath will be gradually lessened by the necessity of swearing at one time, "that John Trot broke the ranks," at another "that James Budge would not ground his musket." . . . The frequent imposition of oaths has almost ruined the morals of this unhappy nation, and of a nation without morals, it is of small importance who shall be king.

Johnson was no doubt thinking of the number of oaths which his father had to take, as a civic official of Lichfield. But, for obvious historical reasons, a disapproval of loyalty oaths had been part of the Tory complex of political attitudes since 1689.

The Anglo-Hessian and Anglo-Russian treaties of 1755 were complementary to the Militia Bill.[25] In the face of imminent French aggression, there were three ways by which British military strength could be augmented: by an increase in the number of the regular forces, the "standing army," an action so politically dangerous that Newcastle could venture on it to only a limited extent; some sort of militia scheme, such as that which had just been defeated; and the negotiation of military aid from allied nations, in return for financial assistance. The last plan was pursued: Hesse-Cassel agreed to provide from eight to twelve thousand troops for the British service, and Russia undertook the military protection of Hanover, both in return for substantial British subsidies. "A system of subsidies" was violently opposed by the powerful group headed by Pitt and Temple; and Johnson, although in his commentary he gives the arguments on both sides, leaves no doubt that his own sympathies are with the opposition. "The reception of mercenaries into our country" is, he says in a memorable phrase, "the desperate remedy of desperate distress." He has no doubt that requirements of defense can be met by a native militia. His rhetoric is somewhat reminiscent of an American midwestern isolationist arguing against lend-lease in 1940:

That we are able to defend our own country, that arms are most safely entrusted to our hands, and that we have strength, and skill, and courage equal to the best of the nations of the continent is the opinion of every Englishman who can think without prejudice and speak without influence; and therefore it will not be easy to persuade the nation, a nation long renowned for valour, that it can need the help of foreigners to defend it from invasion.

Later in the year, in a short, condemnatory review of a ministerial pamphlet entitled *The Conduct of the Ministry Impartially Examined,* he pooh-poohs the invasion scare:

In one of his pages he [the author of the pamphlet] just mentions the invasion with which we were threatened in the beginning of the year, over which, however, he chuses to throw a total veil. Surely he would not have us forget the alarm which frighted some of our women to strong waters, and our parliament to Hanoverian troops. Let us not forget the flat-bottomed boats, built, I suppose, in the clouds, and now lost in the clouds again. Again, let us not forget that when any nation is to be fleeced, it is first to be frighted.[26]

At the same time, Johnson published several vigorous defenses of Admiral Byng, executed for his insufficiently vigorous prosecution of a naval action off Minorca, who, it was thought, was being sacrificed as a scapegoat for the incompetence of Newcastle, Anson, and the Admiralty.

On these three matters Johnson is more or less on the same side as Pitt was at the time; but only, I think, by coincidence. When in 1757 Pitt compromised his differences with Newcastle and took over the conduct of the war, he pursued it to a successful conclusion in a spirit of dedicated fervor—and with the aid of an extensive system of subsidies. Although Johnson could later sometimes allow his feeling to be carried away by the splendor of the "glorious years" under Pitt—"It being observed to him, that a rage for every thing English prevailed much in France after Lord Chatham's glorious war, he said he did not much wonder at it, for that we had drubbed those fellows into a proper reverence for us, and that their national petulance required a periodical chastisement" [27]—his more sober thoughts are expressed in two remarkable commentaries published in the first and fourth numbers of the *Literary Magazine.*

"An Introduction to the Political State of Great Britain," [28] the opening essay of the *Magazine,* is a brilliantly written analysis of British colonial and foreign policy from the days of Elizabeth to those of George II. The astonishing thing about it, for the modern reader, is its objectivity, its hardheadedness, its freedom from the least tinge of nationalistic sentiment. It is, indeed, an essay in the economic interpretation of history,[29] and it paints so unflattering a picture of Britain's motives in her dealings with other nations that its publication in like circumstances during a twentieth-century war would not improbably result in the author's being interned for the duration.

The key paragraph is this: "No mercantile man, or mercantile nation, has any friendship but for money, and alliance between them will last no longer than their common safety or common profit is endangered; no longer than they have an enemy who threatens to take from each more than either can steal from the other." And Johnson leaves no doubt that Britain, since the time of Elizabeth, has been such a mercantile state. Modern British history—"the present system of English politics"—began, Johnson says, at that time (it will be remembered that the Whigs regarded Queen Elizabeth almost as one of themselves). Three things happened in Elizabeth's reign: "We began . . . to extend our trade"; "we then likewise settled colonies in America . . . we seem to have snatched them into our hands upon no very just principles or policy, only because every state, according to a prejudice of long continuance, concludes itself more powerful as its territories become larger"; and "the protestant religion was established." Yet Johnson is not inclined to give much weight to religious conviction as a motivating force in international relations, by comparison with the desire for commercial gain. The Dutch, he says, have been regarded as the "natural" allies of the British: "we have, it is true, the same interest, as opposed to France, and some resemblance of religion, as opposed to popery, but we have such a rivalry, in respect of commerce, as will always keep us from very close adherence to each other." Only one motive is stronger than the desire for commercial advantage, the instinct for self-preservation. When the French invaded Holland in the late seventeenth century, the Dutch "were obliged to dismiss for a time their love of money, and their narrow projects of private benefit, and to do what a trader does not willingly at any time believe necessary, to sacrifice a part for the preservation of the whole." [30]

The essay contains some interesting judgments on British domestic history. James I appears much as he did in the *Ob-*

servations on Macbeth: "he was a man of great theoretical knowledge, but of no practical wisdom." Charles I properly tried to oppose the growing might of France and Holland; "but for this end, it was necessary to build a fleet, and a fleet could not be built without expense: he was advised to levy ship-money, which gave occasion to the civil war." (Johnson carefully abstains from saying that it was right to levy ship-money). Cromwell, "who perhaps had not leisure to study foreign politics," Johnson finds, made a bad mistake in supporting the French rather than the Spanish in Flanders. Charles II "never disturbed himself with remote consequences." The judgment on James II is significant: "He was not ignorant of the real interest of his country; he desired its power and its happiness, and thought rightly that there is no happiness without religion; but he thought very erroneously and absurdly, that there is no religion without popery. . . . The necessity of self-preservation . . . impelled the subjects of James to drive him from the throne." Queen Anne is cryptically designated "the then darling of England." It cannot be said that this series of considered judgments shows Johnson as a blind admirer of the Stuarts.

The international history of the seventeenth and eighteenth centuries Johnson is inclined to interpret essentially in terms of English resistance to French aggression, or, what amounts to much the same thing in his mind, French competition with English commercial expansion. It was about the time that England discovered her destiny as a trading nation, in the reign of Elizabeth, that France too, under Henri IV, acquired grandiose notions: "The French . . . were in this reign taught to know their own power . . . they began to take an air of superiority which they had never pretended before . . . to consider themselves as masters of the destiny of their neighbours." Johnson is distinctly anti-Gallican (an epithet the *Literary Magazine* later applied to itself) and severely censures Walpole for his appeasement of France, for making "those our friends by servility whom nothing but power will keep quiet." This was, of course, the line taken by the opposition during the 1730's and 1740's; and by following it Johnson should be led to the Tory dilemma of having to praise William III and Marlborough for their vigorous opposition to France and to condemn the makers of the Peace of Utrecht. Actually, he glosses over these aspects of British history with some casuistical skill: without saying that Marlborough's policy of action was mistaken, he emphasizes that Marlborough chose to neglect the navy and fight a land war, "which he knew well how to conduct, both to the honour of his country, and his own profit"; as for the Peace of Utrecht, he confines himself to belaboring the Whigs for their inconsistency—"those who clamoured among us most loudly against it, found it to their interest to keep [it]"—without mentioning the converse inconsistency of the Tories.

Emphatic as Johnson is that the primary aim of British foreign policy must be to keep the French subdued, he puts this proposition forward with no particular display of patriotic emotion; he does not cite, as a nineteenth- or twentieth-century writer probably would, high moral reasons for thinking that the British *ought* to resist French aggression. As he expounds the situation, it is simply a physical or economic fact that an expanding France and an expanding Britain cannot both occupy the same space in America or elsewhere, and since Johnson and his readers happen to be British, by the accident of birth, presumably they must wish to see Britain win, purely out of motives of self-interest. The direction which even these motives take, among the contending countries, is dictated at least in part by the facts of economic life: French commerce constitutes so serious a threat to England's because of the combination of plentiful natural resources and the low standard of living of her workers: "The fertility of their country furnishes the French with commodities: the poverty of the common people keeps the price of labour low." Holland is forced to become a trading nation because of the scantiness of her own natural resources. This amoral and deterministic approach to the Seven Years' War comes rather as a shock to the reader accustomed to the moral and patriotic emotion with which it is usually treated by British and American historians. It may well be possible, of course, that that emotion is justified; nevertheless, the Johnsonian, not to say Marxist, approach is at least momentarily refreshing.

If a balance must be struck, however, in assessing the relative merits of England and France as they are presented in the essay, it would appear that Johnson gives the French dogs the best of it. There is one interesting passage, perhaps the only one to be encountered in Johnson's writings, that is apparently in praise of the advantages of unanimity among the citizens of a state. Johnson is commending Colbert, Louis XIV's great minister:

It must be considered that Colbert had means of acting which our government does not allow. He could enforce all his orders by the power of an absolute monarch; he could compel individuals to sacrifice their private profit to the general good. . . . Where no man thinks himself under any obligation to submit to another, and, instead of co-operating in one great scheme, every man hastens through by-paths to private profit, no great change can suddenly be made; nor is superior knowledge of much effect, where every man resolves to use his own eyes and his own judgment, and every one applauds his own dexterity and diligence, in proportion as he becomes rich sooner than his neighbour.

This is, of course, rather like the sort of comment that used to be made during the second World War about the superior efficiency of the administrations of Hitler and Mussolini, except that the British and American publicists who made it invariably concluded with the pious remark that though inefficiency is a necessary concomitant of democracy, democracy is of course worth it. Johnson does not add such a proviso. Whether its absence is significant is hard to decide: Johnson maintains a tone of such lofty detachment throughout the piece that one is reluctant to make any deductions from it about his personal preference. It is consistent, however, with the Lockeanism in *Irene* and elsewhere that he finds the characteristic of individual enterprise to be its political conservatism—"When . . . everyone hastens through by-paths to private profit, no great change can suddenly be made"— and that revolutionary measures are associated with authoritarianism and the all-powerful state.

The praise that France receives from Johnson for the administration of her American colonies is less equivocal. The central thesis of the essay is what may be called Johnson's theory of colonies, and the key to that theory is the position of the aboriginal inhabitants of the colonized territory. If there is one aspect of Johnson's political thinking that is clearly defined and that does not vary from his earliest to his latest writings, it is his distrust of the foreign invaders of a land and his sympathy with those who originally occupied it. These feelings were expressed in *A Voyage to Abyssinia,* in the *State of Affairs in Lilliput,* in the *Life of Drake;* it appears now in his writings of 1756; it appears in his condemnation of Negro slavery, in his adoption of the Negro Frank Barber and his bequest of his estate to him; it will appear again in his writings of the 1770's and will explain his attitude toward the American colonists.

Johnson sees no virtue in a nation's founding colonies. Britain's American settlements of the time of Elizabeth were "snatched . . . upon no very just principles of policy" because other states were doing the same thing; because "every state . . . concludes itself more powerful as its territories become larger"—a "prejudice" for which Johnson finds no justification. These settlements increased in the reign of James I, when "multitudes who were discontented with their conditions in their native country, and such multitudes there will always be, sought relief." Emigration is a form of escapism, which Johnson always distrusts. France founded her settlements in the "cold, uncomfortable, uninviting region" of Canada, only to "provide a drain into which the waste of an exuberant nation might be thrown"; or perhaps only because of "that impatience of doing nothing to which mankind perhaps owes much of what is imagined to be effected by more splendid motives."

If, however, a colony has been founded, it should be administered with a view to encouraging it in the only useful function it can have for the mother country—that of providing a secure market for the commodities of the mother country's trade. For this reason the bonds between them must be kept close: "These settlements, when they are once made, must keep a perpetual correspondence with the original country to which they are subject, and on which they depend for protection in danger, and supplies in necessity." The French colonies in America have been better administered than the English: "As they have . . . had the happiness of a government by which no interest has been neglected, nor any part of their subjects overlooked, they have, by continual encouragement and assistance from France, been perpetually enlarging their bounds and increasing their numbers." By contrast with the English colonies, they have had good governors: "To be a bankrupt at home, or to be so infamously vicious that he cannot be decently protected in his own country, seldom recommends any man to the government of a French colony." Above all, the French-Canadian colonists have used the Indians decently: "Instead of endeavouring to frighten the Indians away, they invite them to intermarriage and cohabitation, and allure them by all practicable methods to be-

come the subjects of the King of France." Johnson regrets
that the Spanish, on first occupying America, had not "either
the urbanity or the policy to have concilated them by kind
treatment, and to have united them gradually to their own
people." The opportunity was lost by foolishness and cruelty,
and now can never be recovered.

The far-sightedness and humanity of Johnson's ideal of a
colonizing population conciliating and assimilating the ab-
origines instead of destroying and exploiting them are easier
for the modern student to appreciate than for the seven-
teenth- and eighteenth-century settlers. This ideal Johnson
again enunciates in the fine peroration of the essay:

[The French-Canadians'] great security is the friendship of the
natives, and to this advantage they have certainly an indubitable
right; because it is the consequence of their virtue. It is ridiculous
to imagine that the friendship of nations, whether civil or bar-
barous, can be gained or kept but by kind treatment; and surely
they who intrude, uncalled, upon the country of a distant people, ought to consider the natives as worthy of common kindness, and content themselves to rob without insulting them. The
French, as has been already observed, admit the Indians, by intermarriage, to an equality with themselves; and those nations with
which they have no such near intercourse, they gain over to their
interest by honesty in their dealings. Our factors and traders,
having no other purpose in view than immediate profit, use all
the arts of an European counting-house to defraud the simple
hunter of his furs.

These are some of the causes of our present weakness; our
planters are always quarreling with their governor, whom they
consider as less to be trusted than the French; and our traders
hourly alienate the Indians by their tricks and oppressions, and
we continue every day to show by new proofs that no people can
be great who have ceased to be virtuous.

Such is the pessimistic conclusion of Johnson's opening
blast on the subject of the war in America. Three months
later he renewed the attack in "Observations on the Present

State of Affairs." [31] He surveys the events leading up to the declaration of war in a tone of Olympian disdain. "Both nations," he says, "clamour with great vehemence about infractions of limits, violations of treaties, open usurpation, insidious artifice, and breach of faith." He regards all this as mere cant: the contest is a naked struggle for power between two unscrupulous adversaries. The French and the English are fighting for territories "to which, I am afraid, neither can show any other right than that of power, and which neither can occupy but by usurpation, and the dispossession of the natural lords and original inhabitants." "Such is the contest," he concludes, "that no honest man can heartily wish success to either party." The parties for whom he reserves his sympathy are the Indians, whose treatment is described with indignation: "It may indeed be alleged that the Indians have granted large tracts of land both to one and to the other . . . if they were extorted by violence, or induced by fraud; by threats, which the miseries of other nations had shown not to be vain, or by promises of which no performance was ever intended, what are they but new modes of usurpation, but new instances of cruelty and treachery?"

Several paragraphs of Johnson's finest invective follow on the treatment of the Indians by the British colonists. The Indian grants of land can only have been the product of *force majeure:* "if indeed any such cessions were made, of which we have no witness but those who claim from them; and there is no great malignity in suspecting that those who have robbed have also lied." To those colonies which were established more peaceably than others, Johnson concedes "no other merit than that of a scrivener who ruins in silence, over a plunderer that seizes by force." The French, he repeats, have the advantage in the struggle: "They are subject to a governor commissioned by an absolute monarch . . . designs are therefore formed without debate, and executed without impediment. They have yet more martial than mercantile ambition, and seldom suffer their military schemes to be entangled with collateral projects of gain." And "the favour of the Indians which they enjoy . . . we ought to consider with other thoughts; this favour we might have enjoyed, if we had been careful to deserve it." But on the whole, "The American dispute between the French and us is . . . only the quarrel of two robbers for the spoils of a passenger." It is a tribute to the political tolerance of the eighteenth century to reflect how quickly such a defeatist tract would be suppressed at the beginning of a great national war today.

Johnson's unflattering view of the American colonists has an evident relation to the opinions that he was to express twenty years later, when these colonists declared their independence of Britain. Two other pieces that Johnson published in the *Literary Magazine* make that relation even clearer. In June 1756 the magazine printed a long letter from an American of Huguenot extraction on the grievances of the American colonies against Britain. They are much the same grievances as were to form the substance of later revolutionary manifestoes: the appointment of incompetent governors, neglect of defense, failure to encourage emigration to the colonies, and, in particular, restrictions on colonial trade. Johnson appended to this in the magazine a set of slashing "Observations," [32] based on the same theory of colonies he had expressed in his longer pieces. "I do not attempt to prove that all the restraints laid on the Americans are prudent," he concedes. "I have not in general a favourable opinion of restraints, which always produce discontent and an habitual violation of laws, and perhaps seldom contribute much to the end proposed. But whether wise or not, they may undoubtedly be just." Johnson is willing, that is, to argue the American question on the basis of expediency, but he refuses to hear any talk of "justice," "natural rights," and so on, which formed the stock-in-trade of the American polemists, and which strikes Johnson simply as cant. The colonists owe their own property to their unjust deprivation of the original inhabitants of the country of *their* natural rights, and cannot come into a court of justice with clean hands. On what grounds of self-interest, then, should Britain do the colonists favors? One argument of "Gallo-Anglus," that they provide a dumping ground for undesirables, Johnson quickly dismisses:

I do not very clearly see the consequence that, because there are lands in America, there need be no beggars in England. Our beggars are not beggars because we want land, but either by impotence, idleness, ignorance of the arts of life, or misfortune. Those who are impotent will not be much mended by the voyage. . . . What cure, except hunger, or a whip, there is in America for idleness, the inhabitants of that country must inform us.

He finds mass emigration no solution to the ills of a country: "It ought to be considered that every inhabitant gained to the colonies is lost to the mother country. . . . The strength of every country consists in the number of people proportionate to its extent, and it is not the populousness of a nation that produces beggars and strollers, but want of due regulation."

But Johnson's most telling point is the simple one, the colonies' "importance is the consequence of the restraints which he condemns; for if our colonies did not consume our manufactures they would be to us of no importance or value, nor should we have any interest in defending them more than any other body of exiles or fugitives." It is a perfectly clear and logical position, and its natural consequence is that, if the colonies are willing to take over the responsibility for their own defense and unwilling to accept the mother country's regulation of their economy, they should be independent. That Johnson sees this consequence is apparent enough in his long review of Lewis Evans' *Geographical . . . Essays . . . Containing an Analysis of a General Map of the Middle British Colonies in America*.[33] Quoting Berkeley's "Westward the seat [sic] of empire takes its way," Johnson observes the development of America: "There is no reason to doubt that the time is approaching when the Americans shall in their turn have some influence on the affairs of mankind, for literature apparently gains ground among them. A library is established in Carolina; and some great electrical discoveries were made at Philadelphia." But he strongly deprecates Evans' contention that the British should fight to wrest the Ohio valley from the French:

We shall then have an addition of land greater than a fourth part of Europe. This is magnificent in prospect, but will lose much of its beauty on a nearer view. An increase of lands without increase of people gives no increase of power or of wealth. . . . Since the end of all human actions is happiness, why should any number of our inhabitants be banished from their trades and their homes to a trackless desart, where life is to begin anew?

As always, Johnson judges political questions in terms of the happiness of the individuals involved.

The final paragraph is important:

The fear that the American colonies will break off their dependence on England, I have always thought, with this writer, chimerical and vain. Yet though he endeavours for his present purpose to show the absurdity of such suspicions, he does not omit to hint at something that is to be feared if they are not well used. Every man and every society is intitled to all the happiness that can be enjoyed with the security of the whole community. From this general claim the Americans ought not to be excluded: but let us not be frightened by their threats; they must be yet dependant: and if they forsake us, or be forsaken by us, must fall into the hands of France.

When the French power in North America was crushed a few years later, Johnson's last argument no longer applied. There was no longer any valid reason, on his own premises, why the American colonies should not cut their ties with Britain, nor any reason why Britain should seek to restrain them from doing so, if Britain were unable to control their economy; nor do I think that Johnson ever expressed any profound objection to their doing so or much regret for their having done so. But his last words on the matter were not written until 1775.

3. THE END OF AN ERA (1757–1760)

A fully detailed treatment of the political references in the multitude of Johnson's other writings of the late 1750's would be too long to be attempted in a survey of this kind. They consist mainly of detached *obiter dicta:* although, like everything else Johnson wrote, they are thought-provoking, they include no extended dissertations on political topics such as those in the early numbers of the *Literary Magazine.* But a brief sampling of them may be of value.

Of Johnson's many other contributions to the *Literary Magazine* besides those already discussed, the most impressive in length among those of political interest is his *Memoirs of the King of Prussia,* known to posterity as Frederick the Great.[34] In 1756 Frederick had almost reached the peak of his spectacular rise to fame, and become a phenomenon that naturally interested Johnson and his readers. Frederick later provided Carlyle and Macaulay with fine opportunities for moral variations on political themes. We are inevitably disappointed to discover that Johnson neglected to make similar use of the opportunity: Frederick would have furnished a splendid text for an antihero-worshiping tract from Johnson. But fond as he was of moralizing, Johnson did not regard it as the primary object of biography; moral lessons might indeed come out of biography, but the duty of the biographer was above all to present the facts. And his life of Frederick is almost severely objective, apart from a number of derogatory remarks about kings in general:

The studies of princes seldom produce great effects, for princes draw with meaner mortals the lot of understanding.

Princes have this remaining of humanity, that they think themselves obliged not to make war without a reason. Their reasons are indeed not always very satisfactory.

Moderation in prosperity is a virtue very difficult to all mortals; forbearance of revenge when it is within reach is scarcely ever to be found among princes.

Another contribution to the magazine was a review of Thomas Blackwell's *Memoirs of the Court of Augustus*,[35] where Johnson finds, "among other affectations," "a furious and unnecessary zeal for liberty, or rather for one form of government as preferable to another. This indeed might be suffered, because political institution is a subject in which men have always differed, and if they continue to obey their lawful governors, and attempt not to make innovations for the sake of their favourite schemes, they may differ for ever without any just reproach from one another." If distrust of "a furious and unnecessary zeal for liberty" is proof of Toryism, this passage might be cited to show that Johnson's Toryism, in this sense, existed before George III's accession to the throne. But the same distrust was clearly expressed a dozen years before in the *Life of Savage,* and implied in the charity sermon for Henry Hervey Aston and in the *Life of Roscommon.*

Of Johnson's two greatest works of the late 1750's—*Rasselas* (1759) and the *Idler* (1758–60)—the same general observation may be made as was made of the *Rambler,* that they deal primarily with the problems of psychology and morality that underlie political attitudes rather than with political questions themselves. But the *Idler* is richer in specifically political discussions than the *Rambler*. The best known such paper is *Idler* 10, where Johnson makes fun of political credulity, in the shape of Tom Tempest the Jacobite, and Jack Sneaker the Whig. The nomenclature rather favors the Jacobite. But apart from that, it would be difficult to say whether the Whig or the Jacobite dog gets the better of it. Tom

is a steady friend to the house of Stuart. . . . He is of opinion that, if the exiled family had continued to reign, there would have neither been worms in our ships nor caterpillars in our trees. . . . He believes that king William burnt Whitehall that he might steal the furniture; and that Tillotson died an atheist. . . . He considers the new road to Islington as an encroachment on liberty, and often asserts that *broad wheels* will be the ruin of England.

Johnson's satire on Tom's hostility to technological progress is noteworthy; Johnson himself was consistently a friend to such innovations. But Jack, the doctrinaire Whig, is certainly no more perceptive: "He has known those who saw the bed into which the Pretender was conveyed in a warming pan. . . . He considers a standing army as the bulwark of liberty; thinks us secured from corruption by septennial parliaments. . . . He cannot believe that the Nonjurors are so quiet for nothing; they must certainly be forming some plot for the establishment of popery; he does not think the present oath sufficiently binding."

Idler 65 contains the famous characterization of the Whigs John Oldmixon and George Duckett, who questioned the authenticity of the first edition of Clarendon's *History,* as "the two lowest of all human beings, a scribbler for a party and a commissioner of excise." *Idler* 20 presents a parody on the differing accounts an English and a French historian would give of the taking of Louisburg; *Idlers* 7 and 30, a general condemnation of journalists, especially in time of war—"I know not whether more is to be dreaded from streets filled with soldiers accustomed to plunder, or from garrets filled with scribblers accustomed to lie"—that contrasts strangely with his earlier praise of "diurnal historiographers" in *Rambler* 145. *Idler* 73, a rather conventional condemnation of riches, begins with the striking reference to "a nation like ours, in which commerce has kindled a universal emulation of wealth, and in which money receives all the honours which are the proper right of knowledge and virtue."

Three main political themes can perhaps be distinguished in Johnson's writings of the last years of the reign of George II. One is condemnation of the military. Some animus against the army has been noted in his earlier writings and attributed to Tory prejudice arising from the exploits of Cromwell and Marlborough. But the abundance in the *Idler* of satire against soldiers in general is probably rather a manifestation of a widespread antimilitaristic tradition, of many centuries' standing, among Western intellectuals. It is very improbable that Johnson or his friends suffered much from "streets filled with soldiers accustomed to plunder" or that a military existence was as productive of evils as he chose to picture it. The traditional judgment on the *Idler* is probably correct, that it sacrifices intellectual acuity to the wish to amuse, and it certainly makes more use of intellectual clichés than almost anything else Johnson ever wrote. The most charitable thing that can be said about these attacks is that they were perhaps intended to stimulate greater military efficiency at a time when the British forces certainly needed it; they occur only in the earlier *Idlers* and disappear after the news of the military successes of 1759 begins to come in.

At any rate, military incompetence gave Johnson an opportunity for indulging his perpetual delight in *écraser l'infâme:* the impromptu speech on the subject of the Rochefort expedition [36] in 1757 that he is supposed to have composed for a member of "a certain respectable *talking* Society" shows him in his old slashing form of the 1730's:

> They went out, and they are come back again, not only without doing, but without attempting to do anything. . . . It is fit that this miscarriage, whether it be the effect of treachery or cowardice, be detected and punished, that those whom, for the future, we shall employ and pay may know they are the servants of a people that expect duty for their money, that will not be mocked with idle expeditions or satisfied with an account of walls that were never seen and ditches that were never tried.

If anyone has thought that Johnson's condemnation, the year before, of "a furious and unnecessary zeal for liberty" indicates that he is mellowing into authoritarianism, this insistence that the government are the people's servants and accountable to the people may reassure him. He goes on, in a fine outburst of democratic indignation, to say that even old George II's peace of mind is subordinate to the people's:

> It is said, an objection expresses some distrust of the king, or may tend to disturb his quiet. An English king, Mr. President, has no great right to quiet when his people are in misery; nor does he show any great respect to his sovereign who imagines him unwilling to share the distresses as well as the prosperities of his subjects. . . . It is the misfortune of a king that he seldom, but in cases of public calamity, knows the sentiments of his people. It is commonly the interest of those about him to mislead him by false intelligence, or flatter him by soft representations. It is therefore fit, when the people are injured, the people should complain, and not trust the sycophants of a court with their cause or their sentiments.

All this talk of "the people's" miseries and the people's right to direct complaint is not too unlike the language of the earlier stages of the American and French Revolutions.

Johnson's most thoughtful discussion of "the military mind" is the little piece entitled "On the Bravery of the English Common Soldiers." [37] Written, presumably, after the great victories of Minden (July 1759) and Quebec (September 1759), it represents perhaps some sort of amends made by Johnson for the early *Idlers*. "Our nation may boast," he says, "beyond any other people in the world, of a kind of epidemic bravery, diffused equally through all its ranks. We can show a peasantry of heroes, and fill our armies with clowns, whose courage may vie with that of their general." Johnson marvels, as so many intellectuals since him have done, that courage is not the exclusive property of the intellectually well-endowed. What, he wonders, are the causes of this "plebeian magnanimity"? The success of other armies, notably the Prussian, is due to "discipline and regularity," characteristics eminently not those of the British soldier. What has he to fight for? "Liberty and property," the fashionable cry of the professional patriots? "Property they are . . . commonly without. Liberty is, to the lowest rank of every nation, little more than the choice of working or starving."

Johnson's explanation of the phenomenon of "plebeian magnanimity" is that "It proceeds . . . from that dissolution of dependance which obliges every man to regard his own economic character. While every man is fed by his own hands, he has no need of any servile arts; he may always have wages for his labour; and is no less necessary to his employer than his employer to him. While he looks for no protection from others, he is naturally roused to be his own protector." In other words, it is the result of a system of economic individualism. It springs from "neglect of subordination." The economic overtones of this word as Johnson uses it should always be kept in mind; it connotes, we have seen, a society "where one part of the community is sustained and accommodated by the labour of the other"; "difference of property is necessary to subordination." [38] Johnson was no more able than most people to reconcile his attraction to the two poles of individualism on the one hand and a social existence ("subordination") on the other. It was clear to him that with the advance of science and technology, in which he was so keenly interested, the world was necessarily tending in the direction of ever more complex social and economic organization, where the need of "subordinating" the individual's self-regarding desires to the happiness of the whole was becoming more and more apparent. Yet his own personal instincts were on the side of individual self-expression, and he was able to perceive that, on the field of battle at least, English individualism was in the long run equal to the efficiency of French and Prussian regimentation. His conclusion is uncertain and unsatisfactory, though perhaps no more unsatisfactory than that of anyone else who has ever attempted to solve this seemingly insoluble problem:

From this neglect of subordination I do not deny that some inconveniences may from time to time proceed: the power of the law does not always sufficiently supply the want of reverence, or maintain the proper distinction between different ranks; but good and evil will grow up in this world together; and they who complain, in peace, of the insolence of the populace, must remember that their insolence in peace is bravery in war.

Another important theme that runs through Johnson's writings of this time (as of other times) is that of humanitarianism. In the preface that he wrote in 1760 (at the request of that intransigent Whig and Miltonian, Thomas Hollis) for the *Proceedings of the Committee Appointed to Manage the Contributions for Cloathing French Prisoners of War*,[39] he puts forward a moving appeal for charity to the enemy. Two papers in the *Idler* (22 and 38) paint a vivid picture (almost a century before Dickens) of the miseries caused by the inequitable laws for regulating imprisonment for debt at the discretion of the creditor; they are wrong in principle, for "the end of all civil regulations is to secure private happiness from private malignity; to keep individuals from the power of one another." In *Idler* 17, he devotes a few paragraphs to a fiery execration of vivisection. But the most bitter invective Johnson ever wrote against man's inhumanity to man, against the horrible absurdity of war—invective which even the author of the fourth book of *Gulliver's Travels* hardly surpasses —is the original *Idler* 22, which in the collected editions Johnson suppressed. A family of vultures are discussing man, and are lost in wonder when they consider his actions. "When you hear noise, and see fire, with flashes along the ground," the old vulture instructs her young,

hasten to the place with your swiftest wing, for men are surely destroying one another; you will find the ground smoking with blood, and covered with carcasses, of which many are dismembered and mangled for the convenience of the vulture.

But when men have killed their prey, said the pupil, why do they not eat it? . . .

Man, said the mother, is the only beast who kills that which he does not devour, and this quality makes him so much a benefactor to our species. . . .

But still, said the young one, I would gladly know the reason of this mutual slaughter. I could never kill what I could not eat.

My child, said the mother, this is a question which I cannot answer, though I am reckoned the most subtile bird of the mountain. When I was young, I used frequently to visit the ayry of an old vulture. . . . His opinion was that men had only the appearance of animal life, being really vegetables with a power of motion; and that as the boughs of an oak are dashed together by the storm, that swine may fatten upon the falling acorns, so men are by some unaccountable power driven one against another, till they lose their motion, that vultures may be fed.[40]

The decade of the 1750's was not a happy time for Johnson. It saw the death of his wife and his mother, and of old Gilbert Walmesley and his cherished Hill Boothby. With the publication of the *Rambler* and the *Dictionary*, with the award of an honorary degree from the University which as a youth he had been forced to leave, he had at last won what he had so long striven for, public recognition of his talent, only to find, what the neurotically ambitious often find, that "success" turned to ashes in his mouth. The great *Dictionary* he "dismissed with frigid tranquillity . . . having protracted my work till most of those whom I wished to please have sunk into the grave, and success and miscarriage are empty sounds." It is not greatly to be wondered at if, out of this wasteland of the spirit, he should look on the war in which his country was engaged as merely senseless carnage waged for the acquisition of tracts of wilderness that could add nothing to the meager happiness of mankind. It is at this time that the most frequent expressions occur of still another theme in Johnson's political thought—that of the essential unimportance of politics by comparison with the private sources of individual joy and agony. Its chief expression is in *Rasselas:*

Thousands and ten thousands flourish in youth, and wither in age, without the knowledge of any other than domestic evils, and share the same pleasures and vexations, whether their kings are mild or cruel, whether the armies of their country pursue their enemies, or retreat before them. While courts are disturbed with intestine competitions, and ambassadors are negotiating in foreign countries, the smith still plies his anvil, and the husbandman drives his plough forward; the necessaries of life are required and obtained, and the successive business of the seasons continues to make its wonted revolutions.[41]

"The good or ill success of battles and embassies extends itself to a very small part of domestic life," he writes to Baretti: "we all have good and evil, which we feel more sensibly than our petty part of public miscarriage or prosperity." [42] Most familiar are the two lines he contributed to Goldsmith's "The Traveller":

> How small of all that human hearts endure
> The part which laws or kings can cause or cure!

It is just, and mournful, to speculate that Johnson might well have changed his mind and abandoned even this one poor crumb of comfort had he known what progress would be made by posterity in extending the dominion of laws and rulers over human hearts.

Macaulay took Johnson's logic to task about this: "If the happiness of individuals is not affected by political abuses, zeal for liberty is doubtless ridiculous. But zeal for monarchy must be equally so." [43] Though "zeal for monarchy" is hardly an accurate summary of Johnson's political philosophy, it is true enough that Johnson, after uttering these expressions, continued to write and talk vigorously on political matters. But whether or not his doing so is logical, its moral and psychological propriety is so obvious that it seems hardly worth while trying to rescue Johnson from Macaulay's cleverness. Macaulay would no doubt have found equal fault with a medieval saint for preaching contempt for things of this world and at the same time feeding the poor.

The evidence of Johnson's political interests in the later 1740's and the 1750's, the most neglected yet not improbably the most important period in the study of those interests, is so rich and complex as to defeat any attempt at a facile summary. One generalization, however, which was made at the beginning of this chapter, may be usefully repeated here: Johnson's chief concern in these years is evidently not to propagate doctrine but to encourage his reader, the common intelligent Englishman, the "secondary legislator," whose opinion is coming to have more and more weight in political decisions as the century advances, to think these matters out independently, to examine the facts, and above all to distrust cant. Johnson makes the point again emphatically in a review published in the month when the reign of George II ended, a review of William Tytler's *Historical and Critical Inquiry* into the "casket letters" attributed to Mary Queen of Scots.[44] Tytler believes the letters forgeries, and Johnson, after a copious and detailed survey of the evidence presented, is inclined to agree with him.

Johnson, it may be thought, agrees because he is a Tory and hence a partisan of the Stuarts. It is possible, however, to approach the question from the other direction, remembering that he has repeatedly expressed his low opinion of James I, Charles II, and James II—the latter a "dangerous bigot," whose subjects drove him from the throne through the "necessity of self-preservation." Why does Johnson at other times spring to the defense of the Stuarts? He is perfectly explicit. "We live," he begins, "in an age in which there is much talk of independence, of private judgment, of liberty of thought, and liberty of press. Our clamorous praises of liberty sufficiently prove that we enjoy it; and if by liberty nothing else be meant than security from the persecutions of power, it is so fully possessed by us, that little more is to be desired except that one should talk of it less and use it better." The influence of patronage, as well as the power of government, over writers has become negligible: "The writers of the present time are not always candidates for preferment, nor often the hirelings of a patron. They profess to serve no interest, and speak with loud contempt of sycophants and slaves." Johnson himself is a conspicuous case in point. So far, so good. But—

There is, however, a power from whose influence neither they nor their predecessors have ever been free. Those who have set greatness at defiance have yet been the slaves of fashion. When an opinion has once become popular, very few are willing to oppose it. Idleness is more willing to credit than enquire; cowardice is afraid of controversy, and vanity of answer; and he that writes merely for sale is tempted to court purchasers by flattering the prejudices of the public.

"It has now become fashionable," he continues, "for near half a century, to defame and vilify the house of Stuart, and to exalt and magnify the reign of Elizabeth. The Stuarts have found few apologists, for the dead cannot pay for praise; and who will, without reward, oppose the tide of popularity? Yet there remains still among us, not wholly extinguished, a zeal for truth, a desire of establishing right, in opposition to fashion."

Johnson is a defender of the Stuarts because an unthinking contempt for the Stuarts is fashionable, and because all his life he has fought against the abdication of human reason and observation to the power of intellectual fashion, as to authoritarianism in any other guise. What is intellectually fashionable must always be challenged; the particular point at issue is not so important as the fact that it has been accepted in blind obedience to authority. Truth, in the long run, can be attained, right can be established, only by individual human beings thinking and investigating for themselves; men must never surrender their minds to any tyranny; and the tyranny of fashion, the tyranny of public opinion, the tyranny of the majority, as John Stuart Mill was later to call it, is no less vicious and stultifying than the tyranny of rulers, governments, and patrons.

Chapter Seven

THE REIGN OF GEORGE III (1760–1784)

1. "ENGAGING IN POLITICKS" (1760–1770)

YOU know that we have a new King . . ." Johnson wrote on June 10, 1761, to Baretti at Milan. "We were so weary of our old King that we are much pleased with his successor; of whom we are so much inclined to hope great things that most of us begin already to believe them." [1] At first Johnson manifested some of his old distrust of a royal upbringing. "The young man," he continues, "is hitherto blameless; but it would be unreasonable to expect much from the immaturity of juvenile years, and the ignorance of princely education. He has long been in the hands of the Scots, and has already favoured them more than the English will contentedly endure." But this early suspicion that George might be something less than a 100 per cent Englishman soon faded, and by 1770 Johnson was able to lament that the Wilkesites were trying "surely without effect, to alienate the affections of the people from the only king who for almost a century [i.e., since Charles II] has much appeared to desire, or much endeavoured to deserve them." [2] Later, Johnson was compelled to admit that these attempts had, for a time, succeeded: "Sir," he said in 1783, "this Hanoverian family is *isolée* here. They have no friends." But Boswell is right in correcting him: "The very next year after this conversation [when Pitt won the election of 1784] and ever since, the King had as extensive and generous support as ever was given to any monarch, and has had the satisfaction of knowing that he was more and more endeared to his people." [3]

An admiration for George III had, in the eighteenth century, important political implications. Modern historical scholarship has made it clear that he was certainly not a despot, as the average American probably still considers him. George was, under the British constitution as it was understood in the eighteenth century, the permanent and effective head of the executive branch of government, with certain prerogatives which it was his duty to exercise, and which he exercised on the whole to the satisfaction of most of his subjects except the Rockingham-Fox aristocratic Whig "connexion." Their contention was, in the words of the famous Dunning resolution of 1780, that "the influence of the Crown has increased, is increasing, and ought to be diminished." But to whom was the influence thus to be subtracted from the Crown to go? The argument of the opponents of the Rockingham Whigs was that a House of Commons in which Gowers and Ansons, by the expenditure of some thousands of pounds, were enabled to choose whom they pleased as members for Lichfield represented nothing but the guineas of the Gowers and Ansons; if it came to a question of the metaphysical word "representation," the king represented the common Englishman at least as well as did plutocratic Whig noblemen. This, at least, was the view of Goldsmith, in one of the most vigorous rebuttals of the Whig contention that what was good for Russells and Cavendishes was good for England:

> Wealth, in all commercial states, is found to accumulate, and all such have hitherto in time become aristocratical. . . . The possessor of accumulated wealth . . . has no other method to employ the superfluity of his fortune but in purchasing power. . . . But there must still be a large number of the people without the sphere of the opulent man's influence, namely that order of men which subsists between the very rich and the very rabble; those men who are possest of too large fortunes to submit to the neighbouring man of power, and yet are too poor to set up for tyranny themselves. . . . This order alone is known to be the true preserver of freedom, and may be called *the people*.

In such a state . . . all that the middle order has left is to preserve the prerogative and privileges of the one principal governor with the most sacred circumspection. For he divides the power of the rich, and calls off the great from falling with tenfold weight on the middle order placed beneath them. . . . What they may then expect [if his power is diminished] may be seen by turning our eyes to Holland, Genoa, or Venice, where the laws govern the poor and the rich govern the laws. I am then for, and would die for monarchy . . . every diminution of [the sovereign's] power . . . is an infringement upon the real liberties of the subject.[4]

For George III in this context substitute, let us say, a New Deal president of the United States; for the accumulated wealth of Gowers and Russells substitute the accumulated wealth of Wall Street or the National Association of Manufacturers; and the parallel to some modern American political thinking is apparent. Johnson's Toryism is not precisely that of Goldsmith's. Nevertheless they have enough in common to make it appear that Johnson's detestation of George I and George II and his (moderate) enthusiasm for George III cannot be explained adequately in terms of "the waning of Johnson's Jacobitism" or "Johnson's growing fear of democracy." The simplest explanation, and the one that "have-not" Tories like Goldsmith and Johnson might themselves have given, if pressed, is that George I and George II allowed the government of the country to be kept under the thumbs of the Whig plutocracy and George III did not.

Of course, the actual political scene from 1760 to 1784 is much too complex to be interpreted so simply. Whatever George III's intentions, he had to rule in cooperation with one or another of the various power-seeking Whig factions, and with the aid of a few outsiders in politics who owed allegiance to none of the established groups—Bute, Jenkinson, to some degree North and Thurlow. The older professionals, especially of the Rockingham-Fox-Burke group, were extremely irritated to find these amateurs poaching on their preserves, and made much noise about the unconstitutionality of the "King's Friends" as they were called; but their influence and number were exaggerated. The position of the Old Tories, the country gentlemen, became even more ambiguous than it had been in the first half of the century, and in many of the crucial divisions of the House of Commons in this period, Tories are to be found evenly distributed on both sides of the question.[5]

Where did Johnson stand in all this? Did he still consider himself a Tory? In 1770 we find him writing a pamphlet to support a ministry that includes Grafton, Shelburne, Conway, and Gower (the second earl), and rebuking the Tories for their "frigid neutrality." [6] Was he a King's Friend? In 1768 we find him rejoicing that "the Virtue of Oxford has once more prevailed" over "the slaves of power," in that two "old Tory" candidates have beaten Charles Jenkinson, pre-eminently the King's Friend, at the Oxford University election.[7] During the decade of the 1760's we find him associated with Gerard Hamilton, who was neither a Tory nor a King's Friend. We may probably say that he continued to regard himself as a Tory, but an extremely independent one; as a supporter of George III, but free to disagree with the conduct of George's ministers whenever he thought it advisable. He often did so.

The notion that Johnson was a subservient and uncritical adherent to Government policy under George III is quite mistaken. For all his lamentation that factious people did not share his devotion to the king, in practice he could criticize the regime as vigorously as any professed opponent of it. Of the various ministers who from time to time enjoyed the king's confidence, he found Bute "a theoretical statesman—a book minister," who "thought this country could be governed by the influence of the Crown alone"—Johnson, then, apparently did not think it could be.[8] Of George Grenville, Johnson wrote the famous description (which North's ministry made him cancel): "Let him not, however, be depreciated in his grave. He had powers not universally possessed: if he could have got the money he could have counted it." [9] As Hill points out, this is equally a thrust at Grenville's predecessor as Chancellor of the Exchequer under Bute, the Tory Sir Francis Dashwood, who could not even have counted it. He decried the "feudal gabble" of the great Chatham, "for whom it will be happy if the nation shall at last dismiss him to nameless obscurity." [10] North's administration, from 1770 to 1782, is regarded as having been peculiarly the personal administration of the king; for it and for North, Johnson reserved invective as vigorous as that which he had used against Walpole in the 1730's. "I believe Lord North is no friend to me," he confided to Boswell as early as 1772; by 1773 he was describing North as having "a mind as narrow as the neck of a vinegar cruet." [11] On the date of North's fall from office there appears the pregnant entry in Johnson's diary: "The Ministry is dissolved. I prayed with Francis, and gave thanks." But the expressions of Johnson's "mean opinion of that ministry," as Boswell describes it, are too numerous to cite. "I am glad the Ministry is removed," Johnson summed it up. "Such a bunch of imbecility never disgraced a country." [12]

Curious as it may seem, Johnson's reported opinions of the main opposition group of Whigs are less severe than those just quoted. With three of its leaders, Shelburne, Burke, and Fox, he was personally friendly. Shelburne he described as "a man of coarse manners, but a man of abilities and information. I don't say he is a man I would set at the head of a nation, though perhaps he may be as good as the next Prime Minister that comes" [13]—which, by comparison with his opinions of North and Grenville, may be taken as a compliment. Johnson's high personal regard for Burke is well known, though he vigorously disavowed Burke's political thinking: "I remember being present," he told Boswell, "when he shewed himself to be so corrupted, or at least something so different from what I think right, as to maintain that a member of parliament should go along with his party right or wrong. Now, Sir, this is so remote from native virtue, from scholastic virtue, that a good man must have undergone a great change before he can reconcile himself to such a doctrine."[14] Against the political principles of Charles James Fox, radical Whig and enemy of George III par excellence, Johnson is not recorded to have uttered a word of disapproval.[15] It is not the least paradoxical fact about the "great Tory" that his last recorded utterance on politics, made after the younger Pitt, to the satisfaction of both king and people, had triumphed over the Foxite Whigs, was "I am for the King against Fox; but I am for Fox against Pitt."[16] "Blind Toryism" seems no more appropriate a description of Johnson's politics after the accession of George III than before it.

Although Johnson wrote little for the public on politics during the 1760's, the decade was nevertheless an active one for him politically. The famous pension was awarded to him in the summer of 1762 by Lord Bute, apparently at the instigation of the canny Alexander Wedderburn. Boswell insists that the government's motive was purely altruistic, and he quotes Bute as saying, "It is not given you for anything you are to do, but for what you have done."[17] Yet Johnson's name is so conspicuous an anomaly on the list of writers in receipt of government pensions awarded for political reasons that it is easy to understand the general public's unwillingness to believe that the award to Johnson was entirely unconnected with politics. Does Bute's "what you have done" refer only to the *Dictionary,* or does it include some of Johnson's previous political writings? The memory of the attacks in the *Literary Magazine* on the Pittite policy of war might have been grateful to Bute, who in 1762 was endeavoring to bring the war to an end. Is it possible that some political writing even more specifically tending to support Bute's policies was done during the obscure years of the late 1750's and has not yet come to light?

More probably, the Government was less interested in doing a service to Johnson or to literature than to itself. The whole incident of the pension has always been a little puzzling; but the psychology behind it becomes clearer when we realize that, contrary to the usual notion, the Tories, at the accession of George III, were not suddenly overwhelmed with partisan enthusiasm for the new king. They preferred him to George II, of course; yet they were by no means ready to abandon at a moment's notice their traditionally aloof and critical attitude toward the central executive. "Though George III was willing to take loyal tories into his service, as he told Pitt in 1765, few of them came; some of them cold-shouldered him, others were useless." [18] It was therefore a matter of some self-congratulation for Bute and Wedderburn to have arranged this striking public testimony of good will between the Government and the great independent Tory writer. Bute was probably quite sincere in disclaiming any thought of demanding any further *quid pro quo;* it was enough of a triumph that Johnson should have accepted the pension at all. Johnson, for his part, must have known, when he accepted it, what he was letting himself in for; nevertheless, he was willing, for the sake of bolstering the credit of the new regime, to subject himself to the inevitable storm of abuse from its opponents. He was equally sincere in determining that his acceptance of the pension should in no way interfere with the independence of his pen.

In spite of the official protestations, one member of the Bute circle, at least, seems to have thought that Johnson might be available for literary assistance to the government.

This was the shrewd Charles Jenkinson, who himself had
made his way into prominence by his political pamphleteer-
ing, becoming successively Bute's Under-Secretary of State
and his private secretary, and, after Bute resigned in 1763,
Secretary to the Treasury under his successor Grenville. One
of Jenkinson's duties seems to have been to act as a kind of
unofficial minister of propaganda to the government. In this
capacity, he arranged an appointment with Johnson in October 1763, and presented him with a set of papers "concerning
the late negotiations for the Peace" of Paris.[19] This manu-
script Jenkinson had prepared two years before but had not
published, and he presumably wanted Johnson to bring it up
to date or use it as material for a pamphlet in justification of
the controversial Peace.

Nothing happened, however, except that at some unspeci-
fied time Johnson complained to Gerard Hamilton that "his
pension having been given to him as a literary character, he
had been applied to by the administration to write political
pamphlets; and he was even so much irritated that he declared his resolution to resign his pension." [20] After waiting
for two years, Jenkinson, now temporarily returned to private
life, at last requested Johnson to return the papers. Jenkinson's letter, though concluding with an elegant compliment
on Johnson's edition of Shakespeare, just published, seems a
trifle short: "About 2 years ago I put into your hands some
papers concerning the late negotiations for the Peace. If you
have no further use for them, I should be obliged to you if
you would return them to me . . ." and in the next paragraph informs him, unnecessarily and pointedly, that since he
is no longer Secretary to the Treasury, he has "no longer the
payment of the Annual Stipend which you receive from the
Crown." [21] The next day, under cover of a letter of massive
courtesy, Johnson returned the papers "carefully preserved,
and uncommunicated to any human being"—and, may one

guess, unread? "I once hoped to have made better use of them," Johnson says, but perhaps this is mere politeness.[22] The papers rest in the British Museum, still unpublished and perhaps unread. Three years later we find Johnson rejoicing that "The virtue of Oxford has once more prevailed," when Jenkinson is defeated at the polls by the Tory Sir Roger Newdigate.[23]

In 1765, however, with the much-postponed edition of Shakespeare off his hands, Johnson seems to have been more willing to turn again to political matters. At least three projects that we know of in which he was engaged in the later 1760's are of political interest.

The first of these is his collaboration with Robert Chambers, whom he had known at least as early as 1754, when Chambers was a seventeen-year-old student at Oxford. Chambers had contributed to the *Literary Magazine* under Johnson's editorship,[24] studied law under Blackstone, in 1762 was appointed Vinerian Fellow at Oxford, and in May 1766, when only twenty-eight, succeeded Blackstone as Vinerian Professor of Common Law. With the formidable precedent of Blackstone's *Commentaries* to compete against, young Chambers turned for help to his distinguished friend. Chambers did not actually begin to lecture until March 1767, but as early as December 1766 we find Johnson writing to chide him for idleness: "Come up to town, and lock yourself up from all but me, and I doubt not but lectures will be produced." [25] The date of Johnson's prayer "Before the Study of Law," September 26, 1765,[26] seems early to connect it with this work; but by this time Blackstone may well have indicated his intention of retiring and Chambers been unofficially selected to succeed him.

The Johnsonian portions of Chambers' Vinerian Lectures, which E. L. McAdam has segregated and collected,[27] form the clearest and most important statement of Johnson's fundamental political views extant. They deserve to be studied carefully and in detail; but it is apparent from even a quick reading that they contain nothing inconsistent with what may be gathered from his other political writings. The basis of political and social organization is human and historical, not divine or theoretical. Historical inquiry must be brought to bear on hypotheses about the origin and nature of government, and in such inquiry Johnson recommends unceasing skepticism:

It may not be improper in this place to caution young inquirers into the origin of our government against too great confidence in systematical writers or modern historians, of whom it may justly be suspected that they often deceive themselves and their readers when they attempt to explain by reason that which happened by chance. . . . In surveying the confusion of remote and obscure ages, we must be often content with slight hints and uncertain conjectures; and great care is to be taken that no man too hastily improve hints into systems. . . . Knowledge is always promoted by inquisitive industry, and almost always retarded by systematic dogmatism.[28]

Tested by adequate historical standards, patriarchal and contractual theories of government fail; Johnson mentions them only as curiosities. How little he was a believer in the divine right of kings may be gauged by the following account:

In that age of prejudice and ignorance . . . it was necessary to invest the king with something of a sacred character that might secure obedience by reverence and more effectually preserve his person from danger of violation. . . . The inauguration of a king is by our ancient historians termed consecration; and the writings, both fabulous and historical, of the middle ages connect with royalty some supernatural privileges and powers.[29]

This implies on Johnson's part a purely secular view of the ceremony of coronation, a view which even today in Britain is not officially accepted; the term "consecration" is official, and the spiritual significance of the ritual is regarded as of

great importance. Johnson also devotes considerable attention
to the popular theory of the "Gothic" origin of the English
constitution, and though more skeptical about the political
virtue of the Teutons than some of his contemporaries,[30] he
is willing to concede that at the time of the Northern invasions they "established new governments of a peculiar form,
from which (though after many and great alterations) the
present constitutions of most of the states in Europe are derived." [31]

For his own part, Johnson sets up a pragmatic and hedonist
basis for government:

By whatever means political bodies were first *framed,* they are
clearly *supported* by these two foundations: 1. a desire of social
life, to which both reason and instinct (if I may be allowed the
expression) incline men; and 2. a certain rule of obedience established in every State, to which every member of it chooses rather
silently to submit than to exchange the protection and pleasures
of society for the solitude and horrors of a desert.[32]

These two basic postulates, it may be noted, come from
Hooker, whose two foundations of a human Commonwealth
are "the one a natural inclination whereby all men desire
sociable life and fellowship; the other, an order expressly or
secretly agreed upon touching the manner of their union in
living together." [33] Johnson continues,

Society implies in its nature an interest common to many individuals, a pursuit of the highest degree of happiness that can be
obtained and enjoyed by any number, great or small, which that
society comprises. To the happiness of the whole, it will be frequently necessary to sacrifice the happiness of a part. . . . There
is therefore a necessity of some *governing* power, by which those
who are inclined to be happy at the cost of others may be compelled to their part of the general task,—and of a *public wisdom,*
by which private judgment shall be directed and controlled.

It is interesting to meet here the phraseology of the American
Declaration of Independence—"the pursuit of happiness"—

and the Utilitarian theory of "the greatest happiness of the greatest number." [34]

The striking thing about Johnson's political system as expounded here and elsewhere is how extremely *radical*, how economical of postulates, it is. It throws out divine sanctions; it throws out natural rights and natural law; it ignores Burkean ideas of prescription and the organic nature of the state; and insofar as it recognizes tradition, it seems suspicious of it. It is a determinedly secular, rational, and hedonist theory, difficult to distinguish from Bentham's and Mill's. To be sure, in its rigid subordination of the individual to not only the "governing power" of the state but also the "public wisdom" of society, it seems to touch Hobbes on the one hand and certain authoritarian political theorists of the nineteenth and twentieth centuries on the other; but Johnson seems more constantly aware than do those writers that the happiness of a society is the sum total of the happiness of the individuals in it.

But that sum total is small at the best—Johnson remarks, in one of his grimmest sayings, on "the constitution of things ordained by Providence, by which man is so formed and disposed that he can suffer more than he can enjoy" [35]— and the implied purpose of Johnson's state is to try to share out that happiness with at least some attempt at equality. The following sentence, one of the most magnificent Johnson ever wrote, is worth quoting not only for the baroque grandeur of its style, but for the fervency of its humanitarian and egalitarian sentiment:

When we consider in abstracted speculation the unequal distribution of the pleasures of life, when we observe that pride, the most general of all human passions, is gratified in one order of men only because it is ungratified in another and that the great pleasure of many possessions arises from the reflection that the possessor enjoys what multitudes desire, when it is apparent that many want the necessaries of nature, and many more the comforts and conveniences of life, that the idle live at ease by the fatigues of the diligent and the luxurious are pampered with delicacies untasted by those who supply them, when to him that glitters with jewels and slumbers in a palace multitudes may say what was said to Pompey, *Nostrâ miseriâ tu es magnus,* when the greater number must always want what the smaller are enjoying and squandering, enjoying often without merit and squandering without use, it seems impossible to conceive that the peace of society can long subsist; it were natural to expect that no man would be left long in possession of superfluous enjoyments while such numbers are destitute of real necessaries, but that the wardrobe of Lucullus should be rifled by the naked and the dainties of Apicius dispersed among the hungry, that almost every man should attempt to regulate that distribution which he thinks injurious to himself and supply his wants from the common stock.[36]

Johnson goes on to grant that such anarchy would lead to even more misery than before, and that there must be laws protecting private property. But at the back of all his political thinking there is the feeling that it is wrong for any one individual to be allowed unlimited opportunity to increase his own happiness at the expense of that of others, and that it is a prime function of the state to set limits to such opportunity. In brief, Johnson's conception of the function of government is not very different from that found in many versions of Victorian and modern rationalist socialism; or, what is much the same thing, in medieval theological conceptions of society, with the theology omitted.

From these fundamental principles Johnson goes on to derive the elements of law, which need not directly concern us here. But the Johnsonian portions of the Lectures contain remarks on many other topics related to the study of his political ideas—remarks on history in general, on the political history of England (especially medieval history), on feudalism, on Parliamentary representation, on the status of the Crown, on international law. It is impossible to go into all these in detail. We might notice one *obiter dictum* that explains a good deal in Johnson—"Rebellions and civil wars are the greatest evils that can happen to a people"; [37] an interesting comment on the place of wealth in the "gradation" of society—"of all kinds of superiority that of riches is most notorious and least disputable. It has been alleged by modern politicians [e.g. Burke?], and alleged with reason, that rich men ought to be more trusted than others by the public because they have more to lose by bad administration. We are not, however, too readily to imagine that the institutions of our savage ancestors were founded in deep research or refined ratiocination"; [38] and, finally, his remarks on the American colonies, remarks which are in harmony with what he had said on the subject ten years before and was to say ten years later. Has the British legislature the right to tax the American colonists? Morally, yes; for it is right that the Americans share in the expense of defending themselves. And legally, yes; the objection that the Americans are not represented in Parliament fails, on the consideration that a great number of British who are not represented nevertheless pay taxes.

Johnson's prayer "before the study of law" was dated in September 1765. In November of the same year he composed another prayer, headed, in his diary, "Engaging in Politicks with H———n." [39] "H———n" was William Gerard Hamilton, a minor politician who had had a rather curious career. Twenty years younger than Johnson, the son of a Scottish lawyer, he was educated at Winchester, Oxford, and Lincoln's Inn. He entered Parliament at the age of twenty-five, a protégé of Hardwicke and Henry Fox, and started his political career auspiciously with a brilliant speech on the Russian and Hessian treaties (1755). He never repeated this performance, though he spoke competently in the Irish House of Commons, where he sat from 1761 to 1764, as Chief Secretary for Ireland during the Earl of Halifax's lord lieutenancy. He returned to England in 1764, having lost his post in the Castle intrigues of the Irish Whigs, but soothed with a sinecure appointment that gave him an annual income of £2,000 for the rest of his life. He continued to sit in the British House of Commons and to take a dilettantish interest in politics, without apparently accomplishing anything else of note.

Exactly in what Johnson's "engaging in politicks" with Hamilton consisted is uncertain. The only concrete evidence of it that has survived is a few pages of notes entitled "Considerations on Corn" that Malone found among Hamilton's papers and published in 1808.[40] In discussing the possible date of these, Malone points out that in 1766 there was a shortage of grain, the price had risen high, and there was much public turbulence as a result. In September, during the Parliamentary recess, the Chatham government, in an attempt to relieve the situation, had by order-in-council proclaimed an embargo on the export of grain. A confused mass of legislation for the control of the grain trade was in force, and it was a nice legal question whether the King-in-Council had the authority to impose the embargo when it did. On November 19, 1766, Johnson wrote to Chambers at Oxford to "enquire what are the reasons for which Dr. Blackstone thinks the late embargo to be not legal, as I hear he does. It always seemed legal to me." [41] Apparently Johnson was mistaken about Blackstone's opinion, and the great jurist agreed with him that the executive decree was legal. Nevertheless the incident provided the opposition with a chance to make political capital, and when a bill was introduced in the next session of Parliament to indemnify the ministers for any possible illegality of their action, there was a great deal of high-flown oratory about arbitrary measures and flouting the authority of Parliament, particularly designed to embarrass the Chathamite group that prided itself on being the "friends of the people."

Malone dates Johnson's paper November 1766, apparently for no better reason than that the session of Parliament in which the matter of the embargo came up began in that month. But, it should be noted, Johnson's "Considerations" deal only incidentally with the embargo; they are primarily a discussion of a different matter, the advisability of paying an export bounty on grain. The principle of subsidizing grain for export had been discussed outside Parliament for some time, notably by the pioneer economist Charles Smith in pamphlets printed in 1758 and 1759, and reprinted in 1766 and 1767.[42] As far as the scanty evidence goes, the question of subsidization does not seem to have been the subject of much Parliamentary debate in the 1766–67 session, but in subsequent years it came up frequently. The necessity of revising the grain control legislation became, in fact, one of Burke's favorite topics, and in 1773 he and Governor Pownall and others were successful in passing revised legislation. Burke's arguments in these debates of 1768 to 1773 are curiously close to those of Johnson's "Considerations," and remind us that from 1759 to 1765 Burke had been Hamilton's research assistant. The arguments of both Johnson and Burke are protectionist in nature, and advocate the continuation of government control and subsidization of agriculture, in opposition to Charles Smith's free-trade views on the subject.[43]

More evidence of Johnson's activities in connection with Hamilton may some day come to light, though Malone is probably right in thinking that Johnson did no more than "enter into some engagement with Mr. Hamilton, occasionally to furnish him with his sentiments on the great political topics that should be considered in Parliament." [44] Of Johnson's work in another area of political activity at about the same time, we have only the evidence of two of Johnson's letters to Robert Chambers. On December 11, 1766, he writes,

"If you could get me any information about the East Indian affairs, you may promise that if it is used at all, it shall be used in favour of the Company," and on January 22, 1767:

The affairs of the East Indies are to come at last before the parliament, and therefore we shall be glad of any information about them. We are likewise desirous of the papers which have been laid before the House, which can be no longer secret, and therefore, I suppose may be easily granted us. We will pay for transcribing if that be any difficulty. What other papers shall be put into our hands, shall be used if they are used at all in defence of the company. Help us, dear Sir, if you can.[45]

The complicated political background of this project has recently been described in detail by Lucy Sutherland.[46] The Seven Years' War had freed the East India Company from French commercial competition in India, and thus enormously increased its potential wealth; at the same time it had placed the Company in a position of quasi-sovereignty over India, delegated to it by the British Crown; and both circumstances rendered it liable to a much greater measure of Government intervention than before. The first step in this intervention was taken by the imperially minded Chatham, though as Miss Sutherland points out, it was probably more in the nature of a raid on the Company's treasury by a financially embarrassed administration than a manifestation of deliberate imperialist policy. In the end, because of divisions in Chatham's cabinet and a complicated network of alliances of financial interest and power between various groups in the Company and various political groups, the action proved abortive and ended in a compromise. But the threat of Government interference was at first a powerful one; and when Chatham's follower, Alderman Beckford, shortly after the opening of the session in November 1766, moved for a Parliamentary investigation into the affairs of the Company, and

a little later, for the tabling of its papers (which Johnson refers to in his letter of January 22), the Directors of the Company were seriously alarmed; something of this alarm is re-
flected in the urgent tone of Johnson's letters.

On whose behalf is Johnson acting in this negotiation?
Who are the "we" who want copies of the tabled papers and
will use them "in defence of the Company"? Why was Chambers in a position to obtain copies of the papers? [47] Chambers
appears to have had connections of some kind with India, for
in 1773 he was appointed judge of the Supreme Court of
Bengal. Another possibility is that Johnson may have been
acting with the so-called Johnstone group, who were extremely active at this time in opposing the Chathamite "raid."
Its leading figure was John Johnstone, who had been a high-
placed Company official in Bengal, and had been dismissed
by Clive on his return to India in 1765 as governor of that
province. Clive, who at present maintained a precarious ascendancy among the Directors of the Company, was an ally of
Chatham and Shelburne. Joined with John Johnstone in opposing him were his brothers, Governor George Johnstone
and Sir James Johnstone, both MP's and acquaintances of
Johnson, and his uncle Lord Elibank, with whom Johnson
was friendly at least as early as January 1765.[48] Acting as liai-
son between the Johnstones and Edmund and William Burke
(who were speculating in East India Company stock and
hoped for a rise in its price, which a Government raid would
prevent) was George Dempster, MP, with whom Johnson
had been acquainted as early as 1763.[49] Also connected with
this opposition to Government intervention was Henry Vansittart, who had been replaced by Clive as Governor of Bengal, and with whose brother Robert Vansittart, Chambers'
colleague as Regius Professor of Civil Law at Oxford, Johnson was very friendly. Partly because of Burke's interest in

the matter, the cause of the Company against the Government was strongly supported in Parliament by the Rockingham Whigs.

If any writing or editing was done by Johnson as a result of this activity, it has not yet come to light.[50] But Johnson's many and important connections with people involved in Indian politics are worth noting for their own sake. As well as those just mentioned, the mutual admiration of Johnson and Warren Hastings, whom Johnson met sometime between 1764 and 1769, is well known. When his friend Chambers, in 1782, found himself in danger of being recalled by Parliament from his judgeship in India (his superior Sir Elijah Impey had just been recalled and impeached), Johnson kept a close watch on the Parliamentary scene on his behalf.[51] At some time, perhaps in the 1750's, Johnson even thought of migrating to India himself, with Joseph Fowke.[52] The events of 1767 help to explain Johnson's detestation of Clive—"a man who had acquired his fortune by such crimes that his consciousness of them impelled him to cut his own throat." [53] It is curious, though, that British exploitation of the natives in India does not seem to have aroused such strong passion in Johnson as did the exploitation of the American Indians, though he expressed his disapproval of it.[54]

But Johnson's acquaintance among politicians and politically minded laymen was vast, and the full story of all his "engagements" in politics, minor and major, will probably never be told. The political affiliations of Henry and Hester Thrale, with whom Johnson was so intimate, deserve a note.[55] Neither was, as various commentators have assumed, a Tory. Henry Thrale was brought up as an intimate of the Temple-Grenville-Lyttelton clan, to which he was distantly related (his father, Ralph Thrale, was a first cousin of Lady Cobham). After two unsuccessful attempts to get into Parliament, in 1754 and 1760, he finally succeeded in being chosen for Southwark at a by-election in 1765, and retained the seat at subsequent elections in 1768 and 1774, but was defeated in 1780, shortly before his death. His Parliamentary career was undistinguished; after 1770 he seems to have been a consistent supporter of North, and before that time (presumably) of Grenville. Johnson acted as a kind of political mentor to him throughout their association, campaigning for him personally in the Borough, and writing election publicity for him.[56]

Mrs. Thrale was at least as much interested in politics as her husband was, and Johnson tells how, in the 1780 election when Thrale was too ill to campaign for himself, she "ran about the Borough like a Tigress seizing upon every thing that she found in her way." [57] Her father, John Salusbury, had been a client of the Earl of Halifax, and had received a small "place" from him in the government of Nova Scotia. As a child and young woman, she was well acquainted with Halifax's circle; indeed the Earl himself helped to arrange her marriage with Thrale.[58] When she was twenty-one, she wrote political squibs for the newspapers, attacking the Bute ministry, and her tutor Arthur Collier playfully designated her "vilissima Whiggula." As both the followers of Grenville and those of Halifax eventually drifted into support of the North administration, there was little cause for disagreement between the Thrales and Johnson on political matters in the 1770's.[59]

But it should not come as a surprise to learn that the great bulk of Johnson's politically-minded friends were, strictly speaking, Whig, not "old Tory." The fact did not seem to worry Johnson greatly. He would sometimes growl at John Taylor's Whiggism, and occasionally get into a dispute with him about the dead-and-buried issue of Jacobitism. Yet that difference did not prevent him from writing Taylor long letters on politics, from advising him on his political relations with his patrons, the Whig Dukes of Devonshire, or even

from writing sermons on political subjects for Taylor to de-
liver.[60] Those who have been deceived by Johnson's anti-
Whig outbursts into seriously believing that he could hardly
bear the sight of a Whig have been the victims of one of the
great hoaxes of literary history.

2. THE PAMPHLETS OF THE 1770'S

When Johnson's political activities are mentioned, most
readers think first of the four pamphlets that he composed
between 1770 and 1775 in support of certain policies of the
administrations of the Duke of Grafton and Lord North. Understandably, they caused Johnson a great deal of notoriety.
He had begun to be regarded as the Grand Old Man of English letters, the great moralist, a landmark of the British cultural scene, expected to pontificate solemnly and judiciously
on suitable occasions—the familiar apotheosis of the older
writer in Britain. It perhaps amused Johnson to puncture
this legend by indulging himself in a last youthful outburst
of political invective in the manner of his twenties. The shock
to the reading public was spectacular, and from all sides the
expressions of hurt reproach came in: "When a man who has
rendered himself eminent by his productions in morals, and
in polite literature, engages in political contentions . . . it
may reasonably be expected of such a writer that he should
distinguish himself not by party violence and rancour, but by
moderation and wisdom. . . . You have written in a manner
utterly unworthy of a great, or liberal, or philosophic
mind."[61] And many unkind things were said about his pension. But the role of *enfant terrible* probably gave more pleasure to the sixty-year-old Johnson than that of the oracle of
expected platitudes.

To the serious student of Johnson's political thought, the
pamphlets of the 1770's, though important, may not seem entirely to deserve the isolated pre-eminence that their notoriety

accorded them. Much of their reasoning about political principles is also to be found in the lesser-known earlier political
writings; and a large proportion of their content is made up
of special pleading about incidents that do not now seem
quite so exciting as they did then.

This is particularly so of the first of the series, *The False
Alarm*. It was published in the dying days of Grafton's administration (he resigned on January 28, 1770), and it was no
doubt inspired partly by Junius' notorious letter to the king
of December 19, 1769, in which, as Johnson says, George III
is "insulted with rudeness and with menaces." Johnson preferred the pamphlet to *Falkland's Islands,* saying, "There is a
subtlety of disquisition in the first that is worth all the fire of
the second." [62] The subtlety may strike the modern reader as
merely misplaced ingenuity. Johnson argues in a lawyer-like
fashion for the constitutionality of the House of Commons'
action in declaring Colonel Luttrell elected for Middlesex in
place of the ineligible Wilkes, in spite of Wilkes' having received a larger number of votes than Luttrell. He is indefatigable in finding precedents to support the House's action,
and in disqualifying the precedents advanced by the other
side. That he is not altogether successful in convincing us that
the House acted constitutionally is to be expected, in view of
the highly indefinite nature of the British constitution. It may
be added that, on the other hand, the "rights" of electors under such a constitution are equally difficult to determine.

It is generally asserted by critics of Johnson that on this
occasion, as on others, he is fighting on the side of prerogative
and against democracy. To be precise, he is arguing for the
right of the House of Commons to determine procedure in
questions regarding its own composition.[63] If the House of
Commons is regarded as "the representatives of the people,"
then Johnson, in exalting its powers and privileges, is assuming a normally Whig or democratic position. If it be

argued, as it has been, that in 1769 the unreformed House was not really representative of the people, it must be asked, when did it become so? In 1832, when the working class remained unfranchised? In 1884, when half the adult population continued to be excluded from the franchise because of their sex? Was the House not equally unreformed in 1642 and 1689, when Whig writers rejoice that the will of the people, speaking through the House of Commons, triumphed? "Representation of the people" is, in fact, a highly metaphysical notion, and the history of British politics seems to show that any group which sets itself up as the guardians of the rights of the people may decide to exalt or ignore the House of Commons as it finds expedient. Not long after the Wilkes affair, in 1788, we find Charles James Fox and other radical Whigs urging the Prince of Wales to assume the power of the Crown by his own volition and prerogative, and denying that Parliament has any right whatever to interest itself in the devolution of the royal power.

But Johnson will not be drawn into a long argument involving hypothetical "rights" of any particular element of society. He simply declines to treat political matters within the Whig frame of reference, in the Whig terminology. To his steadfastly empirical mind, the fundamentals of politics (as we have seen in his enunciation of them in the Vinerian Lectures) resolve themselves into concrete matters of expediency and the exercise of power. "The first laws had no law to enforce them; the first authority was constituted by itself," [64] he insists, getting rid at once of metaphysical Whig notions of social compacts and natural rights, and of metaphysical Jacobite notions of the divine right of kings:

We must again recur . . . to the unwritten law of social nature, to the great and pregnant principle of political necessity. All government supposes subjects, all authority implies obedience. To suppose in one the right to command what another has the right to refuse is absurd and contradictory. . . . The Commons must be controlled, or must be exempt from control. If they are exempt, they may do injury which cannot be redressed; if they are controlled, they are no longer legislative.[65]

This seems to be the crux of Johnson's argument in the Wilkes case. Even granting that the House of Commons has acted unfairly in handling the Middlesex election, what legal recourse is possible? If, as it seems, the House is sovereign in matters regarding its own constitution, none. There is then no point in retailing ideological cant about the House's illegally attacking the rights of the people. If the House is the source of law in regard to its own membership, then it cannot act illegally; it is a contradiction in terms to say so. The power of the House in this regard is great, and the possession of such power is always fraught with danger: as Johnson cleverly argues, if the much-maligned Scottish members wished, they could seize an opportunity to form themselves into a quorum and expel all the other members of the House; their action might be unfortunate and inexpedient; but it would not be illegal. Political power is always susceptible to abuse; but for political organization to exist at all, there must be power. In the case of the Middlesex election, the House of Commons is acting *intra vires,* and legally, therefore, the supporters of Wilkes have no case.

As to the fairness and expediency of the action, apart from its legality, the question must be judged in relation to other similar cases. That the House's exercise of its power will never entirely be free from objection is inevitable in the nature of things: "The perpetual subject of political disquisition is not absolute, but comparative good. Of two systems of government, or two laws relating to the same subject, neither will ever be such as theoretical nicety would desire." [66] Granted that the action of the House in the case of Wilkes is open to objection, granted that the electors of Middlesex do have a grievance with regard to their representation, Johnson says, it must be considered in relation to the whole subject of controverted elections. In such cases (with which Johnson, as a Lichfield man, was extremely familiar) injuries are done to the principle of popular representation in Parliament, and have been done for a very long time, the majority party in the House regularly throwing out a candidate of the other party who has received a larger number of votes, and declaring the election of the candidate of their own party, who has received a smaller number. By comparison with all these incidents, the single case of Middlesex in 1769 seems trivial. The alarm that the constitution is suddenly being subverted, that the state is in danger, is a false one. Looking back on the controversy after nearly two hundred years, one may fairly say that Johnson's point is valid. Of far greater importance than the sound and fury raised over Wilkes in assuring that the wishes of voters be respected was the Controverted Elections Act passed in the same year through the efforts of the much-abused George Grenville, one of Wilkes' "persecutors." In *The Patriot,* Johnson was to pay tribute to this important "advance in democracy."

A considerable part of *The False Alarm,* however, is devoted not to argument but to rhetoric and abuse; Johnson, after all, had had much experience in these, and it probably pleased him to have a chance again to exercise his old talent for rolling, resonant denunciation. "These puny controvertists," he calls his opponents, "these low-born railers." He denounces "the sectaries, the natural fomenters of sedition and confederates of the rabble." A "retailer of sedition and obscenity" he denominates Wilkes. His descriptions of the "progress of a petition" and of an election year are little masterpieces of Hogarthian humor:

The year of election is a year of jollity; and what is still more desirable, a year of equality. The glutton now eats the delicacies for which he longed when he could not purchase them, and the drunkard has the pleasure of wine without the cost. The drone lives a while without work, and the shopkeeper, in the flow of money, raises his price. The mechanic that trembled at the presence of Sir Joseph now bids him come again for an answer; and the poacher whose gun has been seized now finds an opportunity to reclaim it.[67]

Johnson is very likely drawing on memories of Staffordshire elections of his youth.

No doubt what most troubles modern readers of *The False Alarm* is Johnson's abuse of "the rabble": "As we once had a rebellion of the clowns, we have now an opposition of the pedlars. . . . The whole conduct of this despicable faction is distinguished by plebeian grossness." [68] "Submission is the duty of the ignorant, and content the virtue of the poor," his hypothetical statesman is to tell the people; "they have no skill in the art of government, nor any interest in the dissensions of the great." [69] Certainly it is unusual to find Johnson preaching to the poor the virtue of contentment with their lot—I do not know of any other place where he does so. But perhaps he should not be too harshly blamed for not being farther in advance of his time: it was not until a century after his death that virtual universal manhood suffrage was introduced in Great Britain, and most of Johnson's contemporaries would have agreed with him that there are limits of ignorance below which the privilege of participating in the government of a country should not be extended.

It is easy to understand Boswell's preference for *Thoughts on the Late Transactions Respecting Falkland's Islands* (1771) over *The False Alarm*.[70] Without the legal "subtleties" of the earlier piece, the *Falkland's Islands* gives a splendidly lucid narrative of the origin of the conflicting claims of England and Spain to that obscure territory.[71] It then expounds and justifies the Ministry's action in accepting a Spanish offer to leave Britain in possession of the islands without prejudice to Spain's claim of sovereignty. This is a position that appeals to Johnson's empirical temper, in effect dismissing the abstract question of right while settling the immediate and important question of physical occupation, and he argues it convincingly. The pamphlet is certainly the best written and no doubt the most generally successful of the four tracts. Toward the end of it he launches into an exuberant attack on the war-mongering of the opposition, who "sit like vultures waiting for a day of carnage," and lays about lustily at Chatham, Grenville, and Junius. His denunciation of war profiteers is memorable: "These are the men who, without virtue, labour, or hazard, are growing rich as their country is impoverished; they rejoice when obstinacy or ambition adds another year to slaughter and devastation; and laugh from their desks at bravery and science, while they are adding figure to figure, and cipher to cipher, hoping for a new contract from a new armament, and computing the profits of a siege or tempest." [72] At the same time he takes the opportunity again to reprobate what he thinks to be the opposition's appeal to the baser elements and instincts of the populace:

Foreign nations, unacquainted with the insolence of Common Councils, and unaccustomed to the howl of plebeian patriotism, when they heard of rabbles and riots, of petitions and remonstrances, of discontent in Surrey, Derbyshire, and Yorkshire, when they saw the chain of subordination broken, and the legislature threatened and defied, naturally imagined that such a government had little leisure for Falkland's Islands. . . . But . . . to fancy that our government can be subverted by the rabble whom its lenity has pampered into impudence is to fear that a city may be drowned by the overflowing of its kennels.[73]

It is no doubt tempting to interpret such remarks, as Professor Sherburn and others have done, as Johnson's revulsion from "the rising tide of democracy." A careful study still needs to be made of the exact nature of English mob activity

in the eighteenth century; but what little investigation has
been done into the question seems to indicate that it is basically a sociological rather than a political one, and that such
demonstrations as those around London at the time of the
Wilkes affair in 1768 and 1769 have more to do with the absence of an effective police force and with problems of over-
crowding and unemployment in the capital than with democracy.[74]

The Patriot, a short piece which appeared before the general election of 1774, is a heterogeneous attack on the "patriots" of the opposition. Johnson's diagnosis of the disease of
"patriotism" shows to what a large extent his dislike of the
tactics of the radicals was the product of his antipathy to cant:

He that has been refused a reasonable or unreasonable request,
who thinks his merit underrated, and sees his influence declining,
begins soon to talk of natural equality, the absurdity of *Many
made for one,* the original compact, the foundation of authority,
and the majesty of the people. As his political melancholy increases, he tells, and perhaps dreams, of the advances of the prerogative, and the dangers of arbitrary power; yet his design in
all his declamations is not to benefit his country, but to gratify
his malice.[75]

The piece includes a defense of the Quebec Act of 1774,
which guaranteed liberty of religious worship and respect for
their civil customs to the French-Canadians. It adds to the difficulty of a neat interpretion of eighteenth-century politics in
terms of "forces of progress" ranged against "forces of reaction" that the Act, praised in modern textbooks as a remarkably advanced and "liberal" piece of legislation, was enacted
by North and defended by Johnson against the attacks of the
American revolutionaries and English Whigs. Johnson mocks
at the contrast between the high-flown libertarian pretensions
of his opponents and their practice: "In an age where every
mouth is open for *liberty of conscience,* it is equitable to shew

some regard to the conscience of a papist. . . . . If liberty of
conscience be a natural right, we have no power to withhold
it; if it be an indulgence, it may be allowed to papists, while
it is not denied to other sects." [76]

Toward the end of *The Patriot* there occurs a paragraph
which neatly sums up Johnson's central position in the last
pamphlet of the group, *Taxation No Tyranny: An Answer to
the Resolutions and Address of the American Congress*
(1775):

To suppose that by sending out a colony, the nation established
an independent power; that when, by indulgence and favour,
emigrants are become rich, they shall not contribute to their own
defence, but at their own pleasure; and that they shall not be included, like millions of their fellow-subjects, in the general system of representation; involves such an accumulation of absurdity
as nothing but the shew of patriotism could palliate. [77]

The argument of *Taxation No Tyranny* has seldom been
taken very seriously. Those who admire Johnson generally
pass over the pamphlet with an embarrassed smile, and
those who do not admire him denounce it as the most shame-
ful and damning piece of evidence of his blind Toryism.
Neither seem to have read it too carefully. It is in the same
style of controversial writing as *The False Alarm*—a closely
reasoned examination of the legal and logical foundations
of the question at issue, interspersed with satire and invective
against those who maintain the opposite position. It was not
a very successful genre, as far as attaining its purpose was
concerned; the exuberant denunciation of the personalities
and motives of one's opponents, a legacy from the more full-
blooded days of political controversy in the early part of the
century, shocked a generation accustomed to a soberer address. But there is fine satire in *Taxation No Tyranny*. There
is the ironic juxtaposition of two passages from the resolutions of the Continental Congress, one a complaint against

the establishment by the Quebec Act of "a religion fraught with sanguinary and impious tenets" among the Canadians, the other an appeal to the same Canadians for support on the ground that "difference of religion will not prejudice them against a hearty amity, because the transcendent nature of freedom elevates all who unite in the cause above such low-minded infirmities." [78] There is the coupling of Chatham's pompous remark, "This glorious spirit of Whiggism animates three millions in America," with some exaggerated speculation on the probable rate of increase of population, to produce "[We are told] that the continent of North America contains three millions, not of men merely, but of Whigs, of Whigs fierce for liberty and disdainful of dominion; that they multiply with the fecundity of their own rattlesnakes." [79] Readers of Pope and Swift would have enjoyed this kind of thing; but it was apparently too strong for the readers of Goldsmith and Fanny Burney. Boswell has recorded how the government itself timorously watered down the original version, and how Johnson was disgusted at the process.[80]

Johnson's opponents were thus furnished with an opportunity to raise their hands in horror at the great man's want of decorum and were relieved from the necessity of pursuing and answering his line of reasoning. But that reasoning deserves attention; it goes to the heart of the theory of colonial expansion and is cogent enough to deserve better than an *ad hominem* reply. There is little in the pamphlet that Johnson does not say elsewhere, but it brings together two separate lines of reasoning employed by him on other occasions—his theory of sovereignty and his theory of colonies. It is one of his best pieces of sustained ratiocination, comparable to that of the review of Soame Jenyns' *Origin of Evil.*

Its main position may be summed up thus:

1. "All government is ultimately and essentially absolute." Sovereignty is, *by definition,* unrestricted; once restricted in any way, it ceases to be sovereign, and whatever so restricts it becomes sovereign.

2. Sovereignty "is not infallible, for it may do wrong; but it is irresistible, for it can be resisted only by rebellion, by an act which makes it questionable what shall be thenceforward the supreme power." (It should be noted that Johnson is not condemning rebellion; he is merely expounding the definition of sovereignty.)

3. Sovereignty, in the British realm, resides in the Parliament of Great Britain; subordinate legislatures, such as those of the American colonies, derive their powers only by delegation from the sovereign legislature, which can resume them when and as it sees fit.

4. It is axiomatic that "the supreme power of every community has the right of requiring from all its subjects such contributions as are necessary to the public safety or public prosperity." More than that, all subjects ("what must grieve the lover of liberty to discover"), by the fact of being subjects, have "ceded to the king and parliament, whether the right or not, at least the power of disposing *without their consent, of their lives, liberties, and properties"* [Johnson's italics].[81]

All this sounds rather terrible, and one can understand how the statement of such propositions in terms so uncompromising should cause good liberals like Joseph Towers to recoil in horror at Johnson's "propensity to defend arbitrary principles of government." But in fact Johnson is defending nothing. He is expounding straightforward constitutional law, as valid today as in 1775. The Parliament of Great Britain *is* legally omnicompetent as regards its subjects; there is, there can be, nothing in law to prevent it, the source of law, from arbitrarily passing at any time an Act of Attainder depriving any British citizen of life, liberty, and property, or from doing so indirectly by the enactment of criminal or financial statutes. The American citizen has no rights that are not subject to alienation by a constitutional amendment.

Johnson is, in fact, in advance of most of his contemporaries in seeing and clearly stating the fact of the omnicompetence of the modern state. He is advocating nothing; but he is relentless in pulling the veil from the eyes of those who refuse to see that things do stand so. And since they do, such concepts as "the laws of nature, the rights of humanity, the faith of charters, the danger of liberty, the encroachments of usurpation," which "have been thundered in our ears, sometimes by interested faction and sometimes by honest stupidity," [82] vanish into mist. Behind the ineffectual disguise of such comforting slogans stands the naked fact of political power.

In light of that fact, American claims for legal redress are seen as invalid.[83] The principle of "no taxation without representation" is fallacious: millions of Britons are taxed yearly without representation and will continue to be.[84] All that has to be discussed is the question of expediency. It is expedient that Americans should help to pay for their own defense; it is not expedient that the present scheme of Parliamentary representation be drastically revised to include American members.

Yet Johnson was well aware that in 1775 the dispute between America and Britain had gone far past the stage of discussion of abstract principles; and after establishing the validity of his own, he passes on, at the end of the piece, to the question of what is now to be done. There were three alternatives. One was the policy actually followed by North's government, to attempt to maintain the sovereignty of the central administration over the colonies by force of arms. Another was the policy advocated by Chatham, to grant effective sovereignty to the colonial legislatures while retaining the outward form of it in London—a species of dominion status. The third, advocated by the Rockingham Whigs, was the grant of independence, nominal as well as virtual. It can be seen that the Chatham compromise would be the least likely to appeal to Johnson in the rationalist mood in which he viewed the American question. He seems, toward the end of the pamphlet, to be oscillating uncertainly between the two positions of coercion and granting independence. He does apparently align himself with the government policy, and suggests that a sufficiently large force of troops be sent "that the rebels may be subdued by terror rather than by violence." But in the final paragraphs of the essay (which, however, are so mangled by government revision that it is difficult to tell how Johnson really wanted it to conclude) the tone of uneasy jocularity in which he discusses the possibility of American independence may well conceal a real belief that this is how the contest will end, and perhaps even a feeling that it will be the best thing for all if it does. Johnson had enough nationalistic pride to feel hurt the first time he saw a ship flying the American colors,[85] just as he could sometimes rejoice in Chatham's leadership of British arms to victory in the 1750's. Generally, however, the Little Englander side of Johnson prevailed; and it is possible, when one considers the indifference he usually expressed toward territorial expansion, that when American independence finally came he may have heaved a Disraelian sigh of relief that the wretched colonies no longer hung like millstones around the neck of Britain.[86]

Since the ostensible purpose of the pamphlet, however, is to justify the government's policy of coercion, can anything now be said in Johnson's favor for having supported that policy? If the matter is regarded as an abstract problem in political theory, a great deal can be said. To take the most obvious analogy, the situation of 1775 was duplicated within the United States itself in 1861, when Lincoln made the decision that Johnson advocated: to enforce the sovereignty of the central government (or, more precisely, the federal constitution) by resorting to arms.[87] If it was right for the Southern states to be denied the power of secession in 1860, it was equally right for the thirteen colonies to be denied the power of secession in 1776. So much for the abstract question of legal right or wrong. As for the question of expediency, in either case one can only speculate. Perhaps it would make for the greatest happiness of the greatest number if two sovereign powers now existed in place of the single nation of the United States. Perhaps it would make for greater happiness in the long run if one sovereign power instead of half a dozen now exercised authority over the English-speaking part of the world. The argument for the expediency of a smaller or a larger number of national sovereignties in the world is still highly pertinent to the welfare of the ordinary citizen (and is likely to become increasingly pertinent), and it seems as far as ever from being resolved. What is clear, however, is that Johnson's central position in *Taxation No Tyranny* is not to be dismissed with a facile sneer; in clarifying and emphasizing the concept of sovereignty Johnson is not behind his time, but so far in advance of it that only now in the twentieth century is the full importance of that concept beginning to be apprehended.

But the mere legal institution of a central authority subsuming local sovereignties, though necessary, is not sufficient for the successful existence of a unified state; it must be accompanied by some sort of psychological identification of the individuals concerned, by their consent to think in terms of that unified state. The military victory of the Union forces in the American Civil War would have been fruitless if the people involved had not been able to come to think of themselves not as Northerners and Southerners, but as Americans. This second step, the supersession of British and American local identity by some concept transcending both, Johnson seems never to have been willing to take. In his theory of colonies, as originally inherited from mercantilist theorists, the only valid reason for the establishment and maintenance of a colony is to add to the economic well-being of the mother country. Johnson strongly differentiates the interests of Britain and America and leaves no doubt that the former are always to be paramount. The American colonies have the duty of "contributing to the wealth of that country which protected them in their helpless state, on condition that they should obey her laws and promote her interest. . . . If any sacrifice must be made . . . what should we sacrifice but a *poor infant colony?*" [88] This was written in 1756. By 1775, Johnson's thinking on such matters was modified slightly, but only slightly: "The Mother-country always considers the colonies thus connected as parts of itself; the prosperity or unhappiness of either is the prosperity or unhappiness of both; not perhaps of both in the same degree, for the body may subsist, though less commodiously, without a limb, but the limb must perish if it be parted from the body." [89]

It can be seen from the last qualification that Johnson is still reluctant to take the final step of fully equating British and American interests; and it may well be argued that it is this psychological obstacle, this exclusiveness, this unwillingness to accept lesser breeds without the law into full community that has been the fatal impediment to many British attempts at colonization and those of some other European nations. On the constitutional, or administrative, implications of British-American relations, Johnson was perfectly correct, and it would be foolish to deny him the credit of seeing them clearly or to deny that it was important to see them clearly. The equally important psychological implications he failed or refused to perceive at all; and this is the more disappointing because Johnson had great capacity for psychological perception. But apparently he was never willing to exercise it on the Americans.

3. THE LAST YEARS (1775–1784)

Something of Johnson's difficulties with this problem of nationalism can be seen in the *Journey to the Western Islands of Scotland*, published in the same year as *Taxation No Tyranny*. Johnson obviously liked the Highlanders of Scotland; their loyalty and warmheartedness appealed to him. "You may guess at the opinions that prevail in this country," he wrote Mrs. Thrale, referring to the '45; "they are however content with fighting for their king, they do not drink for him; we had no foolish healths"—a glance at the English Jacobites, who enthusiastically drank to the king over the water but did not fight for him. Again, speaking of Flora Macdonald's devotion to the memory of Prince Charles, "These are not Whigs." [90] In spite of their difference in language and race, Johnson seems to have been willing to accept the Highlanders as part of the British nation, in a way that he never accepted Americans.

Hence he was greatly worried by the emigration from the Highlands to North America that was going on at the time. "Some method to stop this epidemic desire of wandering, which spreads its contagion from valley to valley, deserves to be sought with great diligence," he wrote.[91] It is perhaps worth noting that Johnson regarded "wandering" in itself as an evil, just as many Europeans of the present day are puzzled and a little alarmed by the willingness of the North American not to root himself for life in any one spot. Johnson fulminates at the landlords and the governmental policies that encourage such migration. He even proposes government subsidization of lower rents: "I know not whether the general good does not require that the landlords be, for a time, restrained in their demands, and kept quiet by pensions proportionate to their loss." [92] At other times he could argue that the emigrants would not really better themselves: "[Emigration] lessens the comfort of living. Men, thinly scattered, make a shift, but a bad shift, without many things. A smith is ten miles off . . . a taylor is far from them . . . it is being concentrated which produces high convenience." [93]

But what is interesting is that in the end Johnson can put himself in the shoes of the Highlander (a thing he was apparently never able or willing to do with the Americans) and see quite clearly why he does wish to emigrate. He describes the squalor of life on Rasay:

The traveller wanders through a naked desart . . . and now and then finds a heap of loose stones and turfs in a cavity between rocks, where a Being, born with all those powers which education expands, and all those sensations which culture refines, is condemned to shelter itself from the wind and rain. Philosophers there are who try to make themselves believe that this life is happy, but they believe it only while they are saying it. . . . For a long time . . . every man was content to live like his neighbour, and never wandering from home saw no mode of life preferable to his own, except at the house of the Laird or the Laird's near relations, whom he considered as a superior order of beings, to whose luxuries or honours he had no pretensions. But the end of this reverence and submission seems now approaching. The Highlanders have learned that there are countries less bleak and barren than their own, where instead of working for the Laird, every man may till his own ground, and eat all the produce of his own labour. Great numbers have been induced by this discovery to go every year, for some time past, to America.[94]

As for the clan system, "The system of insular subordination . . . having little variety, cannot afford much delight in the view. . . . The inhabitants were for a long time perhaps not unhappy; but their content was a muddy mixture of pride and ignorance, an indifference for pleasures which they did not know, and a strong conviction of their own importance." [95]

But when Johnson takes his eyes away from the actual scene before him, the uneasy feeling that emigration is somehow wrong returns. "It spreads mankind," he tells Boswell, "which weakens the defence of a nation, and lessens the comfort of living." [96] ("Whose living?" one must ask.) Again, "In the Hebrides, the loss of an inhabitant leaves a lasting vacuity; for nobody born in any other parts of the world will choose this country for his residence." [97] It would be difficult to say just who would have been seriously hurt by the vacuity, and the arguments about national defense and comfort of living are hard to take seriously. The national pride of other Britons might be wounded by the thought; but it was hardly fair to expect thousands of Highlanders to live out uncomfortable lives on the barren rocks of Skye in order to provide statistics to gratify the imagination of Londoners like Johnson. Johnson seems to be thinking in terms of a metaphysical entity called "Britain" whose welfare is somehow not the same as the sum total of the welfare of the individuals who constitute it. Some such hypostasis is at the bottom of most nationalistic thinking. It is not a fallacy to which Johnson was usually subject, but it seems to account partly at least for his attitude toward the Americans and, to a lesser degree, toward the question of Hebridean emigration.

The last ten years of Johnson's life reveal not too much of value for the student of his political opinions, although his interest in politics remained vivid up to the end. His one great work of the period, the *Lives of the Poets,* contains some amusing glances at the politics of his subjects, such as the attack on Akenside's "unnecessary and outrageous zeal for what he called and thought liberty—a zeal which sometimes disguises from the world, and not rarely from the mind which it possesses, an envious desire of plundering wealth or degrading greatness." [98] But such *obiter dicta* are not very frequent, and not so important in the plan of the *Lives* as the number of times they have been quoted might suggest. It has often been alleged that Johnson's political prejudices adversely affected his judgment of the poetry of some of the writers of whom he treats. It would be difficult, however, to name any one of his poets whose political activities he wholly approves; certainly the attitude he displays toward the political involvements of Swift and Pope is far from one of admiration. The most politically significant passages are those in the lives of Milton, Waller, and Butler, which deal with the Puritan regime, and have been already discussed.[99]

Johnson's letters and the reports of his conversation reveal that he continued to follow the political affairs of his country closely; and what he saw of them did little to lighten the gloom of his declining years. He has nothing good whatever to say about the North administration. During times of military defeat and national humiliation, he hurls imprecations at its "imbecility" and looks back with longing to the days of Walpole and even Chatham; when North finally resigns, he prays with Francis and gives thanks. North is succeeded by Rockingham; Johnson comments, "The men are got in whom I have endeavoured to keep out; but I hope they will do better than their predecessors; it will not be easy to do worse." [100] Rockingham is succeeded by Shelburne and Pitt; when the latter introduces his bill for Parliamentary reform, Johnson says, "I am afraid of a civil war. The business of every wise man seems to be now to keep his ground." [101] Shelburne is succeeded by the coalition of North and Fox: "You . . . do not want to be told that we have now neither power nor peace, neither influence in other nations nor quiet amongst ourselves. . . . I cannot but suffer some pain when I compare the state of this Kingdom with that in which we triumphed twenty years ago. I have at least endeavoured to preserve order and support Monarchy." [102] Fox and North are removed and Pitt succeeds: "The tumult in government is, I believe, excessive, and the efforts of each party outrageously violent, with very little thought on any national interest, at a time when we have all the world for our enemies. . . . Thus Empires are broken down when the profits of administration are so great that ambition is satisfied with obtaining them. . . ." [103] When Pitt triumphs over the opposition, Johnson is only slightly reassured: "Our Parliamentary tumults have now begun to subside, and the King's authority is in some measure re-established." [104] Yet for all that Pitt's victory in 1784 is represented in the history books as the beginning of half a century of almost unbroken Tory rule, there is no evidence of any enthusiasm on Johnson's part. Nor should we expect enthusiasm from Johnson for the son of Chatham and nephew of Grenville, for the favorite candidate of Wilkes and Beckford and the commercial and expansionist interests, for a man who described himself as an "independent Whig" but never as a Tory.[105] Johnson knew better than the nineteenth-century historians how little Pitt represented the old Toryism that Johnson owed allegiance to. It cannot be said that Johnson felt, at the end of his life, that the "great things" he had been inclined to hope, though with reservations, of his new king had come to pass.

The account of Johnson's political life may fittingly be concluded with a notice of two pieces the date of which is impossible to determine but which deserve to be accorded great importance among the expressions of his political beliefs. These are two sermons, Numbers 23 and 24 in the published order, which were "left for publication" by Johnson's friend, the Reverend John Taylor. That they were written by the Tory Johnson to be delivered by the Whig Taylor from his pulpit demonstrates to what a great extent, as Johnson said, "a wise Tory and a wise Whig will agree. Their principles are the same."

The two sermons are complementary. Sermon 23,[106] preached on the thirtieth of January, the great Royalist anniversary, is on the duties of the governed, as Sermon 24 is on the duties of governors. "That the life of man is unhappy," it begins, "that his days are not only few, but evil, that he is surrounded by dangers, distracted by uncertainties, and oppressed by calamities, requires no proof. . . . When such is the condition of beings, not brute and savage, but endowed with reason, and united in society, who would not expect that they should join in a perpetual confederacy against the certain, or fortuitous, troubles to which they are exposed?" Yet it is fallacious to expect the individual's actions to be motivated by a love for society in the abstract. "Such a diffusion of interest, such sublimation of self-love is to all difficult . . . it is to many impossible. . . . No man can live only for others, unless he could persuade others to live only for him. The misery of the world, therefore, so far as it arises from inequality of conditions, is incurable."

The pursuit of self-interest is thus inevitable, and "in the prosecution of private interest, which providence has either ordained, or permitted, there must necessarily be some kind of strife. Where blessings are thrown before us, as the reward of industry, there must be a constant struggle of emulation."

Having thus accepted individualism as the necessary basis of society, Johnson goes on to explain the necessity for its always being kept under control. It may be controlled by individual morality: "This strife would be without confusion, if it were regulated by reason and religion, if men would endeavour after lawful ends by lawful means." What is lawful is "an honest contention for preference and superiority, by which the powers of greater minds are pushed into action, and the ancient boundaries of science are overpast." What is not lawful is personal envy of others; and to this Johnson attributes most public disorder. Even "the ravages of religious enthusiasts" are to be attributed to it: "pure zeal" cannot carry "a man convinced of the truth of his tenets, wishing the happiness of others, and considering happiness as the certain consequence of truth" beyond "warm dispute and earnest exhortation." When men resort to physical violence to support their opinions, it is to be presumed that they are motivated by envy.

Political activities, in particular, are susceptible to such motives. Though far from condemning resistance to despotism—"Many modes of tyranny have been practised in the world, of which it is more natural to ask, with wonder, why they were submitted to so long, than why they were at last opposed and quelled"—Johnson at the same time pleads for tolerance in enduring the necessary imperfections of any government, and for the utmost care in scrutinizing the motives of opposition to government, to make sure that it is not the product of personal resentment rather than of a desire to better the state: "Life is a state of imperfection; and yet every man exacts from his superiors consummate wisdom, and unfailing virtue, and, whenever he sees, or believes himself to see, either vice or error, thinks himself at liberty to loosen the ties of duty, and pass the boundaries of subordination." For when such a spirit of insubordination is once in motion, no one knows where it will stop, and "confusion"—anarchy—may follow very easily: "The great benefit of society is that the weak are protected against the strong. The great evil of confusion is that the world is thrown into the hands, not of the best, but of the strongest." Anarchy inevitably leads to dictatorship: "All certainty of possession or acquisition is destroyed; . . . every man's care is confined to his own interest; and . . . general negligence of the general good makes way for general licentiousness." Johnson then goes on to interpret the Rebellion of the 1640's as an example of this process. Had he lived longer he could have found other illustrations of his thesis that a peaceful society rests precariously on the individual's willingness to subordinate his own individualism to the general good, and if that basis is disturbed, may easily lapse into anarchy, and its inevitable successor, tyranny.

Sermon 24 [107] is addressed chiefly to those who govern. It opens with the striking antithesis (faintly reminiscent of the opening sentence of the *Contrat social*): "That the institutions of government owe their original, like other human actions, to the desire of happiness, is not to be denied; nor is it less generally allowed, that they have been perverted to very different ends from those which they were intended to promote." "Every page of history," Johnson continues, in expansion of this theme,

whether sacred or profane, will furnish us abundantly with instances of rulers that have deviated from justice, and subjects that have forgotten their allegiance; of nations ruined by the tyranny of governors, and of governors overborne by the madness of the populace. . . . Thus have slavery and licentiousness succeeded one another, and anarchy and despotic power alternately prevailed.

He states again the utilitarian end of society:

Man is for the most part unhappy, when subjected, without redress, to the passions of another, or left, without control, to the dominion of his own. . . . No man knows anyone except himself whom he judges fit to be set free from the coercion of laws, and to be abandoned entirely to his own choice. . . . Government is therefore necessary, in the opinion of every one, to the safety of particular men, and the happiness of society.

Johnson then makes three points. First, "it is the duty
of those in authority to promote the happiness of the people."
He dwells emphatically on the heavy responsibility of those
having power: "Their superiority is not to be considered a
sanction for laziness, nor a privilege for vice. . . . They are
not to conceive that power gives a right to oppress, and to
punish those who murmur at oppression. They are to look
upon their power, and their greatness, as instruments placed
in their hands to be employed for the public advantage."
They are sufficiently rewarded for their pains (a shrewd
point of psychology) simply by their own sense of power:
"There is somewhat in power more pleasing than in any
other enjoyment."

Second, he asks "by what means the happiness of the
people may be most effectually promoted" by governments.
For one thing, governments can analyze political questions
with more acumen than they do: "In political, as well as
natural disorders, the great error of those who commonly
undertake either cure or preservation is that they rest in
second causes, without extending their search to the remote
and original sources of evil. They therefore obviate the immediate evil, but leave the destructive principle to operate
again." As for those sources of public happiness which a
government can foster, Johnson gives a Lockean answer:
"That established property and inviolable freedom are the
greatest of political felicities, no man can be supposed likely
to deny. To depend on the will of another, to labour for that
of which arbitrary power can prohibit the enjoyment, is the
state to which want of reason has subjected the brute. To be
happy we must know our own rights; and we must know
them to be safe."

Having made this important "Whig" doctrine the central
point of his theory of government—and there is no reason,

from our records of Johnson's thought, to imagine for a moment that he did not believe it profoundly—he now surrounds it with a number of what may be called Tory qualifications. These important sources of happiness a good government can ensure; but though they are necessary, they are not in themselves sufficient, for happiness. The ultimate sources of happiness are within the individual himself, and no government can provide them:

In a country like ours, the great demand which is forever repeated to our governors is for the security of property, the confirmation of liberty, and the extension of commerce. All this we have obtained, and all this we possess, in a degree which, perhaps, was never granted to any other people. Yet we still find something wanting to our happiness, and turn ourselves round on all sides, with perpetual restlessness, to find that remedy for our evils which neither power nor policy can afford. . . .

I am far from intending to insinuate that the studies of political wisdom, or the labours of legislative patriotism, have been vain and idle. They are useful, but not effectual; they are conducive to that end which yet they cannot fully gain. . . . Every man sees and may feel evils which no law can punish.

Nor are liberty and material security, simply in themselves, necessarily sources of happiness; they must be rightly used: "Liberty, if not regulated by virtue, can be only license to do evil; and property, if not virtuously enjoyed, can only corrupt the possessor, and give him the power to injure others. Trade may make us rich; but riches, without goodness, cannot make us happy." Finally, no political institutions, however cleverly devised, can by themselves guarantee liberty and security:

Let us, however, suppose that these external goods have that power, which wisdom cannot believe, and which experience never could confirm; let us suppose that riches and liberty could make us happy. It then remains to be considered how riches and liberty can be secured. To this the politician has a ready answer, that they are to be secured by laws wisely formed, and vigorously executed. But, as laws can be made only by a small part of an extensive empire, and must be executed by a part yet far smaller, what shall protect us against the laws themselves? And how shall we be certain that they shall not be made without regard to the public good, or shall not be perverted to oppression by the ministers of justice?

This passage is, I think, the key to a great part of Johnson's political thinking. He relentlessly insists, in the Vinerian Lectures, in *The False Alarm* and *Taxation No Tyranny*, and now here, on the fact that when one penetrates beneath all laws and constitutions and systems of checks and balances and statements of "rights," what one finds is one human being in possession of power over other human beings. He insists on it, not because he likes despotism—he has just expressed his detestation of tyranny, and he expresses it in many other places, and his whole life is an expression of it—but because he wishes men to realize that in the long run the character of a society must depend on the character of the individuals who comprise it. Men must not allow themselves to be lulled into forgetfulness of their own individual responsibility for the morality of a state through a blind confidence in institutions and forms, however ingeniously contrived, or to think that, while they behave viciously, those forms will provide them with liberty and security which can only be the products ultimately of their own right behavior. This is neither Toryism nor Whiggism: it is simple fundamental human morality, taught by a thousand doctors, Christian and non-Christian, but seldom related so closely to current political discussion as by Johnson.

He concludes the sermon by asking "How the people are to assist and further the endeavours of their governors," and by insisting again on the responsibilities of the individual:

As all government is power exerted by few upon many, it is apparent that nations cannot be governed but by their own consent. The first duty therefore of subjects is obedience to the laws; such obedience as is the effect, not of compulsion, but of reverence; such as arises from a conviction of the instability of human virtue, and of the necessity of some coercive power which may restrain the exorbitances of passions, and check the career of natural desires. . . .

The happiness of a nation must arise from the combined endeavours of governors and subjects. The duties of governing can be the lot of few, but all of us have the duties of subjects to perform; and every man ought to incite in himself, and in his neighbour, that obedience to the laws, and that respect to the chief magistrate, which may secure and promote concord and quiet. Of this, as of all other virtues, the true basis is religion. The laws will be easily obeyed by him who adds to human sanctions the obligations of conscience; and he will not easily be disposed to censure his superiors, whom religion has made acquainted with his own failings.

Chapter Eight

A RECAPITULATION AND
SOME REFLECTIONS

IT would probably not have come as a surprise to Johnson, who had few illusions about humanity's capacity for error, to learn how far the popular picture of him was to deviate from the reality. The growth of the Johnson legend is a subject too large to be examined in detail here. No doubt elements in Johnson himself made it possible to attach that legend to him; and his fate in being made into the central figure of Boswell's great work of art certainly contributed to its development.[1] But Johnson's chief misfortune was to be caught up in an even larger structure of myth, that of the "Tory." The history of this still lively and influential concept is, again, something for a separate study, which would notice, among other matters, Fielding's Squire Western, Addison's sly portraits of Sir Roger de Coverley and the Tory Fox-Hunter, and Macaulay's brutal and illiterate squire of 1685. The "Dr. Johnson" of legend is one of the most vivid and memorable contributions to the composite portrait. It is not likely, of course, that a revision of the traditional picture of Johnson will cause so sturdy and well-established a stereotype as that of the Tory to dissolve: on the contrary, the durability of the generalized stereotype will help to perpetuate the traditional Johnson; these things reinforce one another. If, however, any student should undertake a serious study of Tory political style [2] as it occurred in living people of the eighteenth century, not in the imagination of polemists, he should be warned in advance that the evidence of Johnson's political and social attitudes found in the records of his life and writings points to a significantly different picture from that of the legend. It may be useful recapitulating some of that evidence here.

If the average modern reader were asked to construct an imaginary portrait of the youth of an arch-Tory, it would probably be that of a pompous and dogmatic young man, accustomed from his earliest years to venerate wealth, birth, position, and authority; convinced of the importance of conformity and taking positive pleasure in conforming; concerned to maintain things as they are, sighing over the past, suspicious of the future, intolerant of the new and strange— a young George Apley of the Midlands. The actual picture of the young Johnson, curious about everything under the sun, eager for experience and knowledge, restless, fiercely independent, rebellious, iconoclastic, skeptical, must be startling to such a reader.

The situation into which Johnson was born, the son of an impecunious bookseller in a small Midland town, was one which entailed on him remarkably few inherited loyalties to preconceived political opinions. The Civil War, in Lichfield, left many potent memories, to be sure; but it was long over, and Johnson's family was not directly involved in its miseries. The politically lively city was far from being a Tory stronghold, and at Gilbert Walmesley's table and from his clever and ambitious schoolfellows in the Grammar School Johnson would have heard a great deal of Whig argument; it is important to notice the great extent to which Johnson's friends and associates, throughout his life, were Whigs; his Toryism may have even been primarily the result of his instinctive rebellion against a preponderance of Whig intellectualism in his youth. If (to follow a not too certain tradition) he inherited from his father a High Church desire to maintain the dignity of the Established Church, this existed together with a large portion of the intense preoccupation of the early Evangelicals and Methodists with individual and personal religion—a preoccupation related to the profound humanitarianism that can be detected in his earliest writings and is basic to his later political attitudes. A man convinced that he is profoundly involved in his neighbor's welfare (though rejecting any hint of coercion, of "sanguinary zeal," in attempting to ensure that welfare) is not likely to subscribe to any theory of government based on laissez faire; on the other hand, a man convinced that the individual is responsible for his own salvation, convinced, also, that individual morality, which rests on religion, penetrates the whole universe of human activity, is not likely to sign away the individual's political responsibility to any system of government smacking of totalitarianism.

The modern student probably needs also to bear in mind that there was no very distinct correlation in eighteenth-century Britain between party and social or economic class—another reason, perhaps, why eighteenth-century British politics resembles twentieth-century American more closely than twentieth-century British politics. Had Johnson been born, say, a century and a half later, the ambitious and discontented son of a struggling bookseller in a Cathedral city, the chances are less likely than they were in his own day that he would have been invited to dinner parties in the Close or been sent to Oxford;[3] and one might have predicted with some assurance that he would have gravitated toward the "left" in politics. But in Lichfield, around 1700, unless one had very strong hereditary ties to either the Royalist or the Puritan tradition, there was no *prima facie* reason of birth why one should support the Tory Captain Richard Dyott, of Freeford, in an election in preference to the Whig Sir Michael Biddulph, Bart., of Elmhurst, or vice versa. Johnson, at any rate, moved with phenomenal ease on any social level,

showing no more embarrassment when dining at Inverary
with the Duke and Duchess of Argyll than at the Three
Crowns with his old schoolfellow Harry Jackson, whom Boswell describes with obvious distaste as "a low man, dull and
untaught," wearing greasy leather breeches.[4] Johnson's own
family connections cover what by modern British standards
would be an extraordinarily large segment of the social scale,
and make it hard to generalize about his natural tendencies
in politics on the grounds of his affiliation with the prole-
tariat, the *bourgeoisie*, or the gentry. Even the conception of
such a division of humanity would probably not have been
too well understood by Johnson. Johnson believed in *rank*,
to be sure; but there is no evidence that he believed in *class*,
which, in later senses of the word, is an entirely different matter.

It is true, also, that Johnson was poor, and that he felt his
poverty, and the poverty of others, keenly. Yet even in modern politics it is not axiomatic that poverty connotes "left"
and wealth "right" in politics. The ambitious poor man
who, like Johnson, manages to cope with the world on its
own terms is naturally not always willing, after success is
achieved or in sight, to have those terms changed; and conversely, many revolutionaries have been men of inherited
wealth or position. But however that may be, there was
certainly no reason in the eighteenth century for the un-
propertied to prefer a Walpole to a Wyndham or a Newcastle to a Bute. Indeed the mob in the earlier eighteenth
century seems to have been oftener Tory than Whig, if only
because Tory demagogues like Sir Lister Holt, with less
chance of attaining office, had less motive than Whig demagogues to preserve public order.

There is no reason, then, to believe that Johnson, at the
time he left Lichfield for London in 1737, had any important
intellectual commitment to a particular set of political

dogmas. He appears (on the evidence of the early draft of *Irene*) to have accepted, along with nearly all his more thoughtful contemporaries, Locke's interpretation of the conservative and individualistic basis of the British political system; and there is no evidence that he ever lost faith in this fundamental concept. More important, however, than his commitment or lack of commitment to specific political theories is his whole cast of mind—curious, empirical, skeptical, emotionally sensitive. The frustration, the poverty and disease, of his boyhood and youth left him with profound and genuine insight into human misery, and with a contempt for benevolent liberal theorizers who, from their ivory towers, set out to rearrange the world with no real knowledge of the sources of the common man's happiness and unhappiness. With Johnson's capacity for emotion and with a little less skepticism, he might have become an excellent revolutionary. Most revolutionaries, however, though radical enough in discarding accepted theories, do so merely to seize on another and more preposterous one. Johnson carried his skepticism further, and comparing proposed systems of government with the realities of human nature saw their fallacies and potentialities for danger easily enough. Yet his skepticism was not of a kind to cause him to lapse into cynical inaction: he had the empiricist's faith that by careful observation and analysis, improvement can be brought about —slowly, perhaps, but certainly; and he had the rationalist's conviction that absurdity and ignorance and obscurantism are absolute evils, to be combated at all times.

If, when Johnson went to London and became involved in politics of the most partisan kind, he found it impossible to avoid having some sort of label attached to him, it is understandable that with his cast of mind he should not have rejected that of Tory. The greatest danger in Johnson's time —as in more recent times—to the individual's power of independent judgment was, he felt, the tyranny of intellectual fashion; Johnson was to assert this view explicitly a few years later.[5] When he came to London, two attitudes toward politics were fashionable in intellectual circles, the liberal Whiggism of men like Lyttelton and Thomson, and the manifestly insincere nonpartisanship of Bolingbroke. The official Whiggism of Walpole's followers, to be sure, was not fashionable; but it was associated with the complacent possession of office and wealth. In the mood of defiant iconoclasm of his early years in London (and with his capacity for irony), it would not have displeased Johnson to be called a Tory— distinctly the least fashionable of political labels, which Addison, most skillfully subtle of propagandists, had indelibly associated with stupid country squires. How little Johnson had in common with the fox-hunting squirearchy may be gauged by the disastrousness of his one certain encounter with them, the affair of Sir Wolstan Dixie. But the label's attractions for the young man seem obvious enough: not only would it shock the smugness of his liberal friends; it committed him to absolutely no fixed political dogma, but left his mind free to range and to draw whatever conclusions it would from what he saw.

Of course, there were certain attitudes that Johnson did share with the traditional Old Tory. Above all, he was a stout partisan of the Church of England, and of the maintenance of its position in the state. This loyalty, more than any other of his political feelings, can be confidently said never to have wavered throughout his adult life. Even in his most vociferously patriot days, when he supported the radical positions of Savage and Henry Brooke, he dissociated himself from their anti-clericalism. His loyalty to the Establishment even included an affection for Whig bishops.[6]

Another political characteristic that Johnson had in common with Midland squires and country parsons (and no doubt the majority of their tenants and parishioners) was a certain amount of what may be called isolationism. Too much can be made, and has been made, of this in Johnson, of course. His curiosity was genuinely stimulated by distant lands and exotic cultures—by Abyssinia, China, the Hebrides, Italy. He held that underneath superficial differences of color and language and customs, human nature was essentially the same throughout the world—he possessed a sincere and thoroughgoing egalitarianism. He felt intense indignation at the sufferings of Negro slaves, American Indians, and Hebridean crofters: indeed he went farther than many modern sympathizers would do in living up to the ideal of racial equality, in virtually adopting the young Negro Frank Barber, educating him as a son (or trying to), and making him his heir. The number of his non-English friends was great. Yet the notion of admitting American colonists or Scotch adventurers to full and equal community with "true-born Englishmen" seems to have repelled him. Perhaps the explanation of this seeming contradiction is simply that the Americans and Lowland Scotch were obviously destined to be successful in the world, and the Negroes and Indians were not.

With what may be called the economic isolationism of the Old Tories (which they shared to some extent with the Old Whigs of the Walpole tradition), Johnson was much more consistently in sympathy. Like theirs, his economic ideas were based on the conception of a small, isolated, economically self-contained state, its economy kept in balance by careful governmental control. This, the normal mercantilist position of the days before Adam Smith, lies at the bottom of a great deal of Johnson's political reasoning.

Much has been written recently about Tory opposition, represented chiefly by Pope and Swift, to the materialistic commercialism of the Whigs, led by Walpole. This view is a

distortion of the real political situation. Walpole and
Townshend, country magnates themselves, were not really
very far from the Old Tory view of a self-sustaining English
economy, in which agriculture was given due importance.
True, they were connected with the three great chartered
companies, the East India and South Sea companies and the
Bank of England, as any administration was bound to be.
But it should not be forgotten that it was precisely because
Walpole was *not* involved (or thought not to be) in the too
enterprising South Sea transactions of the 1720's that he rose
to power. When the great opposition to Walpole developed
in the 1730's, the hard nucleus of it was the independent
trading interests of London and Bristol, whose complaint
was that Walpole was not enterprising enough in providing
them with opportunities of unlimited expansion. "The
enemy of commerce"—variations on this theme recur continually in the violent attacks on Walpole during the
decade preceding his fall. The political leaders of these
interests were men like the West Indies merchant, William
Beckford, and, pre-eminently, William Pitt, whose family
fortune had been founded by his grandfather, an interloper
in the East India trade, who had devoted much of his career
to fighting the monopoly of the Company and finally forced
it to come to terms with him. Eventually the opposition got
their way: Walpole was forced into a war with Spain to
protect the rights of British merchants trading in Spanish
waters, and later it was Pitt who conducted the Seven Years'
War to a successful outcome, and by doing so founded the
British Empire and vastly increased the potential markets
of British merchants. At the end of the century the younger
Pitt set his seal on his father's work, and by making the free
trade economics of Adam Smith part of official government
doctrine ensured the commercial and industrial expansion of
Great Britain in the nineteenth century.

In these extemely important developments, which caused the future of Great Britain to take the course that it took in the next two centuries, Johnson was consistently opposed to the Pittites and expansionism. Little as he and the Old Tories may have liked Walpole, they liked Pitt and his allies much less, and when it came to a choice between Walpole and Pitt, they voted for Walpole. Johnson's note on the Commons debate of February 13, 1741, his *Further Thoughts on Agriculture* and *Considerations on Corn*, his opposition in 1756 to the Seven Years' War, his plan to defend the East India Company against Chathamite attacks in 1766, his preference, at the end of his life, for Burke and Fox (the heirs of Walpole) to the two Pitts, his own tributes to the memory of Walpole—perhaps even his antagonism to America, for the America of 1776 was the creation of Pitt twenty years before—are all part of the same pattern, the defense of the older, self-sufficient Little England against the grandiose imperial conception of England as mistress of the world's commerce, maintaining her markets by military force in every part of the world. If it is a question of supporting older, noncommercial values against a philosophy of commercialism, the antithesis Johnson–Pitt seems to represent the actual state of things much more accurately than the antithesis Pope–Walpole.

Not, of course, that Johnson was opposed to trade and traders in themselves. To the degree that the success of the Pitts represented the victory of the rising middle classes over the older Whig aristocracy, Johnson was probably (on the whole) on the side of the Pitts. Though he might sometimes complain of the decline of the reverence due to rank, his own behavior toward a Lord Chesterfield, Lord Lyttelton, or Lord Bolingbroke hardly tended to increase such reverence. He took a proper pride in his own bourgeois origin; he reprobates Congreve's "despicable foppery" in wishing to be thought a gentleman rather than a writer, and is nearly as caustic in describing Pope's and Swift's demeanor toward the nobility. Like Savage and Goldsmith, he had generally a high regard for the "middle state" of life. In the prefaces to Rolt's *Dictionary of Trade and Commerce* and the *Preceptor* he wishes well to trade, and in the preface to Payne's *New Tables of Interest,* he even rises to the defense of stockbrokers—honest stockbrokers, who "sanctify the accumulation of wealth" by "contributing to the support of good government, the increase of arts and industry, the rewards of genius and virtue, and the relief of wretchedness and want." [7] What he objects to is the extreme danger of allowing the British economy to develop so as to become almost wholly dependent on external trade. To what extent the economic position of Britain in the twentieth century is a confirmation of his prediction is an interesting question.

Sometimes Johnson manifested traditional Old Tory attitudes toward recent history. On occasion he spoke violently of the Puritans, with horror of the Civil War, and affectionately of the Stuarts, though if the word "Jacobite" means one who seriously desired the restoration of the Stuarts to the throne, there is not the slightest evidence that it could ever have been applied to Johnson at any time in his life. But it is always hard to tell just how seriously to take these mementoes of the past which any political party possesses—the Whigs, too, had their own set of historical totems, to which a ritual respect was paid from time to time. Many of Johnson's recorded remarks about the Stuarts and the Puritans seem to belong to this category. When he actually wrote about seventeenth-century history, he arrived at very different conclusions from those observations made on the spur of the moment for the purpose of living up to his reputation and shocking the Whigs. We find him praising in the highest terms such Puritans as Blake and Baxter and such dissenters as Watts; we find him contrasting the rude virtue of William III with the polished double-dealing of Charles II. Indeed, we find derogatory comment about all the Stuart rulers except Charles I, and of him we find no praise.

It should be emphasized, for the benefit of those who assumed that Johnson, as a Tory, must have been a fervent royalist, that though he accepts monarchy as probably the best practical form of government, he treats with derision notions of its transcendent origin and sanction, and indeed seldom mentions monarchs in his writings without some disparaging remark about their personal abilities. This is likely part of what may be called the general intellectual tradition of the West; similar remarks can be found in Bolingbroke and many other contemporary writers, regardless of their politics. It has been suggested that this antimonarchical tradition can be traced back as far as Plutarch, and forward, through the Renaissance and seventeenth and eighteenth centuries, to the general culture of twentieth-century America. Probably Johnson's normal pacifism and his prejudice against soldiers derives from a similar long tradition, although reinforced, as far as the British regular army was concerned, by the Old Tory party line dating from the times of Cromwell and Marlborough.

Johnson's fear of civil war likely stems from a more immediate source than Tory tradition. He was not so much of a pacifist as not to wish, when Britain became involved in a war, that she would win it; nor is it to be overlooked that in 1738 we find him, in effect, calling for the use of force against the Spanish, and in 1775 against the Americans—though in the latter instance, with the hope that they might be overawed without bloodshed, and no doubt regarding it merely as a police action necessary to maintain the fundamental organization of the British state. But his declaration "Rebellions and civil wars are the greatest evils that can happen to a people" comes from the heart. International wars in the seventeenth and eighteenth centuries caused little distress to most Englishmen, whereas memorials of the miseries of the Civil War lay around everyone who grew up in Lichfield. Since recent history had provided so conspicuous an illustration of the tenuousness of the bonds of society, of how easily a social organization can dissolve into anarchy and thence inevitably be transformed into despotism, Johnson's concern that everything within reason be done to preserve "subordination"— social organization—is understandable. It is also understandable that to the Englishmen of the century after Johnson's, when it appeared that nothing could ever shake the stability of the British Empire, Johnson's fears seemed preposterous. Those who live in the twentieth century can better appreciate his thinking than those who lived in the nineteenth.

But of course Johnson's political attitudes go far beyond the conventional ones of Toryism. Among the general characteristics of his thinking that contributed to the formation of those attitudes were his deep humanitarianism, his rationalism, his skepticism, his individualism. His humanitarianism and rationalism combined to produce the crusading Johnson of 1738 and 1739, busy "reforming the world, dethroning princes, establishing new forms of government," intent on ridding England of miseries and absurdities by the simple process of turning out Walpole and bringing in Pulteney. A little more experience in the ways of politicians, and some further development of his innate skepticism—there is no better way of acquiring both than by minutely observing the workings of a popular legislative body—checked some of that exuberance. Yet his sympathy for the underdog, especially for aboriginal peoples exploited by "civilizing" white men, persisted from the time of *A Voyage to Abyssinia* throughout his life, and explains a great deal of his distrust of the Americans, as he makes clear in his essays of 1756. His own strong individualism was always at war with his recognition for the need of social organization and the authority to keep individualism under control. It seems a paradox that Johnson, who was all his life a rebel by instinct, who never submitted to authority except on his own terms, who when he wished could write in a rabble-rousing style worthy of any revolutionary, who horrified Oxford by toasting the next insurrection of the slaves in the West Indies, should so fear rebellion. But is it really a paradox? Rather, is it not natural, and the key to much seeming contradiction in his political views, that he, above all men, should be aware of the potentialities for danger in the individualistic impulse?

But it would be wrong to think that, because he pointed out those dangers, Johnson could ever have preferred any system of government which does not rest on the rational exercise of the minds of free and responsible individuals. It is precisely because he intensely wants this state of things to continue (as he makes it clear in his comments on the Puritan despotism of the 1640's) that he warns against political irresponsibility, which may result in anarchy, which will inevitably result in dictatorship. It is as preposterous to conceive of Johnson's advocating or assenting to the abdication of the individual's political responsibility under a Cromwellian or Napoleonic or Hitlerian or Stalinist totalitarian state as it is to imagine a Victorian liberal like John Stuart Mill doing the same. When he thought it necessary to attack official obscurantism, the suppression by *force majeure* of independent thought and discussion on political matters, as by the Stage Licensing Act, he did so with devastating force. For the rest, his answer, like that of the Victorian liberal's, was in the enlightenment of the ordinary intelligent individual, providing him with a wealth of fact and trying to stimulate him to independent criticism and reflection and to a high sense of his own responsibility in such matters. And a great deal of Johnson's energy throughout his life, especially in his journalistic work for the *Gentleman's Magazine* and the *Literary Magazine,* was dedicated to this purpose of educating the "secondary legislators" of Britain in their duties. By any reasonable modern definition of the word, Johnson was one of the most effectual propagators of democracy in the eighteenth century.

Johnson's rationalism predominates in his theory of the state. For all his profound religious conviction, and his insistence that the individual's religious impulse is the most necessary ingredient in the happiness of society, he nevertheless rigidly excludes theological and supernatural considerations of every kind from his conception of the way government comes into being and operates. Hawkins, whose discussion of Johnson's political views is acute, points out that "he was not so besotted in his notions as to abet what is called the patriarchal scheme, as delineated by Sir Robert Filmer"[8] or other versions of the theory of the divine right of kings. Burke's state, too, is organic in a similar sense, with tradition or prescriptive rights substituted for the divine right as the supralegal entity. To Locke and his liberal successors, natural rights of men and a mystical compact between rulers and ruled constituted the sanctions that were above the state. All these metaphysical entities Johnson summarily rejected: the only sanction for law that he recognized was the omnicompetence of whatever is the sovereign power in the state;[9] and the only sanction for the existence of that power was the willingness of the governed to be governed: "In no government power can be abused long. Mankind will not bear it. If a sovereign oppresses his people to a great degree, they will rise and cut off his head. There is a remedy in human nature against tyranny, that will keep us safe under every form of government."[10] And no doubt it would, were everyone the potential rebel that Johnson was.

Hawkins goes on to point out Johnson's debt to the politi-

cal thought of Hooker. "There can be no doubt," says one
modern analyst of Hooker, "that the nearest approach in his
writings to a definite basis for political authority lies in his
teaching that the force of law is based on the consent of the
governed. Laws must be obeyed, not because they derive their
force 'from the quality of such as devise them,' but because
the power which gives them strength resides in society." [11]
Of course there are many other things in Hooker too. Hooker,
following medieval teaching, is careful to insist that human
society is a divine institution founded on the dictates of the
Divine Will. As Johnson points out, this may be eminently
true, but "The will of God cannot be known but by revelation or the light of reason," [12] and revelation says nothing
about how God wishes the state to function. Where Johnson
chiefly follows Hooker is in basing his scheme of society on
the two postulates, that man is naturally a social animal, and
that obedience to authority is the essence of society. Society
is the state of the individual's willingness to subordinate himself to the happiness of the whole.

"A wise Tory and a wise Whig, I believe, will agree," Johnson said. "Their principles are the same, though their modes
of thinking are different." The meaning of this statement becomes clearer when we consider to what a great extent Johnson's principles of government are those of Locke, who in
turn owed so much to Hooker. Like Locke, he had a strong
prejudice in favor of "life, liberty, and property," and a desire that the individual should be assured of his possession of
them and that they should not be subject to arbitrary deprivation at the whim of a dictator, whether the divinely appointed progeny of a line of patriarchal kings or a demagogue
raised to power by a rabble. The principle of the rule of law
enunciated by Locke, an essentially conservative principle,
is as much Tory as it is Whig.

Yet there was a significant difference between Johnson's

mode of thinking about this principle and that of the Whigs. For the Whigs, the principle rested on natural rights of man or on an original compact between governors and governed. To the realistic Johnson, these were merely pleasant fantasies. The source of law can, by definition, be bound by no law. With this consideration there arises the name of another political writer of whom Johnson's views are inevitably reminiscent—Thomas Hobbes. "Mr. Hobbs the Atheist" is seldom mentioned by Johnson, and when he is, it is with the conventional condemnation. But whether or not Johnson was directly influenced by a reading of the *Leviathan,* his mind was enough like Hobbes' in its strong tendency to skepticism and its distrust of metaphysics to have arrived independently at a similar position. The hard fact is that Johnson's conception of the state as a purely secular and rational institution is at least as atheistic as Hobbes'; indeed Johnson outdoes Hobbes in the rejection of metaphysics by discarding or ignoring the notion of a contract, to which Hobbes adheres. But in their emphasis on power as the central fact of government, to which all rights are subordinate, Johnson and Hobbes are very close.

Hobbes, like Johnson, has been called an extreme Tory, an advocate of authoritarianism, a precursor of totalitarianism, for his contemptuous rejection of the natural rights of man. Yet in their statements of the conditions of government, neither Hobbes nor Johnson is *advocating* anything except clear thinking; they are only trying to dispel the cant which, as they see it, dangerously obscures the reality. Sovereignty and subjection are the necessary conditions of social organization; sovereignty is, by definition, power; in the long run the only recourse from the abuse of power is to resistance by force. To point out that things are so is not to advocate tyranny or submission to tyranny; so far is Johnson from doing so that he can proclaim "Many modes of tyranny have been practised in the world of which it is more natural to ask, with wonder, why they were submitted to so long, than why they were at last opposed and quelled." Rather, by recognizing that both the stability of society and the liberty of the subject rest not on fictitious supralegal rights but on the precarious foundations of mutual consent, those in authority are better able to see the dangers of the abuse of power and those subject to authority to see the dangers of frivolous obstructionism. The result of the adoption of Johnson's view of the nature of government should be an increase in the individual's sense of his own responsibility for the preservation of the welfare of society. And it is this sense of responsibility that Johnson is always seeking to foster. "The Tory," he says, "does not wish to give more real power to Government; but that Government should have more reverence. . . . The Tory is not for giving more legal power to the Clergy, but wishes they should have a considerable influence founded on the opinion of mankind." Johnson does not *like* the use of power by one individual over another; rather, he hopes that if men recognize that the ultimate sanction of government *is* power, they will be able to minimize its use.

It has been seen that Johnson's political views have much in common, as he says himself, with fundamental Whig doctrine of the eighteenth century. To what extent, it may be asked, do they correspond with general Tory doctrine of the time? There is, unfortunately, little other formulated Tory doctrine to compare them with. There is Bolingbroke, of course, if Bolingbroke can be considered a Tory; no more confused and incoherent account of a theory of government was ever written than that of the opening pages of *The Idea of a Patriot King*, with its vague references to divine law, the will of God, God as a limited monarch, natural law, the universal law of reason, and other ill-defined concepts. He states some positions with which Johnson, and many others, would have agreed—the utilitarian purpose of society, the necessity for reverence to government, the inconvenience of an excess of party spirit—but he never approaches the question which to Johnson is the central one, the nature of sovereignty itself. Bolingbroke's Patriot King holds his office by some kind of undefined prescriptive right, but Bolingbroke never considers what may be the consequence if that right is challenged. And the activities which Bolingbroke suggests for his Patriot King sound more than a little *ultra vires*. Johnson, for all his desire to see George III head a strong and effective executive, never forgets that in Great Britain not the king but the King-in-Parliament constitutes the sovereign power.

As far as Tory thinking generally is concerned, Sir William Holdsworth makes the interesting comment that to eighteenth-century Tories "the theory of sovereignty came very much more naturally . . . than to Whigs whose intellectual ancestors were Locke and the authors who believed in the natural rights of subjects"; and he cites, in addition to Johnson, Swift, Atterbury, and, with qualifications, Blackstone.[13] His suggestion that this tendency is inherited from an older Tory belief in the divine right of kings, however, is hard to agree with, particularly if Figgis is correct in setting the divine right theory, as "organic," at the opposite pole from "mechanical" theories of autonomous sovereignty. It seems a far step from saying that the sovereign derives his rights from God to saying that the sovereign derives his rights from no one—or rather that the sovereign has no rights at all, only power. Of course, generalizations based on the postulates of a coherent Tory political theory of the seventeenth century, one of the eighteenth century, and a genetic relationship between them are bound, in the absence of clear evidence for any of these postulates, to be little more than pleasant speculation. But if there is anything in Holdsworth's comment, the explanation may be simply that the Whigs throughout the eighteenth century were saddled with theory, first by Locke and later by Burke (the Burke of the *Present Discontents*), theory which became "official" and hardened; whereas the Tories, being committed to no such official doctrine, being as independent in political thought as they were in political practice, were able to let their minds range more freely, and in the generally secular and rationalist intellectual climate of the age, naturally hit on the solution of discarding *all* metaphysical elements from political theory. In the same skeptical spirit, modern radical political thinkers have rebelled against the same metaphysical natural rights, transmitted from seventeenth- and eighteenth-century Whigs to nineteenth- and twentieth-century liberals, and have conceived theories of government based not upon rights but upon the facts of power. Hence, perhaps, the fellow feeling that some Marxist and Socialist writers have felt for Johnson,[14] since both discard the traditional liberal frame of reference in the discussion of political principles.

The question will also inevitably be asked, what relation has Johnson's Toryism to modern British political Conservatism. It is, at present, a question that cannot be answered. The origin and ideological ancestry of the Conservative party in Great Britain is an extremely complex matter, on which much historical research still needs to be done. It can only be said that if Johnson were to be resurrected today, it is far from certain to what modern party (if any) he would give his allegiance.

A final question, with what justification can modern neoconservative thinkers claim Johnson as one of their own, can be answered with more confidence, since detailed formulations of neoconservative theory do exist. In one of the most thoughtful of these, Robert Nisbet points out that "conservatism, as a distinguishable social philosophy, arose in direct response to the French Revolution," and, using mainly

Burke, Bonald, Lamennais, and Hegel as his sources, discovers eleven characteristic doctrines of modern conservatism.[15] We might consider some of these in relation to Johnson:

Society . . . is an organic entity, with internal laws of development. . . . It has deep roots in the past—roots from which the present cannot escape through rational manipulation.

Johnson would not have subscribed to this. "Organic entity" and "internal laws of development" would have been concepts much too metaphysical for his liking. Although he certainly had a sense of the past and responded emotionally to it, yet his discussion of the relation between society and the past, in the Vinerian Lectures, indicates that he did not feel the past dominates the present to the extent indicated here.

Society cannot be broken down, even for conceptual purposes, into individuals. . . . The individual . . . is but a fantasy, the shadow of a dream. We can never perceive what the rationalist calls "individuals." We see, rather, members of a society—not "individuals" but fathers, sons, priests, church members, workers, masters, and so forth.

With this Hegelian doctrine Johnson would have disagreed most profoundly. The concept of the individual is not merely rationalist, but Protestant—even general Christian—doctrine. Johnson was far too much of a Protestant, as well as a rationalist, to think of society as anything but a collection of individuals, for whom the relation between individual and God is more important than even the relation between individual and society.[16]

. . . the principle of function. Every person, every custom, every institution, serves some basic need in human life. . . . Even prejudice, Burke insisted . . . has . . . the indispensable function of holding together the structure of society.

That "every custom, every institution" fulfills some larger purpose—the old doctrine of the Great Chain of Being—Johnson refuted, in the *Life of Pope* and the review of Soame

Jenyns' *Origin of Evil,* with as much emotional violence as he ever demonstrated. I do not think it can be shown that Johnson ever defended the existence of a prejudice because it *was* a prejudice; he defended it because it had some rational ground that the critic of it had overlooked. It did not, for instance, impress Johnson when Boswell argued that, on the question of slavery, four of the Lords of Session "resolutely maintained the lawfulness of a status which has been acknowledged in all ages and countries, and that when freedom flourished, as in old Greece and Rome." [17] Johnson held no brief for prescription and prejudice when it was clear to him that they were wrong. He asked people to be willing to put up with inconveniences, with "imperfections," in government, for the sake of peace and quiet—but not *because* they were irrationalities; rather *in spite of* their being irrationalities.

The conservative, in reaction to the individualistic Enlightenment, stressed the small social groups of society. . . . The religious groups, family, neighborhood, occupational associations, these, declared Bonald, are the necessary supports of men's lives.

Johnson had small use for the family as a social group; he preferred the impersonality of life in London to the "small social groups" of Lichfield, and he resolutely ignored theories of a patriarchal or familial origin of society. He deplored the weakening of religious associations, partly on political grounds, no doubt, but chiefly, I think, because of the probable harm to the individual. Certainly he did not think of religion as a matter to be participated in by groups.

. . . the indispensable value of the sacred, nonrational, nonutilitarian elements of human existence. . . . To attempt to found society upon the purely secular and upon purely individualistic motivations of pure achievement is ruinous.

It is clear from Sermons 23 and 24 that this is precisely how Johnson *did* attempt to found society. His is a resolutely utilitarian society, and I do not recall his ever having applied the word "sacred" to any political entity, even King Charles I's head.

. . . the principle of legitimacy of authority. Authority is legitimate when it proceeds from the customs and traditions of a people, when it is formed by innumerable links in a chain that begins with the family, rises through community and class, and culminates in the large society.

Johnson would have regarded Burke's founding the "legitimacy of authority" in custom and tradition as unnecessary a fiction as the "natural law" and "divine right" of other writers. Authority needs no other justification than the fact that it is, by definition, necessary to government; and government is justified by its utility to human happiness.

Obviously, then, it is impossible to classify Johnson with those modern conservatives who derive their political attitudes from Burke. And yet it is impossible to deny the designation of conservative to Johnson, who believed "All change is of itself an evil, which ought not to be hazarded but for evident advantage."

The difficulty can be resolved, perhaps, by postulating at least two important and radically different, even opposed, types of the conservative temperament. There are those like Burke, with whom Bolingbroke, Coleridge, Disraeli, and T. S. Eliot may be classed, whose conservatism can be described as idealistic or even Romantic—as Nisbet points out, it was after the French Revolution that it began to flourish vigorously (though it had precursors); and certainly one of its most characteristic (and most appealing) figures was the arch-Romantic Sir Walter Scott. It is attracted by metaphysics— Burke's "sacred rules of prescription" are as metaphysical a notion as any that he ever condemned the Jacobins for maintaining. It has a tendency to idealize history—one recalls Burke's famous description of Marie Antoinette, Bolingbroke's glowing picture of the reign of Elizabeth, Disraeli's historical fantasies, Scott's middle ages—and to project those idealizations into the present and future. It romanticizes the relation of governor and governed, and in its extreme form regards submission to authority as so far from a "necessary evil" as to erect it into a source of positive pleasure. What the dangers of this last tendency are can be discerned from observing the careers of some of the spiritual heirs of Hegel in the twentieth century.

These, like all political tendencies, no doubt represent certain innate and universal elements in human nature. Johnson was not entirely free from them: "There is a reciprocal pleasure in governing and being governed," [18] he permitted himself to say on one occasion—not that he himself ever manifested much pleasure in being governed. But remarks of this tendency are really extremely rare in the records of Johnson's thought. A much more representative attitude is found in his reply to Boswell:

I said, I believed mankind were happier in the ancient feudal state of subordination, than they are in the modern state of independency.—

Johnson. "To be sure, the *Chief* was: but we must think of the number of individuals. That *they* were less happy seems plain; for that state from which all escape as soon as they can, and to which none return after they have left it, must be less happy; and this is the case with the state of dependance on a chief or great man." [19]

On the whole, it seems to me, Johnson is much more a type of what may be called the rational or skeptical conservative, of whom Hobbes, Hume, and Gibbon may be cited as other examples. Perhaps Voltaire also belongs in that category; and it is hard to resist mentioning that fine modern specimen, H. L. Mencken.[20] Their objection to proposals by would-be reformers for the rational reconstruction of an imperfect society is not the Burkean conservative's, that the proposals *are* rational, and that an irrational institution that has existed for a long time is to be cherished. Their objection is rather that on analysis the proposed reforms are at least as irrational as the institution they are designed to replace:

BOSWELL: "So, Sir, you laugh at schemes of political improvement."
JOHNSON: "Why, Sir, most schemes of political improvement are very laughable things." [21]

On the basis of experience (the skeptical conservative finds) the probability is that the confusion arising from an upheaval in the familiar ways of doing things, absurd as they may be, will produce a greater total of unhappiness than will be balanced by the amount of happiness to be produced by the proposed reform. This is a highly rational, not an irrational, attitude.

Further, the skeptical conservative, being a distruster of metaphysics, is likely to do his political thinking in terms of concrete individual human beings rather than of abstract entities and systems. When political action is discussed, he tends to put himself into the position of the individual affected by the action and to ask himself, "Just how, in practice, will this alter my life?" Very often he concludes, like Johnson, that, considering the small proportion of the individual's life they are going to affect very greatly one way or the other, many political squabbles are hardly worth the energy that is expended on them.

As he sees the governed as individual human beings rather than as societies or classes or economic groups, the skeptical conservative also tends to see governments not as lofty abstractions labeled "the will of the people" or "the spirit of the nation," but as fallible, greedy human beings invested with power over other human beings; and, like Johnson, he is likely not to put too much faith in their ability to produce happiness or virtue. Politics thus resolves itself into questions of morality dealing with the relations between individual human beings, questions to be decided by invoking general moral principles. To Johnson all political questions are thus moral questions: politics is no more than a branch of general human morality. The idealist conservative, on the other hand, if the formulations of his creed that have been quoted are authentic, takes more pleasure in contemplating ideas than individuals. If the concept of the individual be rejected entirely, as in the more throughgoing forms of Hegelian statism, the concept of individual moral responsibility, it would seem, must be rejected with it. The result will be to make politics a separate world of its own in which the ordinary principles of morality, as between individual human beings, do not apply and are replaced by other principles of action which transcend them. Such a concept would have seemed to Johnson mere insanity.

As a literary critic, it was Johnson's fate to be sneered at as hopelessly behind the times when, as events were to show, he was in fact far ahead of them. His close attention to the hard facts of a literary text, his sturdy refusal to be led away from them into nebulous generalization, his constant awareness of the intimate relation between literature and morality, which were treated so superciliously by the nineteenth century, have come in the middle of the twentieth, through the influence of Eliot, Leavis, and others, to be the prevailing mode; and Johnson, from being regarded as an amusingly or pitifully "blind" fumbler, has attained a reputation as one of the greatest of English critics, if not the greatest. Conceivably one reason why his reputation as a political commentator suffered is that here too he was in advance of his time. Many of his political judgments, wrong-headed as they seemed to those who took a short view of these matters, have had a disconcerting way of turning out to be true in the long run. His doubts about the morality and usefulness of imperial expansion, his belief that the basis of any successful scheme of colonization must be a respect for the individual human dignity of the native population, his distrust of overzealous missionary activity and the white man's burden, all of which would have seemed impossibly old-fashioned and unimaginative to the enterprising nineteenth-century heirs of Chatham, have been amply confirmed in the twentieth. His skepticism about Great Britain's putting all her economic eggs in the basket of unrestricted commercial expansion, untenable as it seemed in the heyday of Cobden and Bright and the other descendants of Adam Smith, again was shown by the events of the twentieth century to have been eminently justifiable. His rigorously objective analysis of the economic causes of the Seven Years' War, and of British foreign and colonial policy from the sixteenth to the eighteenth centuries, commends itself more to the twentieth than it did to the nineteenth century. Few informed modern scholars would seriously disagree with his verdict that the legal and constitutional arguments advanced by the publicists of the American Revolution can be safely ignored. Most important, perhaps, we have come to see that, as Johnson insisted, the key to the politics of the modern world is the omnicompetent sovereignty of the modern national state; whether we like the fact or not—and Johnson nowhere says that he likes it, merely that it is so—any political discussion which ignores this fact is misleading and dangerous. No one, certainly, will acclaim Johnson as a systematic political theorist, any more than as a systematic literary critic. But as in criticism Johnson's desultory observations are worth half a dozen of the forgotten critical systems his contemporaries were fond of inventing, it may be argued that a similar deficiency in political theory is no great loss. The fine metaphysical theories of the seventeenth and eighteenth centuries which Johnson so resolutely ignored—theories of divine right and natural rights and original compacts and the organic state—have come to possess little more than historical or polemical interest for the twentieth century. In the general discredit of older political theory that now prevails, Johnson's rigorously empirical approach to the facts of political power as it actually exists, troubling his head very little about what theoretical justification can be devised for its existence, may have a certain appeal to the serious student of politics.

If Johnson's approach to political matters seems often very modern, there is also a sense in which it is very old. The complex of political attitudes that I have called "skeptical conservatism" has been little studied, but one has a suspicion that it occurs widely and is of long standing in the culture of the English-speaking world. No one with any practical experience in the matter would deny that, in spite of occasional sudden outbursts of political enthusiasm, the politics of the ordinary citizen, the man-in-the-street, in Britain and America, contains a sizable portion of the feeling that "I'm from Missouri" (or Staffordshire)—of a normal distrust of the glowing professions of career politicians, even thoroughly self-deceived ones; of an unwillingness to jump from a known frying pan into an unknown fire—an unwillingness which is not the product of any Burkean rhapsodizing about the venerable antiquity of the frying pan, but simply of his innate suspicion that most schemes of political improvement are very laughable. It is an attitude that is, almost by definition, unformulated and inarticulate—it is the Bolingbrokes and Burkes, the Rousseaus and Marxes, the people with ingenious theories to propound, who write the books and make the speeches and get the publicity. But insofar as it has a spokesman, it is hard to say who would fill that role better than Johnson, the John-

son who asserted—those who accuse him of a blind distrust of
the people would do well to remember—that "The common
voice of the multitude, uninstructed by precept and unprejudiced by authority . . . in questions that relate to the heart
of man, is, in my opinion, more decisive than the learning of
Lipsius." [22]

APPENDIX A

THIS list includes a number of minor or recently attributed pieces not mentioned elsewhere in the text of this work. It makes no pretensions to completeness.

The earliest surviving piece of prose by Johnson has a distinct political thesis. This is a Latin school exercise, dated 1725, of which R. W. Chapman has reproduced one page in facsimile as a frontispiece to his edition of the *Letters* (1952). It is apparently a "theme" based on a couplet from Horace (*Odes* I, 2), written in another hand on the reverse of the page, "Audiet pugnas vitio parentum / Rara juventus." The piece from which it is taken is one of Horace's patriotic odes; but Johnson's composition, though taking off from the same assertion of the degeneracy of the times, develops in quite another direction than Horace's plea for more imperial leadership by Augustus. Roman imperialism was bad enough, the boy seems to be saying, but that of modern Europe is worse. "Avaritia adeo est insatiabilis"—"Our avarice is so insatiable that, as if the part of the world now known hardly contained enough gold and gems, we seek out new regions unknown to our ancestors and subjugate their inhabitants. Thule is no longer regarded the end of the earth, nor are the equatorial regions supposed uninhabited. The love of gold drives our ships where the Roman standards never"—here the published fragment breaks off. It is clear that Johnson's dislike of the imperial idea was well developed at the age of sixteen.

At Oxford, Boswell tells us (*Life, I,* 60), Johnson was instructed to write an exercise on the Gunpowder Plot (presumably for November 5, 1728). Instead, he turned in a Latin poem entitled "Somnium" (now lost), in which he announced "that the Muse had come to him in his sleep, and whispered that it did not become him to write on such subjects as politics; he should confine himself to humbler themes." Since the Muse's warning had little effect on Johnson at other times, this was probably merely a tactful way of getting out of a distastefully hackneyed assignment: it would be like asking a brilliant young American undergraduate to write an essay on the subject of the Fourth of July.

A letter in the *Gentleman's Magazine* for July 1738, signed "Pamphilus," has recently been attributed, plausibly, to Johnson: see Jacob Leed, *Modern Philology, 54* (1957), 221–9. It is a thoughtful discussion of the theory and practice of "condolence," related to the views Johnson expresses in his essays on epitaphs, and his remarks on *Lycidas*. But its starting point is political—the formal addresses of sympathy to George II by the Houses of Parliament on the occasion of Queen Caroline's death, the insincerity of which Johnson demonstrates; and it ends with perhaps the most devastating of all Johnson's many personal attacks on the king. He has found two speedy means of consolation for his wife's death. One is money, which Parliament has undertaken to supply. The other is not named, but the innuendo is clear—it is his German mistress, Amalie von Wallmoden, whom George, certainly without much regard for the conventional decencies, had recently hurried over from Hanover.

The letter was in reply to the first of a series of "Questions" which the magazine had published the previous month, in order to stimulate discussion among its readers. With Pamphilus' letter appearing so promptly and aptly in reply, it is hard not to suspect that Johnson, involved as he was in the direction of the magazine, framed the questions too. They are obviously drawn up by someone who has been following recent political events closely, and are carefully worded so as to draw either Government or Opposition replies. They inquire, among other things, whether the practice of continuing land forces from year to year (by means of the annual Mutiny Acts) is not the same as keeping up a standing army (which of course it is—the question might be taken either to suggest that the Government is acting unconstitutionally, or to satirize the Opposition's horror at the magic phrase "standing army"); whether the MP's who voted to authorize 12,000 troops for the coming year, or those who voted for 18,000, are the greater patriots and lovers of liberty (see p. 304, n. 46); whether the Government had made "proper application" to the court of Spain on behalf of British shipmen, or whether the Opposition could not judge "what countenance" the Spanish government had given to the *guardacostas* who "plunder our merchants" without calling for confidential diplomatic instructions to be tabled in the House (the opposition had recently moved for this, in order to embarrass Walpole).

A letter to the *Gentleman's Magazine* in January 1739 (pp. 3–4), attributed to Johnson by Hill, has some pointed things to say about political journalism. "Political truth is undoubtedly of very great importance," it begins; ". . . nor do the writers on this subject ever more deserve the thanks of their country than when they enter upon examinations of the conduct of their governors, whether kings, senates, or ministers; when they impartially consider the tendency of their measures, and justify them in opposition to popular calumnies, or censure them in defiance of the frowns of greatness, or the persecutions of power." The writer feels sorry for hack party writers, "when I see the laborious drudgeries they are forced to undergo . . . to say something when they have nothing to say. . . . Some topicks indeed there are, equally copious and easy, by the help of which it costs them very little

pain to fill their pages. The miserable fate of the brave and
resolute Catalans, the life of the great Burleigh, and the history of Bolingbroke are inexhaustible funds of eloquence on
one side, which can only be equalled by the fate of wicked
ministers exemplified in the histories of all ages and nations."
Some think the remedy for such fatuity is the licensing of the
press. This would only "exasperate the evil. Falsehood and
defamation would then circulate unconfronted, under the
protection of a court, and sanction of a licenser."

One of Johnson's notes to his translation of Crousaz' *Commentary* on Pope's *Essay on Man* (1739) is an amusing illustration of his political sensibilities. He contrasts Pope's opening
couplet,

> Awake, my St. John, leave all meaner things
> To low ambition and the pride of Kings,

with Du Resnel's version of it,

> *Sors de l'enchantement, milord, laisse au vulgaire*
> *Le séduisant espoir d'un bien imaginaire.*

"The address of the one," Johnson comments succinctly, "is
the exclamation of a freeman, that of the other the murmur
of a slave." The vigor of the outburst is due not only to Johnson's normal Francophobia, but also to the fact that the object
of Du Resnel's excessive deference is his *bête noire,* Bolingbroke.

To an "Extract of Mr. Gulliver's Memoirs Relating to the
Characters of the Principal Members of the Senate of Lilliput" (*Gentleman's Magazine,* March 1740, pp. 99–103; May,
1740, pp. 227–30), Johnson perhaps contributed a paragraph
slyly satirizing George Lyttelton: see my article "Some Notes
on Johnson and the *Gentleman's Magazine,*" *PMLA, 74*
(1959), 75–84.

In the few paragraphs of original comment that Johnson
contributed to the *Life of Drake* (1740) there are found a dryly

hostile account of the early days of exploration and colonization of the New World; an interesting discussion of the noble
savage, in which he postulates that "happiness and misery are
equally diffused through all the states of human life," suggests
that the terms "civilized" and "barbarian" need to be taken
with a grain of salt, and criticizes naive notions of primitive
virtues—"He that never saw, or heard, or thought of strong
liquors cannot be proposed as a pattern of sobriety"; and a
characterization of the Spaniards, in relation to their treatment of the American Indians, as "those cruel intruders."

In the *Life of Barretier* (1740), Johnson tosses out, without
warning, the striking dictum, "Princes, who are commonly the
last by whom merit is distinguished, began to interest themselves in his success." In a later addition to the Life he concedes that the Margravine of Ansbach had earlier given
Barretier some encouragement; but he does not modify the
wording of the sentence.

In the preface to the *Gentleman's Magazine* for 1740 Johnson says, "We cannot but flatter ourselves with some hope that
our Magazine is such a collection of political intelligence as
Cicero himself would have approved." This is by way of introduction to a contributed essay, beginning with a quotation
from Cicero, on the "Acta Diurna of the Ancient Romans,"
which are taken as a forerunner of the Lilliputian debates.
(This essay has sometimes been attributed to Johnson, but I
think, with Croker, that the style rules it out as his.) The
preface for the 1741 *Magazine* also points with pride to its
political role, repudiating "another equally gross, though
more malicious [falsehood], that we are byassed by party
considerations . . . a calumny which impartiality always receives from the bigots of all parties; nor have we escaped the
censure of that very party whose particular interest we are
said to espouse." It is evidence of that impartiality that, at this
date, it is hard to decide which of the parties can be meant.

In 1741 Johnson probably edited a reprint of a seventeenth-century pamphlet which appeared under the title of *Monarchy Asserted to Be the Best, Most Antient, and Legall Form of Government. In a Conference Held at Whitehall, with Oliver, Lord Protector* (the tendentious title is not Johnson's, but that of the original edition of 1660), and abridged it for the *Gentleman's Magazine* (February) as "A Debate between the Committee of the House of Commons in 1657, and O. Cromwell, upon the humble petition and advice of the parliament, by which he was desired to assume the title of King." I can find no expression of political views by Johnson in the editorial work. Any significance to be found in the bare fact of Johnson's consenting to give considerable time and energy to this piece—apart from the certainty that he needed the money —can be only speculation. Is it possible that he was attracted by the idea of an elective, rather than a hereditary, monarchy, with men like Cromwell, whose abilities Johnson admired so highly, at its head?

Much significant editorial comment is found, however, in an abstract in the *Gentleman's Magazine* (December 1741) of the controversial pamphlet *Considerations upon the Embargo on the Provision of Victual.* The tendency of the comment is protectionist, defending the principle of government control of the export of grain. So is the editorial comment included in a series of abstracts, extending through several numbers of the *Magazine* in 1742 and 1743, of various pamphlets dealing with the question of the export of wool. I suggest that this comment is Johnson's (see my "Some Notes on Johnson and the *Gentleman's Magazine*," *PMLA*, 74, 1959, 75–84) not only because the nature of the economic thinking embodied in the comment corresponds to that which Johnson elsewhere expresses (see Appendix C, below), but also because of the general pungency of thought and expression. Such remarks as "When was it known that men in power, in prosecuting the publick good, neglected the advancement of their own authority?" sound to me eminently Johnsonian. In the same article just referred to, I extend the attributions hitherto made to Johnson of installments of the *Magazine*'s monthly article on foreign history from two to about a dozen. The two already attributed (on internal evidence—see *Life, 1,* 154–5, and *Gentleman's Magazine,* November 1794, p. 1001) express a generally pacifist outlook on the complicated Continental warfare of the time: so, too, does such an ironic remark as this, inserted in the foreign history article for November 1742:

Upon these marches and counter-marches, it has been observed that the maxims of war have been much changed by the refinements of the present times. In the ruder and more heroic ages it was the standing practice to take at all events the first opportunity of fighting; the great rule of conduct at present is never to fight without a visible advantage, which rule, if it be observed on both sides, will for ever prevent a battle.

It is consistent with such thinking that Johnson at this time was projecting a work (perhaps a tragic drama) entitled *Charles of Sweden (Letters,* No. 17)—no doubt an extension of the comments in *The Vanity of Human Wishes* on the futility of Charles XII's bloodstained career.

The main point of interest in a handful of editorial introductions contributed by Johnson (1744) to seventeenth-century pamphlets reprinted in the *Harleian Miscellany* (see my "Johnson and the *Harleian Miscellany*," *Notes and Queries,* July 1958) is that, in contrast to the militant anti-Catholicism and naive royalism of Oldys, the other editor, Johnson's comments are thoughtful, moderate, compassionate, and critical. "One advantage at least will be afforded by the perusal of this piece," says one; "the reader, amidst his indignation at the cruelties and his pity of the hardships which are here recounted, cannot fail to congratulate himself upon the happiness of living at a time when no such miseries are to be felt or such practices to be feared." Again: "The following tract contains a short narrative of the behaviour of these men at the gallows, who were executed for the Gun-powder Plot, of which I know not whether there is any other Protestant relation, and therefore have preserved this, though not very valuable either for its elegance or decency, for it is written in a strain of merriment and insult, which the religion professed by the author does not teach."

A long verse epitaph on Sir Thomas Hanmer, appearing in the *Gentleman's Magazine* for May 1747 (p. 239), has been attributed somewhat uncertainly to Johnson (as Nichol Smith and McAdam point out, though it is said to be a translation or paraphrase of a Latin epitaph on Hanmer, it is really an original composition). Hanmer was Speaker of the House of Commons during the Tory administration of the last four years of Queen Anne, and the writer commemorates this fact in (I think) effective verse:

> Illustrious Age! how bright thy glories shone
> When Hanmer fill'd the chair and Anne the throne!
> Then when dark arts obscur'd each fierce debate,
> When mutual frauds perplex'd the maze of state,
> The moderator firmly mild appear'd.

It is a just comment on the politics of the time, and on Hanmer, whose "old Tory" virtues of honesty and independence might well have appealed to the historian of the "fierce debates" and "mutual frauds" of the early 1740's. That Johnson thought little of Hanmer as an editor of Shakespeare would certainly not, as Boswell seems to suggest (*Life, 1,* 178), have interfered with his appreciation of Hanmer as a politician.

A letter, attributed to Johnson, in the *Gentleman's Magazine* for January 1749 comments scathingly on the wasteful expense of the notorious display of fireworks designed to commemorate the Peace of Aix-la-Chapelle, and on the futility of the War of the Austrian Succession that it brought to a close:

In this will consist the only propriety of this transient show, that it will resemble the war of which it celebrates the period. The powers of this part of the world, after long preparations, deep intrigues, and subtile schemes, have set Europe in a flame, and after having gazed a while at their fire-works, have laid themselves down where they rose, to inquire for what they had been contending. . . . Many cannot forbear observing, how many . . . acres might be drained, how many ways repaired, how many debtors might be released, how many widows and orphans whom the war has ruined might be relieved, by the expense which is about to evaporate in smoke. . . . There are some who think not only reason, but humanity, offended by such a trifling profusion when so many sailors are starving, and so many churches sinking into ruins.

The list of humanitarian projects on which the money might be spent corresponds closely to Johnson's known concerns. It is wryly amusing to note the usual Tory concern for sailors, whereas soldiers, who presumably also suffered in the war, are not mentioned at all. One of Johnson's contributions to John Gwynn's *Thoughts on the Coronation* (of George III; 1761) is very probably the concluding paragraph, which recommends that the Household Cavalry be omitted from the coronation procession, and that the number of infantry lining the streets be reduced,

since it cannot but offend every Englishman to see troops of soldiers placed between him and his sovereign, as if they were the most honourable of the people, or the king required guards to secure his person from his subjects. As their station makes them think themselves important, their insolence is always such as may be expected from servile authority; and the impatience of the people, under such immediate oppression, always produces quarrels, tumults, and mischief.

In a recent article (*Review of English Studies,* new ser. 7,
1956, 367–92), I venture to add another ten or twelve pieces
from the early numbers of the *Literary Magazine* (1756) to the
thirty-two already attributed to Johnson. Some of these reinforce the political positions suggested above, pp. 154–72. We
find him, for example, saying, apropos of the attack on Minorca by the French, "If the distribution of empire were in
my hands, I should indeed rather give up Gibraltar . . . than
Minorca. . . . But I know not whether either is worth its
charge, and by losing them, I am not sure that we shall suffer
anything more than that vexation which accompanies disgrace," and asserting that the Minorquins will, properly, favor
the French in the contest: "The time is now come when it will
appear that oppression is folly as well as wickedness, and that
whoever expects fidelity from a conquered people must send
men like Kane to govern them. A people taxed, harassed, and
insulted will always be desirous of changing their condition,
and the newcomer will always be welcome, since they cannot
fear him more, and they will hate him less" (abstract of Arm-
strong's *History of Minorca, 1,* 11–14). Apropos of British
treatment of the American Indians: "Let us not, because we
owe so much to the generosity of our Indian friends, be so
unreasonably covetous as not to be contented with less than all
that they had to give," and "While the French have been
endeavouring by every artifice that human policy could suggest to establish an interest among them, our Governors there
. . . have for a series of years past taken no care to cultivate
new friendships with the ancient inhabitants, nor has the government been at much expense to cement the old" (*Historical
Memoirs, 1,* 105, 133). He continues to pooh-pooh the invasion scare: "This pamphlet is published to prove what nobody
will deny, that we shall be less happy if we were conquered by
the French. . . . There is no great danger of invasions while
we have the sea covered with our ships, and maintain fifty

thousand men in arms on our coasts" (review of Parkin's *Impartial Account of the Invasion under William, Duke of Normandy, 1,* 186). He delivers a blast against his old enemies the excise commissioners at least as offensive as any of the others now on record: "Why should not all these wretches that live on public misery, commissioners of excise and officers without number, be at once, if it be possible, discarded, and sent to gain a living by honest industry, or to beg it of those whom they are now insulting?" (review of *A Scheme for Preventing a Further Increase of the National Debt, 1,* 188–90).

I end the article by suggesting that Johnson's engagement as editor and chief political correspondent of the magazine was terminated around November 1756, when Pitt took office. Johnson's intransigent opposition to the war was desired while Pitt was in opposition—the more Newcastle's administration was badgered, the better. But now that Pitt was in charge of the "war effort," Johnson's defeatism was out of place.

An important series of five "Observations" on the Seven Years' War, published in the *Universal Chronicle* in August and September 1758 and attributed to Johnson by Boylston Green (*Yale University Library Gazette, 16,* 1942, 70–9) deserve to be better known than they have been (there can be little doubt of their authorship). Green summarizes them thus: "The first three attempt to direct public opinion in the ways of sanity and restraint, condemning equally the excesses of joy and despair. The fourth sharply censures the public for triumphantly celebrating the victory at Louisbourg. An anonymous correspondent, in a letter appearing on September 16, takes exception to the Observator's opinions and implies a lack of patriotism. Two weeks later a rebuttal effectively justifies the author's statements and ends the series." Some typically pungent comments (from the last piece) are worth quoting: "It was often said by the Earl of Oxford that *a knot of idle fellows made a noise in one another's ears at a coffee-house, and imagined the nation to be filled with the same clamour.* This seems to have been lately the case of the English rabble"; "The madness of a nation, at least of the English, seldom lasts long; a week is commonly sufficient to restore them to their senses"; "I hope this zealous writer knows that Cape Breton is only an island." In reply to a statement by the objector that Louisburg is "an ample recompence for the loss of Minorca," Johnson comments, "At Minorca the disgrace was to us greater than the loss."

In Johnson's introduction to *The World Displayed* (1759) appears his most violent condemnation of the activities of the Europeans in expanding their dominion over the rest of the world.

We are openly told that they [the Portuguese] had the less scruple concerning their treatment of the savage people, because they scarcely considered them as distinct from beasts; and indeed the practice of all the European nations, and among others of the *English barbarians* [my italics] that cultivate the southern islands of America proves that this opinion, however absurd and foolish, however wicked and injurious, still continues to prevail. Interest and pride harden the heart, and it is vain to dispute against avarice and power.

Johnson's deepest rancor against exploiters of native populations seems to have been directed against these English sugar-planters of the West Indies: it was the "next insurrection of the Negroes in the West Indies" that he toasted at Oxford; the Negro boy whom he protected, Frank Barber, was from Jamaica. It is worth remembering that the West Indies merchants were a powerful force in English politics in the mid-eighteenth century. Their policy was always to press for greater expansion of British opportunities for trade; and the intercourse between New England and the West Indies was an important economic factor in the movement for American independence.

Along with traders, he condemns the Catholic missionaries:

Being secure of the goodness of the end, they had no scruple about the means, nor ever considered how differently from the primitive martyrs and apostles they were attempting to make proselytes. The first propagators of Christianity recommended their doctrine by their sufferings and virtues; they entered no defenceless territories with swords in their hands; they built no forts upon ground to which they had no right, nor polluted the purity of religion with avarice of trade, or insolence of power.

The reminiscence of Lobo is apparent. Not that "this purpose of propagating truth" has ever "been seriously pursued by any European nation":

When a fort is built, and a factory established, there remains no other care than to grow rich. It is soon found that ignorance is most easily kept in subjection, and that by enlightening the mind with truth, fraud and usurpation would be made less practicable and less secure.

The matter is summed up in Johnson's verdict on the work of Prince Henry the Navigator:

What mankind has lost and gained by the genius and designs of this prince, it would be long to compare and very difficult to estimate. Much knowledge has been acquired, and much cruelty been committed; the belief of religion has been very little propagated, and its laws have been outrageously and enormously violated. The Europeans have scarcely visited any coast but to gratify avarice, and extend corruption; to arrogate dominion without right, and practise cruelty without incentive. Happy had it then been for the oppressed, if the designs of Henry had slept in his bosom, and surely more happy for the oppressors. But there is reason to hope . . . that the light of the gospel will at last illuminate the sands of Africa, and the deserts of America, though its progress cannot but be slow when it is so much obstructed by the lives of Christians.

APPENDIX B

The Sentiments of a Tory

I BELIEVE that the "vindication" referred to on p. 130, above, is the pamphlet entitled *The Sentiments of a Tory in Respect to a Late Important Transaction and in Regard to the Present Situation of Affairs* (London, T. Cooper, 1741). It is listed in the "Books Published" section in the *Gentleman's Magazine* for April 1741, p. 224. I am not so certain of the "celebrated Pamphlet" in which the Tories are challenged to answer for their conduct. It may be *A Review of the Late Motion for an Address to His Majesty against a Certain Great Minister . . . by a Member of Parliament* (London, W. Ward, 1741), in which the writer proclaims (p. 3), "Let Those, who sneak'd upon that Occasion, answer it to the World and their own Conscience"; or, less probably, *Reasons Founded on Facts for a Late Motion,* subtitled *A Letter to a Tory Member* (London, T. Cooper, 1741), in which the challenge is implied, though not stated. These three pamphlets are bound together in a volume bearing the bookplate of George Grenville (the future prime minister), now in the library of Western Reserve University, Cleveland, Ohio. Grenville, who had entered the House of Commons in 1740, was of course a participant in these events.

The Sentiments of a Tory is an illuminating statement of the "liberal" Tory position to which Johnson (since he recommends the work) presumably subscribed at the time, and is probably a valid statement of Johnson's definition of Toryism throughout the rest of his life. Since evidence of the nature of this position is so scarce, it will be worth while attempting a summary of the 63-page pamphlet.

After an introductory note, in which the writer says that though the Tories' support of Walpole has won general approbation from the public, a clear and unheated statement of the Tories' position will commend itself to "the honest men of all parties," who "mean their country well, though they may differ about the means of serving it," the pamphlet launches into a devastating attack on Bolingbroke—"the Shaftesbury of the present age, a man to be sure well versed in the history and interest of parties, since, in the course of his life, he has been of all, and, I believe I may say, at the head of all the capital parties in these kingdoms, I mean Whigs, Tories, and Jacobites, and therefore no man fitter to form this project of a coalition, which was, in short, a project for the putting himself at the head of them again all at once." The writer refutes Bolingbroke's doctrine of "abolishing, or, which is the same thing, uniting all parties; a kind of Methodism in politics, whereby a pretence is made to a higher degree of state-purity than can be reasonably expected among Englishmen. . . . That Patriotism shall perform more than religion ever could, that is, make us all of one mind, is . . . what no man in his senses will believe."

The immediate relevance of this attack is that the opposition Whigs, in reproaching the Tories for not voting with them against Walpole, alleged—e.g. in *Reasons Founded on Facts*—that the Tories could have no real policy or principles, in the Walpole crisis, distinct from those of the opposition Whigs; this view the writer stigmatizes as Bolingbrokism. He then goes on to make a strong plea for the recognition of the existence of a set of distinct Tory principles: "*Tory* and *Whig* are terms that have now a settled meaning, and the moderate men of both parties, I mean such as consult their reason and the constitution, will always acquiesce in such measures as have an evident tendency to the public good. . . . While people profess their real principles, while Tories act like

Tories and Whigs like Whigs, we know what we are doing, and we know the issue of our doings." He defends the Tories against charges of extremism:

The Tories have been very unjustly charged by their enemies with being bigots in respect to religion, and slaves in respect to their political principles, whereas they are extremely free in their opinions with respect to both. They are warm friends to the established Church, not because it is established, but because they look upon it to be the best constituted church upon earth. For the same reason, they are zealous for the good old English constitution, which their reason tells them hath assigned a proper proportion of power to the crown, the nobles, and the people. But though from those motives they are inviolably attached to the settlement in Church and State, yet they are far from supposing that either churchmen or statesmen are infallible. . . . In short, they are for the Church, that they may secure peace hereafter, and for the constitution that they may enjoy it here.

The similarity of this position to that expressed in Johnson's disquisition "Of Tory and Whig" (p. 14, above) is obvious.

The writer now reviews some history. "Men of these principles have been generally speaking the majority in this nation." They were "the greater and the better part of the people in 1641," when they adhered to Charles I. "How they came afterwards to be divided, and, in consequence thereof, to be destroyed, and to be subjected by a handful of their fellow subjects" is well known. "After the constitution was restored in the year 1660, they became apparently the majority again." He defends Charles II's Parliament of 1661 to 1679, though conceding that "that Parliament erred in some things, and was, perhaps, rotten in some of its members, but it was sound at heart, and therefore when the King plunged into corrupt measures, he parted with it and lived to regret it." He then enlarges on the point hinted at here, that the Tories have not been blindly subservient to monarchs. "In the course of the

Civil War the Tories (for such the wiser Cavaliers were)"—a nice distinction—"did their utmost to support the Crown, but by no means inclined to make an absolute conquest of their fellow subjects." Under Charles II "they were for limiting a Popish succession," though against an exclusion. "In 1688, the Tories concurred in bringing about the Revolution, eminently concurred, and therefore they have as just a right to the fruits of it as any other set of men in Britain, whatever some may pretend to the contrary." In the revolution "they took care not to hurt the Constitution, which, in their judgment, is precisely the same now that it was then, the difference of [royal] families excepted."

Coming down to 1741, the writer rebuts the contention of the opposition Whigs that it is illogical of the Tories to have opposed Walpole's policies and yet to refuse to support the motion penalizing Walpole. He does so by a masterly exposition of what is, in effect, the modern doctrine of the role of the opposition in the British Parliament:

There ought to be, especially in parliament, a spirit of enquiry; or, if you will, a spirit of jealousy. Power is a dangerous and intoxicating thing, and those who are possessed of it are but too apt to carry it a little farther than they ought, let them be of what party they will. For this reason there hath been, and I hope there always will be, a party willing to inspect the actions, and ready to control the councils [i.e. counsels?], of every administration. But this is far from doing any hurt to the people in general, to the parliament in particular, or to the administration itself which it opposes. On the contrary, it does good to all, it encourages the people not to submit tamely to any grievances, it keeps up that life and freedom which ought to appear in parliamentary debates, and it serves to restrain men in power from the vain imagination that either they may do what they will or that it is in their power. . . . From all this it follows that men of the strictest honour, men of the greatest loyalty to their prince, men who have the utmost zeal for the constitution, may engage in such an opposition with a view only of coming at truth, of serving their constituents as they ought, and of promoting the true interest of their country, without any selfish views of profit, or personal prejudices against those whom they oppose.

The duty of carrying on this "loyal opposition," the writer continues, should be in the hands of those who are not connected with the administration. (Obvious as this seems today, it was not so in the eighteenth century, when an administration sometimes carried its own opposition within itself—e.g. Pitt and Fox in 1754.) "Having less knowledge of the springs of action, they are the more ready to entertain jealousies even of just and reasonable measures; which however begets no inconvenience, since, from their being opposed and examined, they come to appear just and reasonable, which otherwise they would not have been so thoroughly known to be." Furthermore, "such independent persons are usually applied to by the people, and by such as have, or think they have, as great knowledge in matters of public concern as those who manage them; of which sort of folks there will never be any dearth in a free nation." The obvious candidates for the role of (apparently) permanent opposition are the Tories: "It is on account of their having so seldom the honour to be trusted with any share of power," says the writer, a little wryly, "and their having so generally the honour to be confided in by their countrymen. If, therefore, their conduct in Parliament has been such as, by keeping up a just and moderate opposition, they have maintained our constitution in health and vigour, in what have they done amiss?"

The writer then attacks the opposition Whigs for their inconsistency, making the shrewd point that since most of them were formerly supporters of Walpole at some time or other, it will be difficult for them to decide which of Walpole's measures were treasonable and which not, and for their rancor: "May not men differ about the means of serving their country, and neither side be traitors? . . . If their reasoning was to prevail, censure and impeachments would be the business of every new Parliament, and then where would be the liberty of speaking?" He goes on to plead for the attribution of honorable motives to those who disagree with one on political matters, and against the vindictive treatment of defeated political enemies. (It has been remarked that Walpole's escape from punishment after his downfall is an important landmark in the development of British Parliamentary government. Hitherto severe retribution had almost inevitably been visited upon a fallen minister of any capacity; Walpole himself, as the opposition Whigs gleefully pointed out, had moved the impeachment of Harley—though see p. 312, n. 15. The Tories deserve some credit for the part they played in the 1740's in bringing about a more enlightened way of doing things.)

The pamphlet then asserts that, contrary to the allegations of the opposition Whigs, the Tory tradition is not opposed to the concept of a prime minister:

Our glory, liberty, and trade are chiefly owing to the integrity and wisdom of three great ministers, Burleigh, Clarendon, and Godolphin. . . . The King is at liberty to make use of the councils of any minister; and . . . a minister is at liberty to serve his Majesty in any manner not repugnant to the known laws of the land. . . . To infer from hence, that Tories are servilely or slavishly addicted to the Crown would be a very false consequence; for in truth they are the only people in this kingdom who have extensive notions of freedom, notwithstanding all that has been said to the contrary. Others are for giving vast prerogatives to the nobility [Algernon Sidney and Denzil Holles are cited], or to the people [as Milton and Harrington]; and because this cannot be done but by lessening the power of the Crown, they think and call themselves friends to liberty. But the Tories, following the rule of the Constitution, are for allowing its just rights to the Crown, their legal privileges to the nobles, and that liberty and property which is their birthright to the people.

They think, that since the executive power is in the King by law, he is at liberty to act as he thinks proper, as to the choice of ministers, and use of their councils; provided they are not contrary to the laws, or are not evidently prejudicial to the commonwealth.

The similarity of this to Locke, and to American constitutional theory, is notable.

There follows a close argument about the cases of Strafford, Clarendon, and Harley, summarized in the passage quoted from the *Gentleman's Magazine*. The pamphlet concludes with further exhortation to a spirit of moderation and an abatement of both political hypocrisy and the cynicism consequent on it, which "has brought patriotism itself, the noblest, the most valuable of all civil virtues, to be thought a chimæra. . . . If, in these days, a man opposes power in the mildest terms, and with the most solemn assurances of duty to his prince, he passes with the many for a Jacobite and for a hypocrite with the few." The way to cure the present confusion in public affairs is "to impose silence upon all parties, not by any law for restraining the liberty of speech or the freedom of the press, that would but increase the tumult and augment the confusion; but by doing what is in the power of the people, and in nobody's power but theirs, discountenancing all declamatory applications, and resolving to proceed in so important an affair with that caution and sobriety which it becomes men to shew, who have their country's concerns at heart." This the people will have an opportunity to do in the forthcoming general election, by allotting their votes not on the basis of faction but of merit—and hence, presumably, returning a good number of independent Tory members. The writer also proposes a return to the old system of payment of members of the House of Commons, to ensure greater independence among them (see p. 94, above).

This brief summary does not do justice to what is by any

standard a thoughtful and impressive piece of political discussion. The style of writing, though good, is not Johnsonian. Is it conceivably by William Guthrie, Johnson's senior colleague on the *Gentleman's Magazine* staff? The possible influence of Guthrie on both Johnson's political thinking and Johnson's prose style is something that should be investigated, though no doubt the available evidence is scanty.

APPENDIX C

JOHNSON'S ECONOMIC VIEWS

J OHNSON'S ideas of political economy deserve separate and fuller treatment than they can be given here. But the subject is so intimately allied with his political views that a brief account of them will be attempted.

That Johnson regarded the study of economics as highly important appears from his recommendation of it in the preface to the *Preceptor* (1748):

A discourse has been added upon *trade* and *commerce*, of which it becomes every man of this nation to understand at least the general principles, as it is impossible that any should be high or low enough not to be in some degree affected by their declension or prosperity. It is therefore necessary that it should be universally known among us what changes of property are advantageous, or when the balance of trade is on our side; what are the products or manufactures of other countries; and how far one nation may in any species of traffic obtain or preserve superiority over another. The theory of trade is yet but little understood, and therefore the practice is often without real advantage to the public; but it might be carried on with more general success, if its principles were better considered; and to excite that attention is our chief design.

How greatly interested Johnson himself was in such matters is evident from the multitude of passages in his writings and recorded conversation where he speculates on them. As might be expected, he generally approaches economic questions in an empirical way, drawing largely on his own by no means negligible acquaintance with the world of commerce, and with little or no use of technical terminology (of which little, in any case, then existed): it was, as has been said, an age when every man was his own economist.

But certain basic postulates of Johnson's economic think-ing can easily be detected. There can be no doubt that he was essentially in sympathy with mercantilism, the unsatis-factory name modern writers give to virtually all economic theorizing that preceded Adam Smith. The list of text books that Johnson recommends to the student of the *Preceptor* consists of standard mercantilist treatises: Thomas Mun's *England's Treasure by Forraign Trade, or the Ballance of our Forraign Trade is the Rule of our Treasure* (1664); Sir Josiah Child's *A New Discourse of Trade* (1690); "Locke upon Coin"—i.e. *Some Considerations of the Consequence of Lowering the Interest and Raising the Value of Money* (1691) and two later monetary treatises, published when the gov-ernment of William III was undertaking the reform of the currency; the numerous publications of Charles Davenant; *The British Merchant,* a series of periodical tracts compiled in 1713, in answer to Defoe's *Mercator* and opposing Boling-broke's proposed commercial treaty with France; a *Diction-naire de commerce* (no doubt Savary's); and "for an abstract or compendium," Joshua Gee's *The Trade and Navigation of Great-Britain Considered* (1729). The long subtitle of the last may be quoted to show the tendency of most of these treatises: "Shewing that the surest way for a nation to in-crease in riches is to prevent the importation of such foreign commodities as may be rais'd at home. That this kingdom is capable of raising within itself, and its Colonies, materials for employing all our poor in those manufactures which we now import from such of our neighbours who refuse the ad-mission of ours. . . ."

The Britain that Gee and most of the others visualize is a self-contained, protectionist, carefully regulated state, its in-ternal economy and its trading relations with the rest of the world controlled by the government for the greatest benefit of the inhabitants of Great Britain. This conception, of course, more or less underlay British governmental thinking from medieval times until the official adoption of free-trade principles in 1846, principles which were again abandoned in 1931. The recrudescence of ideas of a planned economy in the twentieth century we all know. In Johnson's time, ideas of laissez-faire economics were just beginning to circulate; the two most important landmarks were Mandeville's *Fable of the Bees* (1714), and, much more important of course, Adam Smith's *Wealth of Nations* (1776). Johnson testified that Mandeville "opened my views into real life very much," and Anna Seward and Birkbeck Hill are probably right in equating Johnson's arguments on behalf of "luxury" with Mandeville's doctrine. "You cannot spend money in luxury without doing good to the poor," Johnson said; ". . . for by spending it in luxury, you make them exert industry" (*Life, 3, 291*). Being not too fond of exertion himself, Johnson ought to have seen the obvious fallacy in making the necessity of exertion, the "creation of employment," a good in itself; unless of course he was going on the Puritan assumption that industry *is* a virtue in itself, presumably because it is unpleasant (see p. 150, above). Johnson once mentions Adam Smith favorably (*Life, 2, 430*); but Birkbeck Hill, a good Gladstonian Liberal for whom free trade is little less than divine truth and Adam Smith its evangelist, decides that Johnson could not have understood him: "his ignorance . . . remained as deep as ever."

Perhaps; yet Johnson was well aware of some refutations of free trade argument. In *Further Thoughts on Agriculture,* published in the *Universal Visiter* for March 1756, he puts forward very clearly the choice that faced Britain in the mid-eighteenth century, of encouraging its population to continue to feed itself and retain a reasonably well-balanced economy, or else to commit itself fully to a policy of industrial and commercial expansion. "Commerce," Johnson declares,

however we may please ourselves with the contrary opinion, is one of the daughters of Fortune, inconstant and deceitful as her mother; she chooses her residence where she is least expected, and shifts her abode, when her continuance is in appearance most firmly settled. . . . It is apparent that every trading nation flourishes, while it can be said to flourish, by the courtesy of others. We cannot compel any people to buy from us, or to sell to us. A thousand accidents may prejudice them in favour of our rivals; the workmen of another nation may labour for less price. . . . Experience has shown that there is no work of the hands which, at different times, is not best performed in different places. . . .

Manufactures, indeed, and profitable manufactures, are sometimes raised from imported materials, but then we are subjected a second time to the caprice of our neighbours. The natives of Lombardy might easily resolve to retain their silk at home, and employ workmen of their own to weave it. And this will certainly be done when they grow wise and industrious, when they have sagacity to discern their true interest and vigour to pursue it.

This is remarkably prophetic. The great industrial expansion of Britain in the late eighteenth and early nineteenth centuries was made possible by Britain's temporary superiority in technology over the rest of the world; when the world caught up with British technology, it did indeed find it better to retain its raw materials and manufacture them at home than to pay the British for their services in processing them. Johnson summed up his view poetically in the four concluding lines that he contributed to Goldsmith's *The Deserted Village* in 1770; I give them here with the three preceding lines by Goldsmith:

> Teach erring man to spurn the rage of gain;
> Teach him, that states, of native strength possest,
> Though very poor, may still be very blest;

That trade's proud empire hastes to swift decay,
As oceans sweep the labour'd mole away;
While self-dependent power can time defy,
As rocks resist the billows and the sky.

The *Considerations on Corn* that Johnson wrote for Gerard
Hamilton in the 1760's (p. 198, above) is again an argument
against a free market in grain and a plea for the retention
of government control of the grain trade and subsidization
of farmers if necessary. In this, as has been noted, Johnson
agreed with Burke and the Rockingham Whigs, the heirs of
Walpole, the agrarian section of the Whigs.

Johnson's views on colonies follow directly from his economic views. The only point in founding a colony can be to
widen the scope of the mother country's economy; but to do
so its economy must be strictly controlled and integrated with
that of the mother country. A colony economically independent of the mother country is a contradiction in terms; hence
Johnson's contempt for any policy toward the Americans that
tried to mediate between strict economic (and hence political) control by Britain on the one hand and complete independence on the other.

The great representative of British commercial and imperial expansion in the eighteenth century was Chatham, and
the great disciple of Adam Smith was his son, the younger
Pitt. It is natural enough, then, that Johnson should seem
to distrust the Pitts even more than he did the Walpole-
Rockingham official Whig succession.

NOTES

ABBREVIATIONS

Gleanings   Aleyn Lyell Reade, *Johnsonian Gleanings*, 11 vols. privately printed, 1909–52.

Letters   R. W. Chapman, ed., *The Letters of Samuel Johnson*, 3 vols. Oxford, 1952.

Life   James Boswell, *The Life of Samuel Johnson*, ed. G. B. Hill, rev. L. F. Powell, 6 vols. Oxford, 1934–50.

Miscellanies   G. B. Hill, ed., *Johnsonian Miscellanies*, 2 vols. Oxford, 1897.

Poems   D. Nichol Smith and E. L. McAdam, Jr., eds., *The Poems of Samuel Johnson*, Oxford, 1941.

Works   *The Works of Samuel Johnson*, London: *1–11*, 1787; "supplementary" vols. *12, 13,* 1787; *14,* 1788; "*15,*" 1789.

PREFACE

1. *Georgian Oxford: University Politics in the Eighteenth Century* (Oxford, 1958), p. v.

2. H. R. Trevor-Roper, "The Country-House Radicals" and "The Social Causes of the Great Rebellion," in *Men and Events* (New York, 1958), pp. 179–88, 195–205. What became of these impoverished squires after the turmoil of 1640–60 was over? Trevor-Roper closes his detailed study of them at this point and is content to repeat the conventional reading of the political history of the rest of the Stuart period. "It [the Great Rebellion] was the blind revolt of the gentry against the Court, of the provinces against the capital. . . . Ultimately . . . they gave up the effort, accepted back the old political system, and sank into political quietism. They might still grumble about Court and City: but, instead of arming themselves with radical ideas, they

consoled themselves with conservative ideas: they became high-flying tories, preachers of non-resistance and divine right. . . . They became the royalist Anglican 'young squires' of the Convention and Cavalier Parliaments, the squires of the October Club, the high-flying non-resisting Tories. It is from then, and then only, that the country houses of England have been, as they have seldom ceased to be, conservative."

But have they? When, over a century later, we find 61 knights of the shire voting *for* Dunning's motion "that the influence of the crown has increased, is increasing, and ought to be diminished" and only 9 against it (Sir Lewis Namier, "Country Gentlemen in Parliament, 1750–84," in *Personalities and Powers*, London, 1955, p. 76), we wonder whether the political style of the country houses has really changed very much from the days of the Long Parliament. The fact is that the politics of the landed gentry has been subjected to close scrutiny for only the two periods—that of the early seventeenth century, by Trevor-Roper, and that centering on 1760, by Namier and his co-workers. At both times the country gentry are seen to be turbulent, independent, resentful of the authority of the central government. What their political attitudes were between these two periods awaits further investigation as searching as that of Trevor-Roper and Namier: both historians have taught us the uselessness of relying on the textbook clichés on the subject. (A continuation to 1714 of Robert Walcott's *English Politics in the Early Eighteenth Century*, Cambridge, Mass., 1956, which deals with the period 1701–08, would be extremely valuable.)

Much of the difficulty stems from the word "conservative." Was the holding, in 1680 or 1709, of the doctrines of nonresistance and divine right (if in fact the country gentlemen did hold them), was Jacobitism itself, really a manifestation of political conservatism? One thinks of Thackeray's fictional Bolingbroke (in *Henry Esmond*), preparing to restore James Edward to the throne: "And what happened to his grandfather? Our great King came from Huntingdon, not Hanover. . . . Let him come and we'll keep him, and we'll show him Whitehall. If he's a traitor let us have him here to deal with him. . . . Are all Oliver's men dead, or his glorious name forgotten in fifty years? . . . God save the King! and, if the monarchy fails us, God save the British republic!" Not inconceivably this represents the political psychology of the October Club better than the accounts in the standard histories. Surely it is naive to think of these tough country squires suddenly undergoing a mass intellectual conversion to the theories of Filmer: they approved of the Pretender as probably more amenable to their wishes than was George of Hanover; much political "ideology" is of this nature. Is this conservatism? Perhaps the end result of a careful study of the politics of the country gentlemen between the Trevor-Roper and the Namier periods will be the conclusion that the concept of a fundamental dichotomy between "conservative" and "progressive" political thinking is not really a very useful one on which to base histories of political ideology. It is, after all, a comparatively recent concept, popularized, if not invented, by Burke and Macaulay to serve the interests of their own political group.

The North American analogue to the politics of the English small landed gentry may well be the politics of the farmers of the western plains, so fruitful in "radicalism" and isolationism and antagonism to the rascals in Washington and New York and Toronto. As for "conservatism," it has been argued, with some plausibility, that Sen. Joseph McCarthy traced his political lineage from Bryan, La Follette, and the populists.

3. *The Vision of Theodore.*

4. E. L. McAdam, Jr., *Dr. Johnson and the English Law* (Syracuse, N.Y., 1951), p. 99 (from the Vinerian Lectures on the English Law).

1. INTRODUCTION

1. George Sherburn in *A Literary History of England,* ed. A. C. Baugh (New York, 1948), p. 1001.

2. My eye falls on the following remark in a recent book of criticism: "Bradley speaks of her [Jane Austen's] 'moralising tendency' and sees in her work a close connection to Dr. Johnson. Actually, however, it is just her moral complexity which gives sharpness to her themes. Johnson himself held to a rigorous orthodoxy in politics, in religion, and in his social ideas." That no full-length study has ever been made of Johnson's religious, social, or (up until now) political ideas is, it seems, no deterrent to the currency of such pronouncements.

3. See p. 130.

4. *Life, 5,* 269; *4,* 139.

5. "Memoirs of the King of Prussia" (1756), *Works, 4,* 537.

6. "On the Bravery of the Common English Soldiers" (1760?), *Works, 10,* 288.

7. E.g. Sir Lewis Namier: *The Structure of Politics at the Accession of George III,* 2 vols. London, 1929; *England in the Age of the American Revolution,* London, 1930; and "Monarchy and the Party System" and "Country Gentlemen in Parliament, 1750–84," in his *Personalities and Powers,* London, 1955. Also Wolfgang Michael, *Englische Geschichte im achtzehnten Jahrhundert,* 5 vols. Berlin, Leipzig, Basel, 1896–1955; Romney Sedgwick, ed., *Letters from George III to Lord Bute, 1756–1766,* London, 1939; Herbert Butterfield, *George III, Lord North, and the People,* London, 1949; Richard Pares, *King George III and the Politicians,* Oxford, 1953; Robert Walcott, *English Politics in the Early Eighteenth Century,* Cambridge, Mass., 1956; John B. Owen, *The Rise of the Pelhams,* London, 1957; John Brooke, *The Chatham Administration, 1766–1768,* London, 1956; Ian R. Christie, *The End of North's Ministry,* London, 1958; J. H. Plumb, *Sir Robert Walpole: The Making of a Statesman* (Vol. 1 of a projected 2-volume work), London, 1956; Lewis M. Wiggin, *The Faction of Cousins: A Political Account of the Grenvilles, 1733–1763,* New Haven, 1958.

8. "Little now remains of this rigmarole" was the *Times Literary Supplement's* epitaph on it, reviewing the effects of the "Namierian revolution" after a quarter of a century: "The Namier View of History" (August 28, 1953), p. xxii.

9. Review of Mahon's *War of the Spanish Succession,* in *Essays,* ed. F. C. Montague (3 vols. London, 1903), *1,* 531. When Macaulay is not engaged in promoting his thesis, he can give a reasonably accurate account of the politics of the time, as in the essays on Chatham and Horace Walpole, where the Tories appear not as the deliberate sponsors of reaction but as the relatively harmless and disinterested country squires they were. But when propaganda is needed for the cause of nineteenth-century Whiggism, no absurdity is too great for his pen.

10. Macaulay, essay on Sir James Mackintosh (ibid., *2,* 72–4): "The History of England is emphatically the history of progress. It is the history of a constant movement of the public mind, of a

NOTES [PP. 5-6] 289

constant change in the institutions of a great society. . . . We have often thought that the motion of the public mind in our country resembles that of the sea when the tide is rising. Each successive wave rushes forward, breaks, and rolls back; but the great flood is steadily coming in." The introduction of the Victorian notion of progress into politics (and the identification of it with Whiggism) can be traced back to Burke's *Thoughts on the Present Discontents* (1770). The classic rebuttal of Macaulay's view of history is Herbert Butterfield, *The Whig Interpretation of History*, London, 1931.

11. Michael, *Englische Geschichte im achtzehnten Jahrhundert*, *4, 31, 33*: "Even if one tries to get a clear picture of how those who belonged to the two parties were distributed between city and country, one finds that the older formula no longer applies. The expressions 'landed interest' and 'moneyed interest' no longer indicate the true state of affairs. . . . Whig doctrine and Tory doctrine no longer exist. At the most, the parties are still a little encumbered with their past, with their traditions. But otherwise they are free in their activities and plans. They can take up any position they please with regard to every new question that arises in politics. . . . Basically it is merely a question of the possession of office, and the party that is 'out' is always discontented." Michael is speaking of the period around 1720.

12. It has long been customary to say that the American constitution, with its provision for the separation of the legislative and executive powers, was a departure from the British system, originating in or fostered by Montesquieu's misreading of British political history. So, e.g., Sir James Bryce, *The American Commonwealth* (2 vols. New York, 1910), *1, 283, 28*: "It was natural that a foreign observer should underrate the executive character of the British parliament. . . . [The view of the framers of the American constitution] was tinged . . . by recollection of the influence exercised by King George the Third, an influence due to transitory causes . . ." It would seem, in light of the work of Namier and others, that Montesquieu, Blackstone, and the Founding Fathers were more accurate interpreters of the actual state of affairs in the Britain of their time than their nineteenth-century critics imagined.

13. I have always found it astonishing that the average American student, who seems reasonably satisfied with the Constitution

he lives under—at least, there are no signs of a serious movement
to scrap it—should acquiesce so meekly in the standard British
interpretation of eighteenth-century politics, which postulates
that anything tending to make the executive "responsible to" the
legislative branch is laudable and progressive, and that the contrary is bad and reactionary. In practice, of course, what has
happened in countries using the modern British system is that
the legislature ("the representatives of the people") has tended to
become a rubber stamp in the hands of the executive; this issue
has been raised in Canadian elections of the 1940's and 1950's.
Whether this tendency or the opposite is the more "democratic"
is a nice question. The issue between Montesquieu and Burke is
still extremely alive.

14. "In point of fact, Bute was the product of an unimpeach-
ably Whig upbringing": Sedgwick, *Letters from George III to
Lord Bute*, p. xliii. Lord North, as Keith Feiling says (*The Second
Tory Party*, London, 1938, p. 100), "was neither a Tory nor a follower of Bute."

15. "Toryism about 1750 was primarily the opposition of the
local rulers to central authority, and vanished wherever members
of that class entered the orbit of Government": Namier, *England
in the Age of the American Revolution*, p. 211. As Owen points
out (*The Rise of the Pelhams*, p. 67), this is to oversimplify, at
least for the period of the 1740's and earlier, when "not all country gentlemen were Tories, and not all Tories were country gentlemen." There were Tory members from the professional and
commercial classes, and there were Whig country gentlemen.
However, for the purposes of this study, the approximation is
close enough.

16. William Coxe, *Memoirs of . . . Sir Robert Walpole* (3
vols. London, 1798), *1*, 656.

17. Perhaps the division between what may be called the
"rural" and the "urban" outlook (not to be confused with the
contemporary terminology of "court" and "country," which mean
little more than "government" and "opposition"—though perhaps the choice of these names has more significance than is
generally conceded) is as important a fact in early eighteenth-
century politics as the traditional division of Whig and Tory. It
is tempting to postulate a fourfold political structure, analogous
to the familiar fourfold pattern ascribed to the modern American

political scene, with party lines in reality drawn as often horizontally as vertically.

	ENGLAND, 1715–1760		UNITED STATES, ca. 1945	
	Whig	*Tory*	*Democrat*	*Republican*
Urban (internationalist, commercial, "intellectual")	Carteret Pulteney Chesterfield Stanhope	Bolingbroke Wyndham	Northern (Roosevelt)	Eastern (Dewey)
Rural (isolationist, agrarian, traditionalist)	Townshend Walpole	Shippen; the "country gentlemen"	Southern (Byrnes)	Western (Taft)

On this, see Edward Wortley Montagu's interesting notes on the structure of politics at the accession of George I (in *The Letters and Works of Lady Mary Wortley Montagu*, ed. W. Moy Thomas, 2 vols. London, 1861, *1*, 135–41): "To understand the House of Commons it is necessary to know that there has [been] of late years always two sorts of Whigs and two of Tories. . . . The Country Whigs and Country Tories were not very different in their notions, and nothing has hindered them from joyning but the fear that each have of the others bringing in their whole party." For "Country Whigs and Country Tories" read "Southern Democrats and Western Republicans" and the last sentence becomes a useful guide to American politics of the 1940's and 1950's. Wortley Montagu's analysis concludes with the pregnant question, which he leaves unanswered, "WHAT IS A COUNTRY GENTLEMAN?"

18. These and the following figures are from Namier, "Country Gentlemen in Parliament," pp. 73–7.

19. *The Letters of Junius*, ed. John Wade (2 vols. London, 1890), *1*, 215 (Letter 23). George Lyttelton vouched for Egremont: "When Sir Thomas [Lyttelton] expressed uneasiness about the possibility of political contamination in travelling with the son of the Tory leader Sir William Wyndham, George hastened to assure him that Mr. Wyndham was 'a very good Whig, as well as a very pretty gentleman'": Rose Mary Davis, *The Good Lord Lyttelton* (Bethlehem, Pa., 1939), p. 26. Egremont's sister was married to George Grenville.

20. Richard Pares, *King George III and the Politicians* (Oxford, 1953), p. 55: "He [Pitt] seems to have been responsible—

even earlier than Burke—for the vogue of calling a bad whig a tory."

21. See Appendix B, p. 272, for a Tory rejection of Bolingbroke in 1741.

22. *Miscellanies, 1,* 172.

23. See p. 2, above. Johnson's complaint of the Tories' "frigid neutrality" on the matter of Wilkes is borne out by the vote on his expulsion, February 3, 1769: 24 knights of the shire voted for expulsion, 23 voted against, and 33 abstained from voting: Namier, "Country Gentlemen in Parliament," p. 74.

24. "Who were now the 'Tories'? The younger Pitt never used the name and after his death his successors went merely by that of 'Mr. Pitt's friends' (apparently George Canning was the only one who occasionally called himself a 'Tory')": Namier, "Monarchy and the Party System," p. 34.

25. *Life, 4,* 117 (italics mine).

26. *Life, 3,* 174.

27. J. B. Sledd and Gwin Kolb, "Johnson's Definitions of Whig and Tory," *PMLA, 67* (1952), 882–5; Benjamin and Dorothy G. Boyce, "Dr. Johnson's Definitions of 'Tory' and 'Whig,'" *Notes and Queries* (April 1953), pp. 160–1.

28. *Life, 1,* 296, 544. For the history of the Gower incident see pp. 38 ff.

29. *Life, 1,* 38; *4,* 39; *3,* 113; *1,* 43. Notice, too, the additions that Boswell makes to his original journal entry in 1763 when he incorporates it in the *Life* (1791):

> Johnson showed that in our constitution the King is the head, and that there is no power by which he can be tried; and therefore it is that redress is always to be had against oppression by punishing the immediate agents [*Boswell's London Journal,* ed. F. A. Pottle (New York, 1950), p. 292].

> JOHNSON. Sir, you are to consider, that in our constitution, according to its true principles, the King is the head; he is supreme; he is above every thing, and there is no power by which he can be tried. Therefore it is, Sir, that we hold the King can do no wrong; that whatever may happen to be wrong in government may not be above our reach, by being ascribed to Majesty. Redress is always to be had against oppression, by punishing the immediate agents [*Life, 1,* 423–4].

In the *Journal* the remark is a straightforward exposition, for Goldsmith's benefit, of the well-known legal principle that the Crown is exempt from prosecution, a point not of politics but of jurisprudence. In Boswell's elaboration in the *Life,* by the addition of such words as "supreme" and "Majesty," it sounds vaguely like a declaration of divine-right politics. To make the mythical Johnson qualify "constitution" by "according to its true principles" is a brilliant touch.

30. And therefore foreign to English party tradition. See Pares, *King George III and the Politicians,* p. 73, n. 1: "Thinking the English factions made a lot of fuss about little or nothing, they [the Scottish politicians] could have no scruples about selling their votes to the Government of the day, in return for personal advantages for themselves or sectional advantages for Scotland. Exactly the same thing would happen today if Great Britain were to join the U.S.A.: knowing and caring nothing about the differences between Democrats and Republicans, the British members of Congress would be, for a time, a disturbing and demoralizing force . . ."

31. "Poverty of sentiment in men who considered themselves to be company for the parlour, as he called it, was what he could not bear" (*Miscellanies, 1,* 293).

32. *Life, 2, 212.*

33. *Life, 1, 430.*

34. "Dr. Johnson said of himself, 'I am not uncandid, nor severe: I sometimes say more than I mean, in jest, and people are apt to think me serious' " (Murphy, in *Miscellanies, 1,* 357). "It is much to be wish'd, in justice to Dr. Johnson's character, that the many jocular and ironical speeches which have been recorded of him had been mark'd as such, for the information of those who were unacquainted with him" (Frances Reynolds, in *Miscellanies, 2,* 271).

35. Number 10.

36. *Such, Such Were the Joys* (New York, 1953), pp. 7, 9.

2. THE MIDLANDS BACKGROUND

1. *Life, 5, 61-2.*

2. *Works, 10,* 340 ("A Journey to the Western Islands of Scotland"); A. T. Hazen, "The Cancels in Johnson's *Journey,* 1775,"

Review of English Studies, 17 (1941), 201–3. Johnson's protest had no effect; the lead was removed and slate substituted.

3. *Life, 1,* 273. Croker asks plaintively, "What can this mean? What had the whigs to do with removing the smoky hearths from the centre of the grcat halls to a more commodious chimney at the side?" (ed. *Life,* 1831, *1,* 260, n. 2). For an answer, see pp. 18–20, above.

4. *Works, 10,* 501–2 ("Journey to the Western Islands").

5. I have drawn heavily on Stebbing Shaw, *History of the Antiquities of Staffordshire* (2 vols., London, 1798–1801) and Sir Josiah C. Wedgwood, *Parliamentary History of Staffordshire* (3 vols. 1919–33, in William Salt Archaeological Society, Collections for a History of Staffordshire) for the historical material in this chapter.

6. Shaw, *1,* 64; *2,* 3–4. See also D. H. Pennington and I. A. Roots, eds., *The Committee at Stafford, 1643–45: The Order Book of the Staffordshire County Committee,* Manchester, 1957.

7. Namier, *England in the Age of the American Revolution,* p. 230.

8. Wedgwood, *2,* 83–4, quoting from Proceedings before the Court of High Commission, January 1637/8.

9. *Life, 3,* 326. Aleyn Lyell Reade, *Gleanings, 3,* traces bonds of relationship between Johnson and the Skrymshers of Norbury. A cousin, Edwin Skrymsher of Aqualate, was Whig (i.e. Exclusionist) MP for Stafford in the Oxford Parliament of 1681; this may be thought to cancel out the significance for Johnson's politics that Reade seems to find (*3,* 23) in the fact that another Skrymsher was "nurse to James II." A second cousin of Johnson's on his mother's side, John Robbins, was Whig MP for Stafford 1747–54. The great fox-hunting squire Hugo Meynell, whom Reade also finds related to Johnson through the Skrymsher connection, was Whig MP for Lichfield in 1761, unseating his Tory opponent, John Levett, the mortgagee of Johnson's house (*Letters,* Nos. 19–22, 26; see below, p. 297, n. 35). Johnson's third pupil at Edial, "Mr. Offley," was a son of the Offley Crewe family (now Marquesses of Crewe), of whom it has been said that "they have been Whigs for three hundred years" (Wedgwood, *2,* 195).

10. Johnson's opinion of the great High Churchman is worth noting: in the *Life of Blake,* he records Blake's "disapprobation of Bishop Laud's violence and severity" (*Works, 4,* 359); and in

the *Life of Cheynel,* he pairs Laud with that acrimonious Puritan
—"Had Cheynel been equal to his adversary in greatness [i.e.
rank and power] and learning, it had not been easy to have found
either a more proper opposite; for they were both, to the last
degree, zealous, active, and pertinacious" (ibid., p. 504). Johnson
disliked "zealousness"—aggressiveness—in church dignitaries,
whether Anglican like Laud, Presbyterian like John Knox, or
Roman Catholic like Bishop Oviedo (see above, p. 70). The
churchmen he admired were gentle men like Chillingworth and
Baxter.

It is true that in *The Vanity of Human Wishes* Johnson does
justice to the pathos of Laud's downfall, praises his learning, and
reprobates those who put him to death. Yet erudition and martyr-
dom are not the sole qualifications for a good Archbishop of
Canterbury, as Johnson well knew, and, I think, assumed his
readers would know. Many "liberal" historians have agreed with
Johnson that Laud had great abilities, and have found it one of
the tragic ironies of history that the "parts" which at some other
time might have made him conspicuously successful in his office
were at this juncture fatal to him and his cause—a reflection con-
sonant with the thesis of Johnson's poem. And it is surely no
great compliment to Laud that Johnson casts him, along with his
fellow churchman Wolsey, as one of the chief exemplars of the
vanity of merely *human* wishes. One can feel sorry for Laud as a
human being—and for Charles I and Wolsey and Charles XII—
without necessarily approving their public activities; though
Macaulay seems never to have believed this possible. ("Art and
Genius," by the way, weep over Laud's tomb, not, as Macaulay
implies, because Johnson thought Laud personally well endowed
by them, but because he was a great benefactor of Oxford University, the home of Art and Genius.)

11. G. B. Hill, ed., *Lives of the Poets* (London, 1905), *1*, 214–15.

12. On August 24, Johnson wrote to Lucy Porter, "I suppose
you are all frighted at Lichfield and indeed the terrour has been
very general. . . . The [naval] battle, whenever it happens, will
be probably of greater consequence than any battle in our time.
If the French get the better we shall perhaps be invaded, and
must fight for ourselves upon our own ground" (*Letters*, No.
627.1).

13. *Lives of the Poets, 1, 215.*

14. Ibid., p. 157. "How is it that we hear the loudest yelps for liberty among the drivers of Negroes?" occurs in *Taxation No Tyranny*, 1775.

15. *Works, 4,* 503.

16. *Lives of the Poets, 1,* 108. My italics.

17. *Works, 4,* 518.

18. Ibid., p. 376.

19. *Lives of the Poets, 1,* 255, 274.

20. *Life, 4,* 235.

21. *Works, 9,* 173 ("Plan of an English Dictionary").

22. T. H. B. Oldfield, *History of the Boroughs of Great Britain* (3 vols., London, 1792), 2, 97.

23. Wedgwood, *Parliamentary History of Staffordshire, 3,* 212.

24. See Oldfield, 2, 95–6, for a detailed account of how this was done; also Walcott, *English Politics in the Early Eighteenth Century*, p. 15.

25. Wedgwood (2, xxx–xxxi), from whose tabulations this information is taken, supplies the party labels; in some of the earlier elections particularly, there may be a little doubt as to the exactness of the designation of "Whig" or "Tory." I have simplified the electoral history somewhat, omitting such interesting by-elections as that of 1718, when the Tory William Sneyd received 255 votes to 254 for the Whig Chetwynd. The Whig House of Commons of course seated Chetwynd on petition.

26. Ibid., 2, 221.

27. *Gentleman's Magazine* (1747), 383.

28. Wedgwood, 2, 253, from the Anson Papers. The *Morning Advertiser* (June 26, 1747) calls the Duke of Bedford's assailant a "country farmer."

29. Wedgwood, 2, 221.

30. Sir Lister Holt himself, whose candidacy the plaid-covered "Mobb" gathered to support, had furnished 250 mounts for the Duke of Cumberland's forces as they passed through Lichfield in 1745 on their way to engage the Pretender's army. "Indeed, there was scarce a man of any influence in the whole country, who did not exert himself on this occasion [to assist Cumberland]" (John Marchant, *The History of the Present Rebellion*, London, 1746, pp. 209–10). Marchant, to be sure, was a Government propagandist.

31. Wedgwood, 2, 155; Walcott, *English Politics*, p. 86, n. 1.

32. Gower was not, of course, one of the Lords Justices of the kingdom in 1740, as the *DNB* and other reference works report; see the official list in the *London Gazette*, May 10-13, 1740. He later held the appointment on various occasions as a consequence of his office of Lord Privy Seal.

33. Wedgwood, 2, 250.

34. Johnson's personal relations with Anson seem to have been amicable. Mrs. Thrale records a complimentary Latin epigram that Johnson improvised "at my Lord Anson's, when the owner with great politeness walked over the grounds with him" (Katharine Balderston, ed., *Thraliana*, 2 vols. Oxford, 1951, *1*, 213).

35. Wedgwood, 2, 250-66. Some extracts from letters in the Anson Papers given by Wedgwood provide details of interest to students of Johnson's connections:

> Lady Anson to Lord Anson, 7 October 1753: "Capt. Parker [?Porter] who came here with the Levetts upon the news of the opposition at Lichfield [in the forthcoming general election, where Thomas Anson was again a candidate] told Mr. Anson that he was convinced that young Levett was very well affected to the Government, and wanted only a satisfaction that he should be well received, etc., to make him quit his party on this occasion. . . . Upon this it was thought very worth while to know what terms he would think of asking.

John Levett, son of Theophilus Levett, town clerk of Lichfield—both were close friends of Johnson—later stood for Lichfield as a Tory in the election of 1761; but how uncertain his Toryism was is amply evident here. Johnson, reporting to Baretti (*Letters*, No. 142) on his visit to Lichfield in the winter of 1761-62, complained, "My only remaining friend has changed his principles, and was become the tool of the predominant faction." My guess is that the unidentified renegade was John Levett.

> Thomas Anson to Lady Anson, 9 October 1753: "Capt. Porter and Mr. Mence are now with me and inform that their [the Tories'] general style is to ask for Sir T[homas Gresley] only, or if they suspect them inclined to me, for him and me; always declaring a great regard for me and intimating that we shall be on very good terms.

Lady Anson to Thomas Anson, Admiralty, April 30 [1754]: "Capt. Porter has just been confirming me in the good opinion I have of your neighbours contracting to the compromise [concerning the election petition]."

Can there be any Captain Porter, connected with the Admiralty and capable of providing the Ansons with the local details of Lichfield politics, except Johnson's stepson, Jervis Henry Porter? If Porter was in the habit of acting as a political agent for the Gower-Anson group, the coolness between him and Johnson is still further explained.

36. Namier, "Monarchy and the Party System," p. 33.

37. It is hard to know what to do with the assertion "Johnson was a Jacobite," which still continues to be made. If "Jacobite" means one who seriously desired the restoration of the Stuart family to the British throne, there is no evidence for its application to Johnson at any time during his life. An examination of the entries in the index to the Hill-Powell edition of Boswell's *Life* under the heading "Johnson . . . Jacobite tendencies" is instructive. There are six of them; they refer to (1) his being touched by Queen Anne at the age of three; (2) the scantiness of his known writings in 1745–46, which Boswell says "some may fancifully imagine" was due to his "sympathetick anxiety" for Prince Charles Edward, but which Boswell attributes to his involvement with the *Dictionary;* (3) his having made the acquaintance of one William Drummond, who was "out" in the '45, but was later included in the general pardon; Johnson "esteemed him as a very worthy man"; (4) Johnson's assertion that "the family at present on the throne has now established as good a right as the former family," but that it is wrong to oblige people to take loyalty oaths on the subject (which is equivalent to indexing under "Communist tendencies" a report that someone in the 1950's objected to the administration of loyalty oaths on the subject of communism); (5) his comment at Derby, when Boswell remarked that the Highland army had reached that point in 1745, "It was a noble attempt"—"noble" referring, I take it, to the magnitude of the attempt, not to its political desirability; (6) a remark that Johnson, when writing the Parliamentary Debates, "always took care to put Sir Robert Walpole in the wrong, and to say every thing that he could against the electorate of Hanover"—as

though Pitt, Pulteney, and Lyttelton were not doing the same thing. If these constitute "Jacobite tendencies," then Johnson shared them with thousands of other perfectly loyal subjects of the Georges, including many good Whigs.

3. THE YOUNG JOHNSON

1. Johnson to Baretti, 21 Dec. 1762 (*Letters*, No. 147). The couplet is Johnson's contribution to Goldsmith's *The Traveller*.
2. *Gleanings, 10, 3*.
3. Sir John Hawkins, *Life of Samuel Johnson* (London, 1787), p. 3.
4. *Life, 1, 37*. Boswell quotes an extremely cryptic remark of Johnson's, within the framework of much Boswellian ornamentation: "Had not his own father complied with the requisition of government (as to which he once observed to me, when I pressed him upon it, 'That, Sir, he was to settle with himself'), he would probably have thought more unfavourably of a Jacobite who took the oaths" (*Life, 2, 322*).
5. Tyers, in *Miscellanies, 2, 339*; *Poetical Works of Anna Seward* (3 vols. London, 1810), *1*, lxx.
6. *The Works of Samuel Johnson* (New Haven, 1958–), *1*, 3–4.
7. It is wrong to insist, with Croker and others (*Life, 1, 36*, n. 5), that "personal animosity" was the only or even the chief reason for the violence of Johnson's attacks on excise. The second part of the definition in the *Dictionary* has not been sufficiently noticed: "a hateful tax levied upon commodities, and *adjudged, not by the common judges of property, but wretches hired by those to whom excise is paid.*" The embodiment of the principle of *droit administratif* in the excise regulations was the subject of much serious political debate throughout the century (as it still is in Britain, in connection with quasijudicial powers granted to other administrative bodies). As late as 1769, Blackstone could write,

When we again consider the various and almost innumerable branches of the revenue which may be . . . the objects of this summary and arbitrary jurisdiction, we shall find that the *power* of those officers of the crown over the property of the people is increased to a very formidable height. . . . The rigour and arbitrary proceedings of excise-laws seem hardly

compatible with the temper of a free nation. . . . A man
may be convicted in two days time in the penalty of many
thousand pounds by two commissioners or justices of the
peace; to the total exclusion of the trial by jury, and disregard of the common law [*Commentaries*, 2d ed. Vol. *4*, 278;
1, 318].

Johnson, then, like many others, was objecting to excise on
Whiggish, or Jeffersonian, principles. Excisemen and their right
of search and entry continued to be a sore point until much
later, as readers of Burns will be aware. In 1782, the Whig administration of Rockingham, Fox, and Burke disfranchised all
excise and customs officials, as being too much subject to the influence of the Crown.

Excise duties were first imposed in Great Britain in 1643, under
the Parliamentarian regime, and were generally associated with
Whiggish governments. Nevertheless it was an act passed by a
Tory parliament and introduced by Harley (9 Anne cap. 11) under which the prosecution of Michael Johnson was authorized.

8. *Life, 5*, 328.

9. See below, Appendix C, for a discussion of Johnson's views
on economics.

10. *Life, 1*, 246; 2, 323.

11. "Temperamentally, he is always in revolt": B. H. Bronson,
Johnson Agonistes (Cambridge, 1946), p. 44.

12. *Works, 10*, 230 (review of Soame Jenyns, *Free Enquiry into
the Origin of Evil*). The reader should look at the whole of the
magnificent passage, if he is not familiar with it. Johnson's definition of "the poor" in his *Dictionary* is interesting—"Those who
are in the lowest rank of the community; those who cannot subsist
but by the charity of others; but it is sometimes used with laxity
for any not rich."

13. *Gleanings, 10*, 195.

14. *Life, 2*, 261.

15. *Works* (1958), *1*, 6. The general question of Johnson's religious position is far too large and involved to try to expound
here. Much work needs to be done on it. As with his political
position, discussion of it has been confused by questions of
terminology—the expression "High Church" during the last
three centuries seems to have borne at least as many different

significations as "Tory." Nor must the term "Evangelicalism" be interpreted narrowly. For instance, Geoffrey Faber (*Oxford Apostles,* London, 1933) emphasizes the indebtedness of Newman's later career to his strongly Evangelical background; like Johnson and Wesley, Newman was converted in youth by a reading of Law's *Serious Call* (Faber, chap. *1,* sec. 3). Another involved question the student of Johnson should be aware of is that of the relationship and rivalry between the Evangelical and the rationalist movements for social reform, in the late eighteenth and early nineteenth centuries. The classic statement of the claims of the rationalist or Benthamite school to superior effectiveness is found at the beginning of Leslie Stephen's *The English Utilitarians.* Yet the first James Stephen was one of the pillars of the Clapham sect; Noel Annan (*Leslie Stephen,* London, 1948) gives an interesting account of the evolution of this line of English reformers from Clapham to Bloomsbury. These intellectual relationships are complex, and one should not allow them to be falsified by presuppositions based on terminology. It seems clear, for instance, that Johnson can be shown to be more closely connected, in the history of the transmission of political and social ideas and attitudes, with such a modern "liberal" as, say, E. M. Forster, than with the essentially Whig ideological background of such a modern "conservative" as Sir Winston Churchill.

16. G. R. Balleine, *A History of the Evangelical Party in the Church of England* (London, 1908), p. 4.

17. Ibid., pp. 69, 149.

18. Another interesting figure is Lord Cairns, Disraeli's Lord Chancellor and nearly his successor as leader of the Conservative Party.

> The coldest of men must have somewhere a fount of emotion, and Cairns found his in evangelical religion. The earnest Nonconformist, who worshipped Mr. Gladstone and identified godliness with Liberalism, was amazed to find the Tory Lord Chancellor, hymn-book in hand, on the platforms of Messrs Moody and Sankey. Members of the Bar, desirous of rising in their profession, used to attend assiduously at religious meetings, in the hope of catching the Chancellor's eye. From his first day at the Bar he refused to work on the Sabbath, and in the stress of his busiest years he rose every

morning early for an hour's prayer and Bible-reading. His intellect—the greatest pure intellect of his day—accepted and was happy in the simple faith of his childhood [John Buchan, *Some Eighteenth Century Byways* (London, 1908), p. 247].

19. *Life, 1,* 68.

20. *Works* (1958), *1,* 10; *Life, 1,* 38, 67.

21. Ibid., *2,* 14.

22. *Miscellanies, 1,* 163.

23. *Life, 1,* 39.

24. Ibid., p. 44.

25. See E. L. McAdam, Jr., *Dr. Johnson and the English Law,* Syracuse, N.Y., 1951.

26. *Life, 3,* 310.

27. *Life, 1,* 73-4. Clifford, *Young Sam Johnson,* p. 337, n. 26.

28. *Life, 1,* 74.

29. Steevens, in *Miscellanies, 2,* 312–13.

30. *Life, 1,* 79.

31. T. H. B. Oldfield, *Representative History of Great Britain and Ireland* (6 vols., London, 1816), *4,* 496–9.

32. *The Post Boy,* June 2–4, quoted by J. L. Clifford, *Young Sam Johnson* (New York, 1955), p. 104. The Close is under episcopal, not civic, jurisdiction.

33. Hill, *Lives of the Poets, 2,* 21 ("Life of Smith").

34. Wedgwood, *Parliamentary History of Staffordshire, 2,* 253, from the Anson Papers.

35. *Miscellanies, 2,* 208.

36. Ibid.

37. *Life, 1,* 83, n. 3.

38. "Reflections on Samuel Johnson: Two Recent Books and Where They Lead," *Journal of English and Germanic Philology, 47* (1948), 86.

39. Johnson's fairly drastic cutting and condensation of some parts of Le Grand's text should be kept in mind; the serious student of the work will compare it with the French original as he goes along. In one place (pp. 248–9 of Le Grand), Johnson's condensation has obscured the probable source of the name of one of the main characters of *Rasselas:* Le Grand mentions a king of Abyssinia named "Imrah" ("Imrach" in the index), and

another named "Ighum-Amlac." Though they do not appear in
Johnson's text, they are no doubt the joint ancestor of Rasselas's
mentor, Imlac. Joachim Le Grand, *Relation historique d'Abis-
sinie*, Paris, 1728; Johnson's translation, *A Voyage to Abyssinia*,
London, 1735.

40. Johnson, *Voyage*, p. vii. Lobo's countrymen who amuse the
reader with romantic absurdities would be, says C. D. Ley in the
preface to *Portuguese Voyages, 1498–1663* (London, 1947), such
earlier writers as Mendes Pinto, whom Johnson would have encountered in Purchas. Johnson goes on to praise Lobo because
"he meets with no basilisks that destroy with their eyes, his
crocodiles devour their prey without tears, and his cataracts fall
from the rock without deafening the neighbouring inhabitants."
These are not merely rhetoric, but references to actual passages in
Lobo (pp. 19, 104, and 101 of the 1735 ed.) Johnson omits to
mention, however, that both Lobo and Le Grand confirm the
existence of the unicorn (pp. 53, 232), though Le Grand goes so
far as to doubt the pharmaceutical efficacy of his horn. Johnson
translates the circumstantial description of the unicorn without
comment.

41. "The initiative in the Roman Catholic missions to Abyssinia was taken, not by Rome, but by Portugal, as an incident in
the struggle with the Mussulmans for the command of the trade
route to India by the Red Sea" (A. J. Butler, in *Encyclopædia
Britannica*, 11th ed., "Abyssinian Church").

42. Robert Bracey, O.P., "Dr. Johnson's First Book," in *Eighteenth Century Studies and Other Papers* (London, 1925), pp. 26–7:
"Possibly Johnson was influenced by Lobo's work in other and
higher directions. For the Catholic religion is seen in Lobo's
Travels in a very attractive light, its missionaries are zealous for
their faith, happy in their setting forth of its doctrines and practice. Was it not perhaps because of his early association with
Lobo that Dr. Johnson became throughout his life distinguished
above all his contemporaries for his kindly, appreciative, and intelligent attitude towards Catholicism?" Commentators seem
generally to have ignored the energetic anti-Catholicism of the
preface. See John Hennig, "Young Johnson and the Jesuits," *The
Month, 182* (1946), 443: "Johnson then contrasts Lobo's and Le
Grand's soberness with the 'sanguinary zeal' of other missionaries." This is a misreading of Johnson's text. In the first place,

Le Grand was not a missionary; in the second place, although Johnson praises Lobo's "soberness" as a *narrator*, he by no means exempts him from his general charge against the Jesuits of oppressive practices as *missionaries*.

43. *Sale Catalogue of Dr. Johnson's Library* (facsimile, London, 1925), Item 587.

44. The only printed version of it is in *Poems*, pp. 336–77.

45. B. H. Bronson, *Johnson Agonistes* (Cambridge, 1946), p. 141.

46. In February 1738, when Walpole saw that the Spanish war demanded by the opposition was inevitable, he asked Parliament for authority to maintain an army of 17,400 men. The opposition immediately moved that the number be reduced to 12,000. The following year the government asked for an annual subsidy of £70,000 to Denmark, which was to provide Great Britain with 6,000 troops for its defense. A large number of the opposition had at this time temporarily seceded from Parliament in protest, so that the measure was easily passed.

47. Boswell states (*Life, 1,* 197) that Johnson himself told him of Yonge's authorship. See, however, *Poems*, p. 247 n.

48. This statement is not intentionally perverse; I am trying to emphasize that we have *no* real evidence of Johnson's specific views, if any, on national politics before the publication of *London* in 1738. Johnson's opinion of Walpole, as I try to show below, did a *volte-face* between 1739 and 1742; why not also between 1736 and 1738? Walmesley, who recommended the play, Garrick, who produced and played the lead in it, and Yonge, who furnished at least part of the epilogue, were the staunchest of Walpolian Whigs, and hardly likely to give such countenance to anti-Whig propaganda.

49. *Poems,* p. 352.

50. *Johnson Agonistes,* p. 141.

51. *Poems,* p. 236.

52. Whether there is any significance in the fact the final version of *Irene* omits the description of the pastoral life, I do not know. If it be suggested that the omission indicates that Johnson's thinking became less Whiggish between 1736 and 1749, it can be urged on the other hand that "where King and People own one common law" in the draft is strengthened to "where common Laws *restrain* the Prince and Subject."

53. *An Essay Concerning the True Original, Extent, and End of Civil Government*, chap. 5, secs. 27, 34. I do not think that Max Weber uses the latter, extremely pertinent statement in *The Protestant Ethic and the Spirit of Capitalism*, New York, 1930. Weber's thesis is of course highly relevant to any discussion of eighteenth-century political ideas in general, and Johnson's in particular (though H. R. Trevor-Roper's reservations about it should be noted—see above, p. 285, n. 2).

54. *Essay*, chap. 19, sec. 223.

55. Samuel Kliger, *The Goths in England* (Cambridge, Mass., 1952), provides an excellent collection of references, although his interpretation of them in terms of eighteenth-century party structure is unsatisfactory.

56. *History of England*, chaps. 1, and 3 (appendix i). The passage in *Irene* is not so anachronistic as Nichol Smith and McAdam assert. The limited nature of the English monarchy existed, according to eighteenth- and nineteenth-century historians, during and long before the Wars of the Roses. Thus Macaulay (*History of England*, chap. 1): "The King could not legislate without the consent of his Parliament . . . could impose no taxes without the consent of his Parliament . . . was bound to conduct the executive administration according to the laws of the land. . . . No candid Tory will deny that these principles had, five hundred years ago, acquired the authority of fundamental rules." Indeed, the Wars of the Roses themselves originated, in effect, in the action by Parliament, fifty years before the time of *Irene*, of deposing Richard II and choosing Henry IV as king. Macaulay, a few pages later, equates the events of 1399 and 1689. There is no reason to think Hume or Johnson would have disagreed with this interpretation.

There *is* a genuine anachronism in the passage in *Irene*— "Where circulating Pow'r / Flows through each member of th' embodied state." The first, and only, critic to take exception to it was, amusingly enough, Samuel Johnson—"A late writer has put Harvey's doctrine of the circulation of the blood into the mouth of a Turkish statesman, who lived near two centuries before it was known even to philosophers or anatomists" (*Rambler*, No. 140).

57. *Essay*, chap. 7, sec. 92.

4. LONDON AND WALPOLE

1. "Johnson in Grub Street," in *An Eighteenth-Century Gentleman and Other Essays* (Cambridge, 1930), pp. 44–5.
2. *Life, 3,* 19.
3. Ibid., *1,* 116.
4. *Works, 4,* 524 ("Life of Cave").
5. Clifford, *Young Sam Johnson,* p. 190.
6. The phrases are those of the psychiatrist Edward Bergler, "Samuel Johnson's 'Life of the Poet Richard Savage' . . ." *American Imago, 4* (1947), 42–63.
7. *The Endless Adventure* (3 vols. London, 1930–35), *1,* 151–8. Oliver's book has been treated somewhat severely by professional historians; but as biography it has certain virtues that should not be overlooked.
8. *Memoirs of the Life and Administration of Sir Robert Walpole . . .* (3 vols. London, 1798), *1,* 757. Walpole's latest biographer, J. H. Plumb, (*Sir Robert Walpole,* London, 1956–), Vol. *1,* is no less susceptible to his charm: "The more I have come to know this great man, the stronger has my admiration grown. . . . He had a heightened awareness both of the world and of men. From this sprang both his exquisite taste and his finesse in human relations. He could live outside his own character. He possessed *empathy,* the quality to get, as it were, into the skin of other human beings, to feel with them" (p. xi).
9. C. B. Realey, *The Early Opposition to Sir Robert Walpole* (Lawrence, Kansas, 1931), p. 44.
10. *Poetical Works of Richard Savage* (London, 1791), *1,* 151–58.
11. Ibid., pp. 109–21.
12. *Miscellanies, 1,* 371. This is Murphy's version of the story. Hawkins makes it take place in St. James's Square.
13. Hawkins, *Life of Johnson,* p. 60.
14. *Life, 2,* 221.
15. See p. 125.
16. Some of this stems from Juvenal, of course. It is an awkward consideration, in any attempt to use the satire of Pope, Swift, and Johnson as evidence of the political climate of the time, that satire is a *genre,* and if you are going to write satire, you must find something to satirize. Since satire was fashionable

in the eighteenth century, every budding poet, whatever his politics, wrote satire and found the state of England deplorable. A few years before *London* appeared, a poet had written

> Turn ages o'er,
> When wanted Britain bright examples more?
> Her learning and her genius too, decays,
> And dark and cold are her declining days.
> As if men now were of another cast,
> They meanly live on alms of ages past.

One might easily set this down as a fine specimen of "the gloom of the Tory satirists" and deduce that the poet was another violent member of the opposition, if one did not know that he was Edward Young (*The Universal Passion*, Satire 3), an unswerving, and pensioned, supporter of the government; the poem ends, in fact, with a glowing tribute to Walpole.

Nevertheless, there is a better case for specific political animus in *London* than in much contemporary satire. Nichol Smith and McAdam have carefully collated the poem with Oldham's version of the same satire of Juvenal, and shown what a great deal of topical political reference Johnson has furnished. "What was [in Oldham's hands] preeminently a social satire . . . becomes in Johnson's hand largely a political satire" (*Poems*, p. 2).

17. In *Rex v. Francklin*, 1731 (*English Reports* 93, Sess. Cas. 220), the printer of the *Craftsman* was tried for seditious libel before a special, rather than a common, jury, requested by the Crown; Walpole's law officers made of the special jury a tool to help them get convictions in such cases. Members of a special jury are chosen from a panel of individuals having substantial property qualifications. The political aspects of the special jury were emphasized as recently as 1947 in the much-publicized case of *Laski v. The Newark Advertiser*, when a special jury found the newspaper not guilty of libel in reporting that the Chairman of the British Labour Party in an election campaign address had advocated the use of violence (see, e.g., Kingsley Martin's *Harold Laski*, London, 1953).

18. That is the traditional expansion of the name in the couplet

> Despise a fool in half his pension dressed
> And strive in vain to laugh at H——y's jest.

I have come to have serious doubts about its accuracy, however. Johnson had "an avowed and scarcely limited partiality for all who bore the name or boasted the alliance of an Aston or a Hervey" (Mrs. Thrale, in *Miscellanies, 1,* 254); I do not know that Lord Hervey was noted for jesting or gaudy apparel; his emoluments as Vice-Chamberlain and later Lord Privy Seal were hardly a "pension"; and not even Pope called Hervey a fool, for he was very far from being one. And was the Thales of the poem likely to be so often in the company of this high officer of the Court, the assiduous attendant of Queen Caroline, that the necessity of laughing at his jests would become a hardship?

It seems to me much more likely that Johnson expected the word to be read "Henley." The Reverend John Henley—"Orator" Henley—was the public buffoon of the time—"the Zany of his age," Pope calls him. An account of his antics is found in Isaac D'Israeli, *Calamities of Authors,* London, 1867. In 1737 Henley was writing *The Hyp-Doctor* in support of Walpole, and receiving a small stipend from the government for doing so. The purpose of the significantly titled *Hyp-Doctor* was "to cheer the spirits of the people by ridiculing the gloomy forebodings of Amhurst's *Craftsman.*" Henley's jests, then, would be a very proper subject to be attacked in a poem concerned to propagate the *Craftsman's* gloomy forebodings. The couplet seems to me altogether more appropriate to such an individual than to the sophisticated and fastidious Lord Hervey, and, the purpose of Henley's jests being what it was, the reading gives the couplet more political point.

19. "Licens'd" was a later substitution for the "silenc'd" of the original edition. There has been some speculation about why the change was made, but no one seems to have observed that *"warbling* eunuchs fill a *silenc'd* stage" is a howler in the same class as "kill the yet unanimated young," which Johnson laughed at in one of his boyish poems.

20. Hill says, "That he wrote the introduction . . . can scarcely be doubted" (*Life, 1,* 502). Medford Evans, "Johnson's Debates in Parliament" (dissertation, Yale, 1933) and Benjamin Hoover, *Johnson's Parliamentary Reporting* (Berkeley and Los Angeles, 1953) seem to concur. Hoover reprints the whole piece (pp. 172–81).

21. In quoting from the *Gentleman's Magazine* throughout this work, I have generally reduced capitalization, and sometimes spelling and punctuation, to modern practice.

22. Coxe, *Walpole*, *1*, 411–12. In the early nineteenth century annual parliaments and the payment of members were regarded as radical, "leftist" measures; they formed two of the points of the People's Charter of the 1840's. The writer of *Sentiments of a Tory*, 1741 (see below, Appendix B), gives a long and reasoned argument for the restoration of the custom of paying members; he seems to feel that it is the cure for most of the Parliamentary evils of the day.

23. *Works*, *14*, 1–36.

24. I should like to repeat that this deprecatory attitude toward the character and abilities of monarchs generally is not, so far as I can tell, merely a temporary aberration of Johnson's, connected with his "Whiggism" of the moment. Other expressions of it occur as late as his life of Frederick the Great (1756) (see above, p. 173); and even in connection with George III, of whom he felt "inclined to hope great things," he believed "it would be unreasonable to expect much from the immaturity of juvenile years, and the ignorance of princely education" (*Letters*, No. 138, June 10, 1761). I know of no evidence, from any period of his life, of an admiration for monarchs generically. They were necessary for the existence of monarchical government, which Johnson regarded as an effective form of administration, but one sometimes feels that he regarded them as necessary evils (see below, p. 317, n. 29, and p. 324). He was certainly no royalist in the sense that Burke, Boswell, and T. S. Eliot proclaim themselves to be.

25. In 1733, Walpole had moved for the alienation of £500,000, to be used for current expenditure, from the sinking fund set up to amortize the national debt. Sir John Barnard declared "that the author of such an expedient must expect the curses of posterity" (Coxe, *1*, 368). Hence, perhaps, the "concern for posterity" that Johnson makes so much of in *Marmor* and the *Vindication*.

26. *Works*, *14*, 37–58.

27. 10 Geo. II cap. 28. The licensing provisions are now incorporated in the Theatre Act, 1843. The licensers are still active: the London newspapers report the prosecution of an unlicensed

performance in which, among other things, an actor is charged with having burlesqued the oratory of Sir Winston Churchill (*Daily Telegraph,* April 17, 1958).

28. See the essays by Caroline Spurgeon and C. E. Vaughan in *Cambridge History of English Literature, 9,* 58–9; *10,* 327–8.

29. Coxe, *1,* 532.

30. *Samuel Johnson* (New York, 1944), pp. 66, 64.

31. Bronson, *Johnson Agonistes,* p. 15.

32. *Works, 4,* 321–8.

33. E. L. McAdam, Jr., "Johnson's Lives of Sarpi, Blake, and Drake," *PMLA, 57* (1943), 466–76.

34. Suarez, *De Legibus,* and Mariana, *De Rebus Hispaniæ,* are listed in the Sale Catalogue of Johnson's library (Items 348, 489).

35. See Mark Pattison, *Isaac Casaubon* (Oxford, 1892), pp. 308–41; D. H. Willson, *King James VI and I,* London, 1956.

36. *The Divine Right of Kings* (Cambridge, 1914), p. 180. See, e.g., John Nalson, *The Common Interest of King and People: Shewing . . . That Absolute, Papal, and Presbyterian Popular Supremacy Are Utterly Inconsistent with Prerogative, Property, and Liberty,* London, 1678. Louis Bredvold, *The Intellectual Milieu of John Dryden* (Ann Arbor, Michigan, 1934), p. 346, writes: "The Jesuits were . . . as we have seen Dryden pointing out, at one with the English Whigs and Dissenters in political theory."

37. *Encyclopædia Britannica,* 11th ed., "James I."

5. THE PARLIAMENTARY DEBATES

1. The Seventh Session of the Eighth Parliament of Great Britain, November 18, 1740, to April 25, 1741; the First Session of the Ninth Parliament, December 1, 1741, to July 15, 1742; the Second Session of the Ninth Parliament, November 16, 1742, to April 21, 1743. In "Some Notes on Johnson and the *Gentleman's Magazine,*" *PMLA, 74* (1959), 75–84, I venture to attribute to Johnson the long and brilliant series of debates on the removal of Hanoverian troops in the British service, *Gentleman's Magazine,* May to December and Supplement, 1744. But these need further study.

2. Three studies of the "Debates" have been made. That by

Birkbeck Hill appears as Appendix A to Vol. *1* of the *Life*, pp. 501–12. There are also two doctoral dissertations: Medford Evans, "Johnson's Debates in Parliament," Yale, 1933; and Benjamin B. Hoover, *Samuel Johnson's Parliamentary Reporting*, Berkeley and Los Angeles, 1953.

3. The question is thoroughly discussed by Evans and Hoover. Most modern historians seem perfectly willing to quote the Johnsonian "Debates" as accurately representing the views of the speakers: see, e.g., John B. Owen, *The Rise of the Pelhams* (London, 1957), and Wolfgang Michael's remarks on the subject, *Englische Geschichte im achtzehnten Jahrhundert, 4,* 107, and *5, passim.*

4. Though of course the modern Parliamentary reporter does a considerable amount of work in correcting grammar, repairing sentence structure, removing solecisms, and generally "improving" the bare words of the original.

5. My page counts are only rough ones, consisting in subtracting the number of a page on which a report begins from that on which it ends, and making no allowance for fractions of pages.

6. *Life, 1,* 506.

7. *Gentleman's Magazine* (March 1742), pp. 117–28; (April 1742), pp. 171–9. The only adequate text of the "Debates" is that of the *Gentleman's Magazine* itself; the later reprints are incomplete and untrustworthy. My quotations follow the *Magazine* text, reducing capital letters and sometimes spelling and punctuation to modern practice, and translating Lilliputian names ("Walpole" instead of "Walelop"). In subsequent quotations, references to number and page of the *Magazine* will be given at the end of each excerpt. "Supp." means the supplementary issue of the *Magazine* that followed the December issue.

The Mutiny Act is, or was until very recently, in British countries, the annual act whereby Parliament authorizes the maintenance of the regular army and provides for its payment and discipline. The force of such acts was specifically limited to one year at a time, that Parliament might keep a close check on the Crown's use of a standing army. The classic discussion is Macaulay's (*History of England,* chap. 11).

8. *Life, 1,* 506.

9. *Miscellanies, 1,* 379. The story is Murphy's. If the remark

were to be taken seriously, it would be a very puzzling one. After all, most of the opponents of Walpole were Whigs, too. The part played by Tories in the Johnsonian "Debates" is very small.

10. See Hoover, pp. 58 ff. The motion was lost, by a vote of 108 to 59. A debate on a subsidiary motion then commenced.

11. *Life of Johnson*, p. 100.

12. "Another place" is the Commons' euphemism for the House of Lords. The "little ornament" is the star of the Order of the Garter, normally reserved for royalty and the higher ranks of the peerage. For some centuries, Walpole's was the only one granted to a commoner, though in recent times it has been conferred on Sir Winston Churchill and Sir Anthony Eden.

13. *Walpole, 1,* 657–69; Hoover, pp. 96–103.

14. Coxe, *1,* 656.

15. But J. H. Plumb has recently cast some most revealing light on these incidents. He shows (*Sir Robert Walpole, 1,* 254–6) that though Walpole, in 1717, was nominally in charge of the impeachment proceedings against Oxford, he and Townshend deliberately sabotaged them, in order to embarrass their leader, Stanhope, with whom they were engaged in a struggle for power. Walpole's rescue of Oxford would be remembered with gratitude by the Harley family and the older Tories, and they now reciprocated.

To those in the know, the proceedings in 1741 must have seemed hilariously funny—or would have, if Walpole's head and fortune had not been at stake: the Whigs demanding vengeance on Walpole for his vindictiveness against the Tory Oxford, and Walpole unable to defend himself by telling the truth—that he had, on the contrary, saved Oxford's neck by double-crossing the Whigs; Oxford's heir now rescuing Walpole by way of repayment, equally unable to tell the truth—which would have been fatal to Walpole—and instead justifying his action as a Christian turning of the other cheek. But probably the younger and less sophisticated participants in these transactions, such as Lyttelton and Johnson himself, were unaware of this secret history, and their interpretation of them in terms of high morality was sincere.

16. *Gentleman's Magazine* (April 1743), 181. It is printed continuously with the preceding debate and report of the division; so if we assume these to have been Johnson's we seem to have no

reason for denying this to him. I give the exact text, as it has not been reprinted before. The indicated ellipsis stands for a reference to an earlier number of the *Magazine,* where lists of the Tory members voting for Walpole or abstaining were published. For the identification of the pamphlets referred to, see Appendix B, p. 272.

17. Johnson's frequent expressions of dislike, throughout Boswell's *Life,* of what may be called "loyalty oaths" also become more meaningful to the reader if he considers modern analogues.

18. Hoover, p. 130.

19. R. C. Jebb, in *Encyclopædia Britannica,* 11th ed., "Thucydides."

20. *Life of Johnson,* p. 514.

21. *Miscellanies,* 2, 309.

22. For a competent treatment of these events see Owen, *Rise of the Pelhams.*

23. *Life, 5,* 339.

24. Hill, ed., *Lives of the Poets, 2,* 393.

25. Ibid., p. 392.

26. Ibid., p. 363.

27. Ibid., pp. 360–1.

28. Ibid., p. 433.

6. THE SECONDARY LEGISLATOR

1. Vol. *13* (1743), preface.

2. *Works, 9,* 419.

3. Ibid., pp. 350–1.

4. Ibid., *10,* 145 ("Observations on the [Present] State of Affairs").

5. Butterfield, *George III, Lord North, and the People* (London, 1949), pp. 8–9.

6. Pp. 128–31. The attribution sometimes made to Johnson of another piece on the subject of the *Memoirs,* in the *Gentleman's Magazine* for March, April, and May, 1742, is erroneous: see Jacob Leed in *Notes and Queries* (May 1957), p. 210.

7. *Letters,* No. 15. Benjamin Hoover's statement (*Johnson's Parliamentary Reporting,* p. 158) that this letter refers to the publication of Anchitell Grey's *Debates in the House of Commons* cannot be right, if, as seems most probable, Letters 16 and

18 are connected with Letter 15. In these Johnson asks for material dealing with events of the reign of George I, whereas Grey's debates run from 1667 to 1694.

8. *Works, 14,* 63–4. See p. 111, above.

9. *A Sermon Preached at the Cathedral Church of St. Paul . . . by the Honourable and Reverend Henry Hervey Aston . . .* London, 1745. The attribution to Johnson was made by L. F. Powell in *The Times,* November 25, 1938. The sermon has been reprinted in facsimile, under the editorship of J. L. Clifford, by the Augustan Reprint Society, Los Angeles, 1955.

10. See the Thirty-Eighth Article of Religion, "Of Christian men's Goods, which are not common."

11. This was apparently a standard argument. See the Whig Bishop Burnet's *Exposition of the Thirty-Nine Articles* (Edinburgh, 1745, 1st ed. 1699), p. 587. See p. 76, above, where Locke says virtually the same thing.

12. *Works, 9,* 419. In the Sale Catalogue of Johnson's library there are listed editions of Locke; Hooker; and (No. 216) Fortescue, *De Legibus Angliæ.*

13. *Lives of the Poets, 2,* 233.

14. *Works, 9,* 223–4 ("Preface to the Dictionary").

15. Ibid., p. 173 ("Plan"); p. 198 ("Preface"). The reference to Hooker is no doubt to Bk. IV, chap. 14, of the *Ecclesiastical Polity:* "Laws, as all other things human, are many times full of imperfection, and that which is supposed behooveful unto men, proveth oftentime most pernicious. . . . But true withal it is, that alteration, though it be from worse to better, hath in it inconveniences, and those weighty."

16. *Works, 9,* 226 ("Preface"). My italics.

17. James Sledd and Gwin Kolb, *Dr. Johnson's Dictionary* (Chicago, 1955); "Johnson's Dictionary and Lexicographical Tradition," *Modern Philology, 50* (1953), 171–94.

18. Lane Cooper, "Dr. Johnson on Oats and Other Grains," *PMLA, 52* (1937), 785–802.

19. *Commentaries* (Oxford, 1766), *1,* 318. See p. 299, n. 7, above.

20. P. 14.

21. Noted by W. K. Wimsatt in *Modern Language Review, 43* (1948), 78–80.

22. See my article, "Johnson's Contributions to the *Literary Magazine,*" *Review of English Studies,* new ser. 7 (1956), 367–92.

23. *Works*, *14*, 216–19.
24. *Literary Magazine*, *1* (May–June 1756), 57–64.
25. *Works*, *14*, 232–8.
26. *Literary Magazine*, *1* (October–November 1756), 340(bis)–51.
27. *Life*, *2*, 125–6.
28. *Works*, *10*, 158–82.
29. It has been suggested to me that Johnson's "objectivity," and his rudimentary economic determinism, have parallels among the mercantilist writers on economics in the seventeenth century, and in the writings of such *philosophes* as Raynal and Voltaire.
30. For some account of Johnson's views on economics see Appendix C, p. 280.
31. *Works*, *10*, 145–57.
32. Ibid., *14*, 227–31. Reprinted in *PMLA*, *65* (1950), 427–35.
33. *Works*, "*15*" (1789), 454–69.
34. Ibid., *4*, 531–80.
35. Ibid., *10*, 185–94.
36. *Gentleman's Magazine* (October 1785), 764–5.
37. *British Magazine*, *1* (January 1760), 37–39. *Works*, *10*, 185–94, and subsequent reprints omit the important word "economic" in the phrase "obliges every man to regard his own economic character."
38. Pp. 150, 153.
39. *Works*, *10*, 283–85.
40. Ibid., *14*, 244–8. The satire, in the last paragraph, is against the Cartesian theory that the lower animals are automata and only man is possessed of sensibility. The doctrine is also satirized in *Idler*, No. 10.
41. Chap. 28.
42. *Letters*, No. 147 (December 21, 1762).
43. *Essays* (1903), *1*, 386 (review of Croker's Boswell).
44. *Gentleman's Magazine* (October 1760), 453–6; *Works*, *14*, 330–41.

7. THE REIGN OF GEORGE III

1. *Letters*, No. 138.
2. *Works*, *10*, 31 (*The False Alarm*).

3. *Life, 4,* 165.

4. *The Vicar of Wakefield,* chap. 19.

5. See above, p. 10.

6. *Works, 10,* 33 (*The False Alarm*).

7. *Letters,* No. 201. For an account of the election see W. R. Ward, *Georgian Oxford* (Oxford, 1958), chap. 14.

8. *Life, 2,* 353.

9. Ibid., p. 135, n. 3.

10. *Works, 10,* 56.

11. *Life, 2,* 147; *5,* 269.

12. Ibid., *4,* 139. It is a pity to spoil Boswell's story, but the thanks Johnson gave on March 20 were more likely for a *Mens sedatior* (see *Works,* 1958, *1,* 315, entry for March 19).

13. *Life, 4,* 174.

14. Ibid., *2,* 223, see also p. 348; *3,* 45; *5,* 36. For an estimate of Burke's political morality from a Johnsonian point of view (with an exposition of the passage quoted here), see G. M. Young, "Burke" in *Today and Yesterday* (London, 1958), pp. 83–109.

15. He said that the mob was right in shouting "No Fox" in the presence of the king, but then unexpectedly changed his mind and agreed with Boswell that the mob was wrong (*Life, 4,* 279).

16. Ibid., p. 292. Another Whig politician who was an intimate friend of Johnson in his last years was the brilliant William Windham, whose *Diary* gives a detailed account of Johnson's final days. Windham was a staunch supporter of Fox until 1794, when with Portland and other "coalition Whigs" he broke with his leader on the question of the prosecution of the war with France. He became Secretary at War in Pitt's cabinet.

17. *Life, 1,* 372–4.

18. Pares, *King George III and the Politicians,* p. 72.

19. Ninetta S. Jucker, ed., *The Jenkinson Papers, 1760–1766* (London, 1949), p. 203.

20. *Life, 2,* 317.

21. Jucker, p. 290.

22. *Letters,* No. 178.2. The suggestion of Chapman (ibid.) and McAdam (*Dr. Johnson and the English Law,* p. 55) that the Jenkinson episode had some connection with Johnson's work for Gerard Hamilton seems unlikely.

23. *Letters,* No. 201.

24. *Letters*, No. 98.1. Chambers' contribution remains unidentified.

25. *Letters*, No. 187.2. A letter (No. 191.1) from Johnson to Chambers referring to "our necessary operations," which McAdam (p. 67) gives as of October 8, 1766, Chapman has now assigned to 1767.

26. *Works* (1958), *1*, 96–7.

27. McAdam, pp. 81–122. Students of Johnson seem not to have been as much impressed as they should be by the distinguished company in which this work of his is found. Blackstone's *Commentaries*, A. V. Dicey's *Law and Public Opinion in England*, and Sir William Holdsworth's monumental *History of English Law* all originated as their authors' Vinerian lectures. To have his legal opinions delivered from the Vinerian chair must have been some compensation to Johnson for the Lord Chancellorship that he missed.

28. Ibid., pp. 91–2, 99.

29. Ibid., p. 93. See, in E. A. and G. L. Duyckinck, *Cyclopædia of American Literature* (New York, 1855), 2, 333, from the table talk of Thomas Cooper (1759–1840), collected in Cooper's "last years" by Colonel D. J. McCord: "Speaking of Dr. Johnson. P. called him a bigot in politics and religion. *Dr. C[ooper].* No! No! In a political conversation which I had with Dr. Johnson he said, 'I believe in no such thing as the *jure divino* of kings. I have no such belief; but I believe that monarchy is the most conducive to the happiness and safety of the people of every nation, and therefore I am a monarchist, but as to its divine right, that is all stuff. I think every people have the right to establish such government as they may think most conducive to their interest and happiness.' "

Cooper, a British radical who migrated to America, was a close friend of Joseph Priestley, through whom he might have met Johnson. See *Life, 4*, 434, where Priestley is quoted as saying, "Several circumstances shew that Dr. Johnson had not so much of bigotry at the decline of life as had distinguished him before." All this means, I suspect, is that before Priestley met Johnson, he concurred in the general notion of Johnson's "bigotry"; when he actually met him and discovered that he was, in fact, open-minded, he decided that Johnson must have changed. These testimonials from two highly intelligent left-wingers, supporters of the American and French Revolutions, are not to be taken lightly.

I cannot resist quoting the continuation of Cooper's remarks, which is perhaps not entirely irrelevant here: "Boswell, continued Dr. C., was the greatest fool I ever knew. He was a real idiot."

30. See above, p. 77.

31. McAdam, p. 88.

32. Ibid., p. 82.

33. *Ecclesiastical Polity*, Bk. I, chap. 10.

34. The phrase seems to have originated as early as 1725, with Francis Hutcheson—the "able and benevolent" Hutcheson, as Johnson calls him (*Life 3*, 53, with erratum).

35. McAdam, p. 110.

36. Ibid., p. 107.

37. Ibid., p. 97.

38. Ibid., p. 103.

39. *Works* (1958), *1*, 98.

40. W. G. Hamilton, *Parliamentary Logick* (London, 1808), pp. 239-53.

41. *Letters*, 187.1.

42. *Three Tracts on the Corn-Trade and Corn-Laws*, 2d ed. London, 1766-67. The book was praised by Adam Smith in *The Wealth of Nations* for its laissez faire views.

43. For the relation of Johnson's "Considerations" to his views on economics generally, see Appendix C, below. For Burke see *Cavendish's Debates*, *1*, 475; *2*, 55-7; *Parliamentary History*, *17*, 1475-82; and the *Annual Register* for the years in question.

44. *Parliamentary Logick*, p. ix.

45. *Letters*, Nos. 187.2, 187.3.

46. *The East India Company in Eighteenth-Century Politics* (Oxford, 1952), chap. 6, "The First Parliamentary Intervention." See also John Brooke, *The Chatham Administration, 1766-1768* (London, 1956), p. 72 ff.

47. And why does Johnson, in London, write to Chambers, at Oxford, for copies of papers that are in London? To be sure, this letter (No. 187.3) was redirected to Chambers in London.

48. *Life, 4*, 281; *Letters*, No. 1132; *Life, 5*, 572.

49. *Life, 1*, 408, 437-42.

50. *A Narrative of the Transactions in Bengal from . . . 1760 to 1764, during the Government of H. Vansittart; published by himself* (3 vols. London, 1766) is the only considerable publication that I know of issued on that side of the controversy. It is, however, little more than an uninspired compilation of documents, and I can detect no trace of Johnson's editorial hand. The preface to John Hoole's *The Present State of the English East India Company's Affairs* (London, 1772), with which Allen T. Hazen (*Johnson's Prefaces and Dedications*, New Haven, 1937, p. 60, n. 2) plausibly suggests Johnson may have helped, has no bearing that I can see on this controversy.

51. *Letters,* Nos. 793.1, 795. Johnson's observation in the latter, "Shelburne seems to be his [Chambers'] enemy," may indicate that Chambers played an important part in the transactions of 1766–67, when Shelburne was promoting the Government's case against the Company.

52. *Life, 3,* 20, 471–2.

53. Ibid., p. 350.

54. Ibid., *4,* 213.

55. See J. L. Clifford, *Hester Lynch Piozzi (Mrs. Thrale),* Oxford, 1941.

56. For instance, a paragraph in the *Gentleman's Magazine* (March 1769), p. 162, attributed to Johnson by Croker (*Life,* 1831, 2, 68 n.), and several "addresses to the electors" of Southwark, noted by Clifford.

57. *Letters,* No. 667.1.

58. As an alternative to McAdam's speculation (*Johnson and the English Law,* pp. 66–7) that Johnson was introduced to Gerard Hamilton by Chambers, I suggest that he more probably met Hamilton through the Thrales. Hamilton was Halifax's Chief Secretary when Halifax went to Ireland at the time of the Thrales' engagement, which he helped to negotiate. Mrs. Thrale's references to Hamilton in *Thraliana* and the *Anecdotes* indicate that they were old acquaintances. It was on an occasion when Hamilton, Thrale, and Johnson were fox-hunting on the Brighton Downs that Hamilton made his famous observation on Johnson's prowess at that sport.

59. After exulting over the victory of the Old Tory (over a King's Friend) in the Oxford University election of 1768 (*Letters* No. 201, and above, p. 192), Johnson concludes with a half-

apologetic paragraph, as if in recognition of the fact that the Thrales might not see eye-to-eye with him in the matter: "Of this I am sure you must be glad, for without enquiring into the opinions or conduct of any party, it must be for ever pleasing to see men adhering to their principles against their interest"—i.e. voting for someone with no hope of ever having patronage to bestow. If "principle" is merely the antithesis of "interest," Johnson's great blast, "Whiggism is the negation of all principle," means very little more than that eighteenth-century Whigs were concerned with political patronage and eighteenth-century Tories were not—which is very much the conclusion that modern historians draw.

60. See p. 223.

61. Joseph Towers, *A Letter to Dr. Samuel Johnson* (1775), in *Tracts on Political and Other Subjects* (London, 1796), *1*, 147–8.

62. *Life, 2,* 147.

63. It would appear that the British House of Commons, two hundred years later, still agrees with Johnson. In the General Election of 1955, two Irish Nationalist candidates received the highest number of votes in their constituencies (Mid-Ulster, and Fermanagh and South Tyrone). They were found incapable of sitting, and their opponents were declared duly elected—exactly what happened in Middlesex in 1769. One member, opposing the action, summed up the situation by reference to the Wilkes case: "Politically, morally, personally and in every way Wilkes was not a fit and proper person to sit in the House of Commons, but . . . the British people won the right for the constituencies to send whatever person they like to send to Parliament. I hope that the House will support the amendment" (Hansard, ser. 5, *544,* House of Commons, cols. 79–80). The House turned the amendment down by a vote of 197 to 63. Johnson would have been amused by this *reductio ad absurdum* of the phrase "won the right."

64. *Works, 10,* 8.

65. Ibid., pp. 8, 12. (See addendum, p. 324.)

66. Ibid., p. 14.

67. Ibid., p. 29.

68. Ibid., pp. 30–31.

69. Ibid., p. 28. In such a remark as this, Johnson's carefully

restricted definition of "the poor" should be borne in mind (see note 12, p. 300, above).

70. *Life, 2,* 147.

71. So lucid that when the question of its ownership came up again after the second World War (Argentina having inherited the claim of Spain), Johnson's pamphlet was reprinted (London, 1948) as a guide to the complex dispute.

72. *Works, 10,* 61.

73. Ibid., p. 77-8.

74. See, e.g., Dorothy George, *London Life in the Eighteenth Century,* London, 1925.

75. *Works, 10,* 81-2.

76. Ibid., p. 85.

77. Ibid., pp. 88-9.

78. Ibid., p. 125.

79. Ibid., p. 96. Had Johnson seen or heard of the "Don't Tread on Me" flag, with its representation of a rattlesnake?

80. *Life, 2,* 313-15.

81. *Works, 10,* 94, 106, 107, 113. Johnson's "king and parliament" in the last sentence is a loose way of saying "the King-in-Parliament," the legislature of Great Britain. It may be useful here to remind American readers that the enactment of a law in England requires (and has required from time immemorial) the assent of the three constituents of "Parliament" (in the larger sense)—the king, the House of Lords, and the House of Commons (though since 1912 the necessity for the assent of the House of Lords has been limited); further, that the legislative powers of the King-in-Parliament are restricted by no written constitution.

82. Ibid., p. 101.

83. R. L. Schuyler, *Parliament and the British Empire* (New York, 1929) appears to settle the question of the legality of Parliament's taxation of the colonies, on the side of Johnson.

84. Ironically, as I write this, the sovereign State of Massachusetts (where Johnson was burned in effigy in 1775 for having written *Taxation No Tyranny*) is engaged in a squabble with its neighboring states through insisting on its right to tax non-residents of Massachusetts who benefit from its services but have no representation in its legislature. It has thrown into prison in Boston a citizen of New Hampshire who refused to

be so taxed (see the Boston *Globe* for March and April 1959).

85. K. C. Balderston, ed., *Thraliana* (1951), *2*, 945.

86. See above, p. 171, for his views on the subject expressed in his review of Evans' *Middle Colonies;* and below, Appendix A, for his willingncss to part with Minorca and Gibraltar.

87. Jefferson Davis' Inaugural Address as President of the Confederate States uses precisely the same arguments for Southern independence of the Union as were used by the Thirteen Colonies for independence of Britain, and does so consciously.

88. See above, p. 169.

89. *Works, 10,* 109. For the mercantilist sources of Johnson's ideas of colonization see, e.g., Joshua Gee, *The Trade and Navigation of Great Britain Considered* (3d ed. London, 1731), chap. 31, "Plantations One Great Cause of Enriching This Nation."

90. *Letters,* Nos. 327, 329.

91. *Works, 10,* 434.

92. Ibid., p. 436.

93. *Life, 5,* 27.

94. *Letters,* No. 329.

95. *Works, 10,* 425.

96. *Life, 5,* 27.

97. *Works, 10,* 434.

98. *Lives of the Poets, 3,* 411–2.

99. Above, pp. 28–32.

100. *Letters,* No. 776.

101. Ibid., 827.

102. Ibid., 835.1.

103. Ibid., 928.

104. Ibid., 942.

105. Feiling, *The Second Tory Party,* p. 166. L. F. Powell (*Life, 4,* 542–3) has exonerated Pitt from the charge, laid by Macaulay, that he may have had something to do with the refusal of the request, in 1784, for a royal grant so that Johnson might go to Italy for his health. Yet Johnson did well not to be disappointed (*Letters,* No. 1008) over an application to a ministry in which the Home Secretary was Tommy Townshend, who on three occasions had virulently attacked Johnson's pension in the House of Commons.

106. *Works* (Oxford, 1825), *9,* 496–506.

107. Ibid., pp. 506–16.

8. A RECAPITULATION AND SOME REFLECTIONS

1. My favorite piece of misrepresentation (or assimilation of Johnson to Boswell) is the concluding sentence of J. B. Bury's article on Gibbon in the *Encyclopædia Britannica* (11th ed): "It is worthy of notice that he [Gibbon] was in favour of the abolition of slavery, while humane men like his friend Lord Sheffield, Dr. Johnson, and Boswell were opposed to the anti-slavery movement." But every Johnsonian has his own collection of such gems.

2. The term is David Riesman's (*Faces in the Crowd,* New Haven, 1952). It implies that interrelation between individual character and political attitudes which is generally disregarded in historical studies of political behavior.

3. If one is to believe the novels of Wells and Forster—and, of course, Hardy's *Jude the Obscure.*

4. *Life, 3,* 463.

5. In the review of the *Account of the Conduct of the Duchess of Marlborough* (see p. 145, above); later, and more emphatically, in the review of Tytler's *Historical and Critical Inquiry* (above, p. 181).

6. Provided they were learned and behaved in a seemly manner: *Life, 4,* 75, and elsewhere. It should be remembered that the "hierarchy" which Boswell insists that Johnson "profoundly revered" was overwhelmingly Whig.

7. Hazen, *Prefaces and Dedications,* pp. 145–6.

8. *Life of Johnson,* p. 504.

9. A contemporary of Johnson whose political theory is based on the concept of sovereignty and whose work Johnson knew is Jean Jacques Burlamaqui. See his *Principles of Natural and Politic Law,* trans. Thomas Nugent, London, 1752; R. F. Harvey, *Jean Jacques Burlamaqui,* Chapel Hill, 1937; *Life, 2,* 430. The concept goes back to the Renaissance writer Jean Bodin.

10. *Life, 2,* 170.

11. E. T. Davies, *The Political Ideas of Richard Hooker* (London, 1946), p. 69.

12. McAdam, *Dr. Johnson and the English Law,* p. 82.

13. *History of English Law* (London, 1903–52), *10,* 529.

14. E.g. S. G. Brown, "Dr. Johnson and the Old Order," *Marxist Quarterly,* October 1937; William Kent, "Dr. Johnson," *So-*

cialist Review, October 1920. See also John Sargeaunt, "Dr. Johnson's Politics," *Bookman* (New York), January 1898; G. B. Hill, "Dr. Johnson as a Radical," *Contemporary Review,* June 1889.

15. "Conservatism and Sociology," *American Journal of Sociology, 58* (1952), 167–75. For other statements of neoconservatism see the writings of Russell Kirk, Peter Viereck, and Clinton Rossiter.

16. Cf. the famous exchange between Coleridge and Harriet Martineau: "Said he, 'You appear to consider that society is an aggregate of individuals!' I replied that I certainly did" (Harriet Martineau, *Autobiography,* Boston, 1877, *1,* 300).

17. *Life, 3,* 213.

18. Ibid., *1,* 408.

19. Ibid., *5,* 106.

20. Another modern figure whose skepticism of metaphysics in political and social thinking seems remarkably like Johnson's is Oliver Wendell Holmes. Cf. with Johnson's statements on pp. 206–7 and 214 the following dictum of Holmes from the judicial bench: "It is only tautologous to say that the law knows nothing of moral rights unless they are legal rights, and from before the days of Hobbes the argument has been public property that there is no such thing as a right created by law, as against the sovereign who makes the law by which the right is created" (Catherine Drinker Bowen, *Yankee from Olympus,* Boston, 1944, p. 317). Mrs. Bowen calls Holmes' approach to political and social questions "straight pragmatism—and brand-new," and applauds Holmes' "phrase, since widely quoted, *'We must think things, not words'* " (pp. 428–9). Readers who recall Johnson's fondness for the antithesis "Words are the daughters of earth, things are the sons of heaven" will smile.

21. Ibid., *2,* 102.

22. *Rambler,* No. 52.

RECENT WORKS CITED

Balleine, G. R. *A History of the Evangelical Party in the Church of England.* London, Longmans, Green, 1908.

Boswell, James. *Boswell's London Journal, 1762–1763,* ed. F. A. Pottle. New York, McGraw-Hill, 1950.

——— *The Life of Samuel Johnson, LL.D.,* ed. G. B. Hill; rev. L. F. Powell. Oxford, Clarendon Press, Vols. 1–4, 1934; 5, 6, 1950.

Bowen, Catherine Drinker. *Yankee from Olympus.* Boston, Little, Brown, 1944.

Bracey, Robert. *Eighteenth Century Studies and Other Papers.* New York, Appleton, 1925.

Bredvold, Louis I. *The Intellectual Milieu of John Dryden.* Ann Arbor, University of Michigan Press, 1934.

Bronson, Bertrand H. *Johnson Agonistes.* Cambridge, Cambridge University Press, 1946.

Brooke, John. *The Chatham Administration, 1766–1768.* London, Macmillan, 1956.

Bryce, Sir James [Viscount Bryce]. *The American Commonwealth.* Rev. ed. 2 vols. New York, Macmillan, 1910.

Buchan, John [Lord Tweedsmuir]. *Some Eighteenth Century Byways and Other Essays.* Edinburgh and London, Blackwood, 1908.

Butterfield, Herbert. *George III, Lord North, and the People.* London: G. Bell and Sons, 1949.

——— *The Whig Interpretation of History.* London, Bell, 1931.

Christie, Ian R. *The End of North's Ministry, 1780–1782.* London, Macmillan, 1958.

Clifford, James L. *Hester Lynch Piozzi (Mrs. Thrale).* Oxford, Clarendon Press, 1941; 2d ed. 1953.

——— *Young Sam Johnson.* New York, McGraw-Hill, 1955.

Davies, E. T. *The Political Ideas of Richard Hooker.* London, S.P.C.K., 1946.

Davis, Rose Mary. *The Good Lord Lyttelton.* Bethlehem, Pa., Times Publishing Co., 1939.

Feiling, Keith. *The Second Tory Party, 1714–1832.* London, Macmillan, 1938.

Figgis, J. Neville. *The Divine Right of Kings.* 2d ed. Cambridge, Cambridge University Press, 1914.

Hill, G. B., ed. *Johnsonian Miscellanies.* 2 vols. Oxford, Clarendon Press, 1897.

Holdsworth Sir William. *A History of English Law.* 13 vols. London, Methuen, 1923–52.

Hoover, Benjamin B. *Samuel Johnson's Parliamentary Reporting.* Berkeley and Los Angeles, University of California Press, 1953.

Johnson, Samuel. *The Letters of Samuel Johnson,* ed. R. W. Chapman. 3 vols. Oxford, Clarendon Press, 1952.

———— *The Poems of Samuel Johnson,* ed. D. Nichol Smith and E. L. McAdam, Jr. Oxford, Clarendon Press, 1941.

———— *Samuel Johnson's Prefaces and Dedications,* ed. Allen T. Hazen. New Haven, Yale University Press, 1937.

———— *The Yale Edition of the Works of Samuel Johnson,* general ed., Allen T. Hazen. Vol. 1: *Diaries, Prayers, and Annals,* ed. E. L. McAdam, Jr., with Donald and Mary Hyde. New Haven, Yale University Press, 1958.

Jucker, Ninetta S., ed. *The Jenkinson Papers, 1760–1766.* London, Macmillan, 1949.

Krutch, Joseph Wood. *Samuel Johnson.* New York, Holt, 1944.

McAdam, E. L., Jr. *Dr. Johnson and the English Law.* Syracuse, N.Y., Syracuse University Press, 1951.

Michael, Wolfgang. *Englische Geschichte im achtzehnten Jahrhundert.* Vol. 1, Hamburg: L. Voss, 1896; 2d ed. Berlin and Leipzig: W. Rothschild, 1921. Vol. 2, Berlin and Leipzig: W. Rothschild, 1920. Vols. 3, 4, Berlin: Verlag für Staatswissenschaft und Geschichte, 1934, 1937. Vol. 5, Basel: Verlag für Recht und Gesellschaft, 1955. [The date 1945 for Vol. 5, given in Pargellis and Medley, *Bibliography of British History: The Eighteenth Century,* Oxford, 1951, seems to be erroneous.]

Namier, Sir Lewis Bernstein. *England in the Age of the American Revolution.* London, Macmillan, 1930.

—— *Personalities and Powers.* London, Hamish Hamilton, 1955.

—— *The Structure of Politics at the Accession of George III.* 2 vols. London, Macmillan, 1929; 2d ed. 1957.

Oliver, F. S. *The Endless Adventure.* 3 vols. London, Macmillan, 1930–35.

Orwell, George [Eric Blair]. *Such, Such Were the Joys.* New York, Harcourt, Brace, 1953.

Owen, John B. *The Rise of the Pelhams.* London, Methuen, 1957.

Pares, Richard. *King George III and the Politicians.* Oxford, Clarendon Press, 1953.

Piozzi, Hester Lynch [Mrs. Thrale]. *Thraliana,* ed. Katharine C. Balderston. 2 vols. Oxford, Clarendon Press, 1942; 2d ed. 1951.

Plumb, J. H. *Sir Robert Walpole: The Making of a Statesman.* London, Cresset Press, 1956.

Reade, Aleyn Lyell. *Johnsonian Gleanings.* 11 vols., privately printed, 1909–52.

Realey, C. B. *The Early Opposition to Sir Robert Walpole, 1720–1727.* Lawrence, Kansas, University of Kansas Press, 1931.

Roberts, Sir Sydney Castle. *An Eighteenth-Century Gentleman and Other Essays.* Cambridge, Cambridge University Press, 1930.

Sedgwick, Romney, ed. *Letters from George III to Lord Bute, 1756–1766.* London, Macmillan, 1939.

Sherburn, George. *The Restoration and Eighteenth Century.* In A. C. Baugh *et al., A Literary History of England.* New York, Appleton-Century-Crofts, 1948.

Sledd, J. B. and Gwin Kolb. *Dr. Johnson's Dictionary.* Chicago, University of Chicago Press, 1955.

Sutherland, Lucy S. *The East India Company in Eighteenth-Century Politics.* Oxford, Clarendon Press, 1952.

Trevor-Roper, H. R. *Men and Events.* New York, Harper, 1958.

Walcott, Robert. *English Politics in the Early Eighteenth Century.* Cambridge, Mass., Harvard University Press, 1956.

Ward, W. R. *Georgian Oxford: University Politics in the Eighteenth Century.* Oxford, Clarendon Press, 1958.

Wedgwood, Sir Josiah Clement [Lord Wedgwood]. *Staffordshire Parliamentary History.* 3 vols. 1919–33. In William Salt Archaeological Society, *Collections for a History of Staffordshire.*

Wiggin, Lewis M. *The Faction of Cousins: A Political Account of the Grenvilles, 1733–1763.* New Haven, Yale University Press, 1958.

INDEX I

Peers are indexed under family name or title, whichever was best known in SJ's lifetime; cross-references have been provided where they seemed useful, as have dates (in italics) of creation of, or succession to, a peerage. Where additional family names have been assumed (e.g. Hervey Aston, Wortley Montagu) the main entry is usually under the original family name (here "Hervey" and "Montagu").

It may be useful to remind readers that holders of courtesy titles of nobility (sons of dukes and marquesses, eldest sons of earls) are not peers but commoners, and are eligible to the House of Commons (e.g. Lord North, MP, eldest son of the Earl of Guilford); and that Irish peers were members of the Irish, not the British, House of Lords, and might also be elected to the British House of Commons (e.g. Viscount Tyrconnel, MP); although some Irish (and Scottish) peers sat in the British House of Lords by virtue of a subsidiary English or (after 1707) British peerage held by them: e.g. the Earl of Shelburne (peerage of Ireland) sat as Baron Wycombe (peerage of Great Britain).

SJ = Samuel Johnson; L'd = Lichfield; Abp = Archbishop; Bp = Bishop; Vct = Viscount; Mss = Marquess. "SJ and" may mean "SJ's dealings with," "SJ's opinion of," "SJ's attitude toward," or "SJ in relation to."

Abingdon, Willoughby Bertie, 3d Earl of (*1692–1760*), 123
Aboriginal peoples, SJ and, 68, 165, 242, 262–3, 270–1. See also Indians, Negroes
Absolutism, political ("arbitrary government," "totalitarianism," "dictatorship," "tyranny"): Locke on, 78–9; Savage on, 86; SJ and, 75–6, 79–80, 86, 233
Abyssinia, 67–72
Academies, literary, SJ and, 152–3
Adams, William (*1706–89*), 60
Addenbrooke, John, Dean of L'd (*ca. 1690–1776*), 23, 41
Addison, Joseph, MP (*1672–1719*): political career, 56; and L'd Grammar School, 56; SJ and, 65; *Cato*, 75; picture of Toryism, 231, 236
Akenside, Mark (*1721–70*), SJ on, 221

Albert, Prince Consort (*1819–61*), Jacobitism, 17
Alfred, King (*849–901*), "Patriot" hero, 90, 97
Americans (generally the British inhabitants of the Thirteen Colonies; sometimes also those of the West Indies): SJ and, 107–8, 161–72, 196–7, 212–21, 237, 239, 242; Declaration and War of Independence ("American Revolution"), 29, 194, 270, 295
Amhurst, Nicholas (*1697–1742*), 308
Andrewes, Lancelot, Bp of Winchester (*1555–1626*), 110
Anglicanism. See Church of England
Annan, Noel, 301
Anne, Queen (*1665–1714*): "touches" SJ, 16, 298; SJ on, 146, 162
Ansbach (Anspach), Margravine of

329

INDEX II

SAMUEL JOHNSON

A. Life

Only events specially dealt with are listed here. A summary biography appears in the *Chronological Table*, p. xiii, above. For the biographical background of specific writings see Section C, below, under the title of the work. For a recapitulation and summary see pp. 231-58 (not indexed in this section).

B. Characteristics and Attitudes

Any such listing is bound to be personal, selective, and incomplete; and many readers will wish to redefine some of the Protean terms used. For SJ's attitudes toward individuals and more specific subjects see Index I under their names. For a recapitulation and summary see pp. 231-58 (not indexed in this section).

347

C. Writings

Quotations from SJ's letters, diaries, and prayers have not been indexed. Dates assigned are those of composition or beginning of composition, when these are known to differ significantly from date of publication. Ed. = edition of; tr. = translation of; * = verse. Italics in a series of page numbers indicate the main discussion of the item.